PRAISE SONGS FOR DAVE THE POTTER

Praise Songs for Dave the Potter

ART AND POETRY FOR DAVID DRAKE

EDITED AND WITH AN INTRODUCTION BY P. GABRIELLE FOREMAN

FOREWORD BY KWAME DAWES   AFTERWORD BY EVIE SHOCKLEY

THE UNIVERSITY OF GEORGIA PRESS   ATHENS

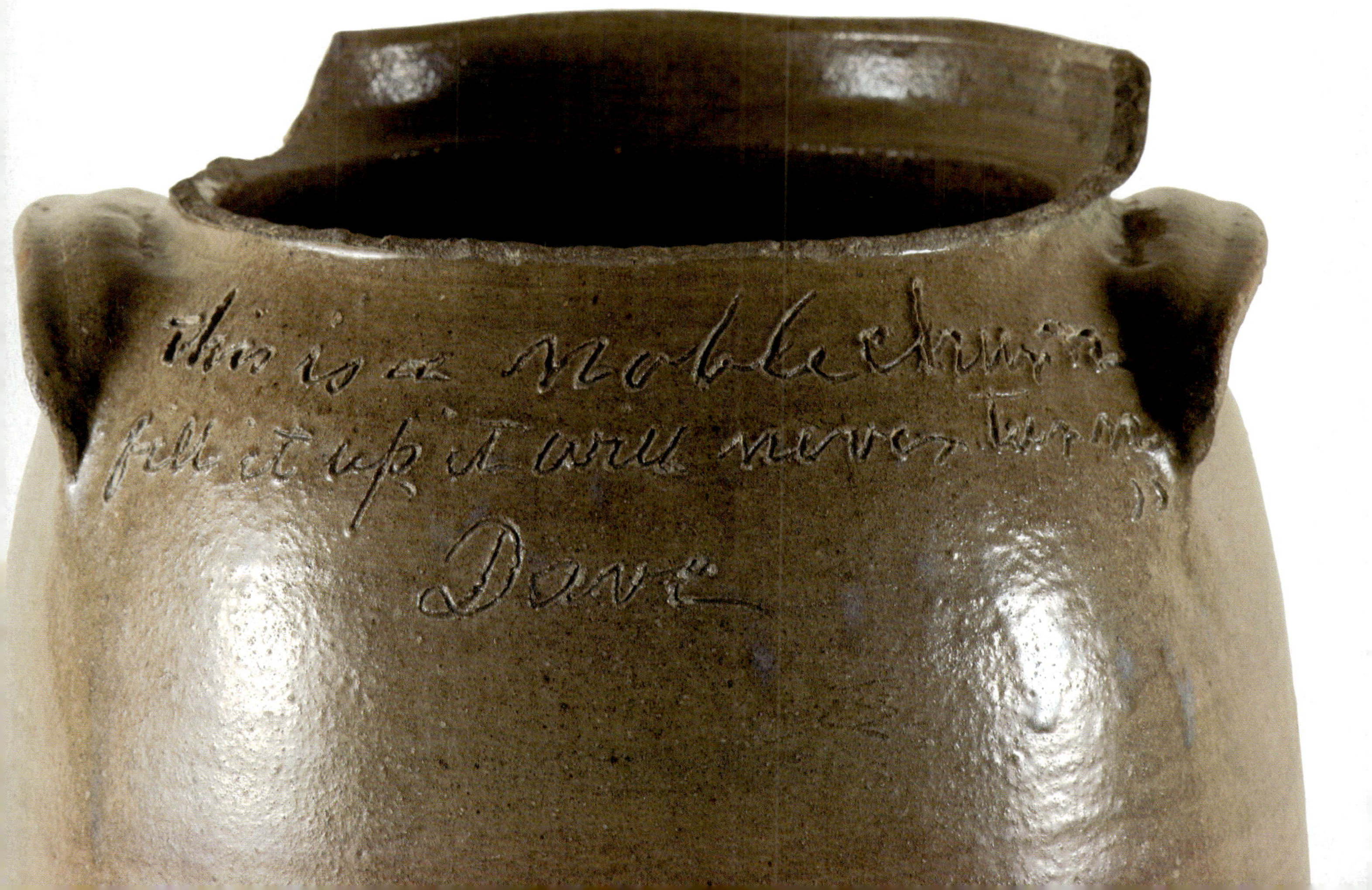

A SARAH MILLS HODGE FUND PUBLICATION

This publication is made possible in part through a grant from the Hodge Foundation in memory of its founder, Sarah Mills Hodge, who devoted her life to the relief and education of African Americans in Savannah, Georgia.

Published by the University of Georgia Press
Athens, Georgia 30602
www.ugapress.org

Designed by Erin Kirk
Set in Arno
Printed and bound by Friesens
The paper in this book meets the guidelines for permanence and durability of the Committee on Production Guidelines for Book Longevity of the Council on Library Resources.

Most University of Georgia Press titles are available from popular e-book vendors.

Printed in Canada
26 25 24 23 22 C 5 4 3 2 1

Library of Congress Cataloging-in-Publication Data

Names: Foreman, P. Gabrielle (Pier Gabrielle), editor. | Dawes, Kwame Senu Neville, 1962– writer of foreword. | Shockley, Evie, 1965– writer of afterword.
Title: Praise songs for Dave the potter : art and poetry for David Drake / edited and with an introduction by P. Gabrielle Foreman ; foreword by Kwame Dawes ; afterword by Evie Shockley.
Description: Athens : The University of Georgia Press, [2022] | Includes bibliographical references and index.
Identifiers: LCCN 2022027193 | ISBN 9780820362496 (hardback)
Subjects: LCSH: Dave, active 1834-1864. | Green, Jonathan, 1955- Sir Dave. | Dave, active 1834-1864—Poetry. | African American arts—Themes, motives.
Classification: LCC NX652.D28 P73 2022 | DDC 700/.451—dc23/eng/20220810
LC record available at https://lccn.loc.gov/2022027193

TITLE PAGE IMAGE: Poetic Vessel, "this is a noble churn," March 19, 1858. David Drake. Greenville County Museum of Art.

To all our relation . . .

and to Lynnette Young Overby

whose vision and leadership served as the

North Star for the collaboration out of which

this book emerged.

Contents

List of Illustrations ix

Foreword. Vessels for Taking Us Home KWAME DAWES xi

Acknowledgments xvii

Introduction. His Page Was Clay: The Cultural Legacies of Dave the Poet/Potter P. GABRIELLE FOREMAN 1

David Drake Verses 21

Exploring Jonathan Green's *Sir Dave* in Context P. GABRIELLE FOREMAN 37

All My Relation Poetry with *Sir Dave* Paintings JONATHAN GREEN AND GLENIS REDMOND 49

Reading Glenis Redmond's *All My Relation* More Closely P. GABRIELLE FOREMAN 97

Black Belonging and Collaborative History Making: A Conversation with Jonathan Green, Glenis Redmond, and P. Gabrielle Foreman 109

Paintings, Poetry, and Place GLENIS REDMOND 139

Dave the Potter: A Theatrical Production Sharing His Legacy LYNNETTE YOUNG OVERBY 159

Black Artists as Cultural Historians: Jonathan Green, Carrie Mae Weems, and David Drake P. GABRIELLE FOREMAN 181

Afterword. A Praise Song for *Praise Songs* EVIE SHOCKLEY 201

Bibliography 207

Contributor Biographies 213

Index 217

Illustrations

David Drake, Poetic Vessel, "this is a noble church" iii

David Drake, Poetic Vessel, "when you fill this Jar with pork or beef" 1

David Drake, Poetic Vessel, "I made this Jar = for cash —" 21

David Drake, Poetic Vessel, "made at Stoney Bluff" 37

Jonathan Green, *Marshland Passage* 44

Relief of the god Ra, First Courtyard of Ramses II, Temple of Luxor 44

Relief of the god Ra with staff 44

David Drake, Poetic Vessel, "I wonder where is all my relation" 49

Jonathan Green, *Edgefield* 54

Jonathan Green, *Young Dave* 56

Jonathan Green, *Dave the Potter* 61

Jonathan Green, *Dave's Market* 63

Jonathan Green, *Sir Dave* 65

Jonathan Green, *Crossroads* 71

Jonathan Green, *Potter's Fragments* 75

Jonathan Green, *Earth to Earth* 78

Jonathan Green, *From Earth We Came* 81

Jonathan Green, *Marshland Passage* 84

Jonathan Green, *Three Vessels* 86

Jonathan Green, *Vessels of Sir Dave* 88

Jonathan Green, *Vessels for Taking Us Home* 90

David Drake, Poetic Vessel, "whats better than kissing =" 97

Ralph Anthony Russell, score from "Three Vessels" 109

Administrative map of South Carolina, c. 1850 139

Jonathan Green, *First Sunday* 144

Jonathan Green, *The Christening* 148

Ralph Anthony Russell, score from "Pretty Little Girl" 159

Ralph Anthony Russell, score from "Field Cotton" 167

"Field Cotton," theatrical production of *Dave the Potter* 167

"Pretty Little Girl," theatrical production of *Dave the Potter* 169

"Sir Dave," theatrical production of *Dave the Potter* 170

"Dave's Market," theatrical production of *Dave the Potter* 171

"Dream of Freedom," theatrical production of *Dave the Potter* 173

"Grave," theatrical production of *Dave the Potter* 174

Ralph Anthony Russell, score from "Shards" 175

"Shards," theatrical production of *Dave the Potter* 176

"Vessels," theatrical production of *Dave the Potter* 177

"Postlude," theatrical production of *Dave the Potter* 178

David Drake, Poetic Vessel, "the Sun moon and — Stars =" 181

Jonathan Green, *Farm Woman* 184

Jacob Lawrence, *The Ironers* 185

Jonathan Green, *Edgefield* 189

Leonardo Drew, *Untitled #25* 192

Jon Mills, photograph of Banksy's *Agency Job (Gleaners)* 192

John Biggers, *Cotton Pickers* 193

Carrie Mae Weems, Untitled (*Boneyard*) 196

Carrie Mae Weems, Untitled (*Ebo Landing*) 197

David Drake, Poetic Vessel, "whats better than kissing =" 201

Foreword

Vessels for Taking Us Home

KWAME DAWES

> I wonder where is all my relation
> friendship to all and every nation
> —DAVID DRAKE

THE SURVIVAL OF "Dave the Potter's" story in South Carolina reminds us of just how complex the delusion of slavery as an innocuous vestige of a "romantic way of life" can be. It is quite likely that for many defenders and apologists of slavery, those who hail from places like Dave's home of Edgefield, South Carolina, where the defense of slavery was a generational and defining ethic and tradition, that the figure of "Dave the Potter" was ample evidence that the enslaved were not always the victims of violence, dehumanization, and cruelty. Instead, in this narrative of historical endearment, they were part of the fabric of the South and members of a shared community. Dave was valued, they said. Dave was celebrated for his art. Dave was coveted. Dave enjoyed certain liberties not afforded to many enslaved people. And Dave was an artist who was allowed to make art that was sought after by white society.

The obscenity of this thinking should be obvious enough. But the fact is that it makes an assumption about this man, about his ability—against all odds—to make art and to demand that he be acknowledged for that art. There is in the biography of Dave the Potter a hopeful narrative—not because it speaks to an oxymoronic "humane slave society," but because it symbolizes a singular moment of defiance, a profound resistance to erasure. We know of Dave the Potter not because he was a great artisan. We know him because he recognized that the society in which he lived, and in which his race was denied both presence and value, required that he signal his presence with a small gesture, the signing of his art.

Dave the Potter was not the only enslaved ceramicist in South Carolina. We know that Black iron workers, builders, architects, and skilled artisans of all sorts existed. Yet Dave the Potter stands out because by signing his work, he was waging a quiet attack on the far-reaching implications of ownership that defined slavery. He was saying, "I made this," which was psychically akin to saying, "I own this." And more grandly he was saying, "Remember me."

Dave Drake was owned. His art was owned. Anything he produced, including children, urns, jugs, and glazed ceramic pieces, were owned by those who owned him. Dave the Potter sought to wrench himself from this ownership by an act of remarkable defiance.

When Dave the Potter was born, around 1800, literacy for the enslaved was illegal. Yet, Dave the Potter wrote inscriptions on his pottery, and he signed his name. He not only defied the law, but he sealed this in art. In "stealing away" the complete power that South Carolina law asserted, he negated their power of erasure.

One suspects that Dave the Potter survived these acts because of the patronage of his owners and others. Patronage—permission, if you will—is the currency of slavery, the troubling action of benevolence that benefits the benefactor. When Phillis Wheatley was published and allowed to write, she was granted the permission—as is the nature of patronage. Her owners emerged as the benevolent ones, the ones responsible for her talent. It was this feature of patronage that troubled the lives of Zora Neale Hurston and Langston Hughes; they struggled with it while producing work despite it. Dave the Potter's life and work remind us of the cost of making art, and the implications of the "permission" that we are given to make art. But Dave the Potter's sense of irony and his defiance against this patronage emerge in his poems.

During the periods when, apparently, Dave the Potter produced no art, it was because he was enslaved by those who did not give him permission to do so. If Dave the Potter lost his leg, it is as likely because of some infraction of slave law as it was because, as the convenient story goes, that he laid down on a railroad track, inebriated, and was run over. When he did make art, it was because owners made it possible for him—they gave him permission. Dave the Potter never stopped being an artist, but the constraints of his human condition, dictated by a country that regarded him as of little value, limited his freedom to make art. Dave the Potter's work exists not as a sign of resilience but as a sign of just how many things created and imagined by the enslaved have not been passed on to us, have been erased, have been prevented from even happening. Art does not persist, not always. The capacity to make art can be squelched and destroyed. A civilization can be deprived of its opportunity to produce great art. And this is the great tragedy of slavery. It constrained the value of Black intelligence to labor only, to the use of Black bodies for just that alone. America failed itself by failing to value the fullness of who enslaved people were.

Dave the Potter's fragments are slivers of this genius, and for this we have to be grateful. For those of us with the opportunity to restore what has been erased, he is a gift, a promise; every piece of ceramic work that has survived represents this possibility, this hope. They exist in museums and galleries and in collectors' homes. Yet there is no indication that ownership of his work, the very thing his signature was meant to assert, is something any of his descendants have inherited.

Yet, the Potter Dave is witty: "Dave belongs to Mr. Miles," he incised on a pot. He reminds us that he knows what slavery means when he declares that his pots are owned by those who own him and who control the means for his labor.

We come to Dave the Potter fully aware that in his existence and in his function as an ancestor for Black artists, he reminds us of just how challenging and unsettling the issue of race is today. The economy of race is a conundrum for Black artists, one that we struggle with and end up feeling compromised by, one we wish to defy as we break its stranglehold. It is the conundrum that brought Zora Neale Hurston to that emotionally and psychically charged place from which to declare: "I do not always feel colored. Even now I often achieve the unconscious Zora of Eatonville before the Hegira. I feel most colored when I am thrown against a sharp white background. For instance at Barnard. 'Beside the waters of the Hudson' I feel my race. Among the thousand white persons, I am a dark rock surged upon, and overswept, but through it all, I remain myself."[1] Hurston believes in a self, but she knows that she is multiselved, and that sometimes the self betrays itself. What Dave the Potter keeps us doing is "feeling our race." Dave's circumstances resonate in Langston Hughes's words: "So I am ashamed for the black poet who says, 'I want to be a poet, not a Negro poet,' as though his own racial world were not as interesting as any other world. I am ashamed, too, for the colored artist who runs from the painting of Negro faces to the painting of sunsets after the manner of the academicians because he fears the strange un-whiteness of his own features. An artist must be free to choose what he does, certainly, but he must also never be afraid to do what he might choose."[2] For Hughes, Dave the Potter would be the great artist who is not afraid to be himself because Dave the Potter is never allowed to be anything else but himself. It is this wrestling that makes Toni Morrison bristle at the suggestion by white critics that her art will not be great enough, or American enough, if she does not finally write about white people—or said another way, until she stops writing about only Black people. I could go on and on talking about what it means for Black artists to negotiate their art in a white space that Hughes describes as "American standardization"; and while he does not spell this out, he knows it means the white American economy, the white American value system, and the white American culture, where galleries owned by whites have to endorse Black art, where fellowships and awards have to be given to Black artists by white individuals and institutions, and where Dave the Potter's work is lauded and praised by white people who own it and who, in a sense, continue to make demands on the meaning of this work.

And, in the end, this is why this project is so beautiful and important. For Jonathan Green, "Sir Dave" is part of a multitude of Black people filled with spiritual power and invention, filled with the capacity to create and re-create, filled with the genius of revelation and intuition and philosophical force, filled also with the capacity to remember. And this army has always been at the fore of his imagination because he grew up in a culture that protected this understanding and that guided him to connect through the lineage of ritual and tradition to his ancestry, to his African beginnings. This is what he celebrates in paintings that wrench Sir Dave from the clutches of American standardization.

And for Glenis Redmond, Dave is the poet voice, keeping in the crafty archival space of the engraving on clay and sealed in glaze that reminds her of the voices of her ancestry—our ancestry, preserved through song, through story, through the work of their hands, and carried to her, saying that this is her inheritance, her legacy, and in this, Dave the Potter reminds her that her song is part of a long and moving chorus of song. We, Black artists, are all searching for precedence, for the evidence that we did not spring up without roots, without an army of holy witnesses, and her poems celebrate this connection.

If I seem to be suggesting that all of this is straightforward and self-assured, then I have failed. I am saying that we can see in Redmond and Green a full understanding that they too have suffered, as we Black artists all have, from the very same thing that Dave the Potter suffered—the need to somehow see the shackles that sought to silence and erase him, and further, to find imaginative ways to defy those shackles, to find a way to speak and to say "I am here."

Gabrielle Foreman, Lynnette Young Overby, and Evie Shockley have added their songs to this cultural anchoring, their songs that collect this deep spirit, this deep understanding of what Dave the Potter means to Black artists. Foreman's brilliant excavation of meaning and her deep dive into the appreciation of what we have left to us in the scattering of history bring together fragments of meaning in Dave the Potter's life and art in a splendid anthem of prayer and praise. Here the lead voice has heard all the requests from the mouths of the congregants and then has allowed her antennae to pick up the waves of unspoken prayers, those groanings too deep for words, so that her own praise is a true gathering for this book.

This is why I have been drawn to Green's titling of one of his *Sir Dave* paintings, *Vessels for Taking Us Home*. This book, these praise songs, even, these are all the vessels that will transport us into the Black imaginary, the African imaginary. And this strikes me as tragically and righteously good. I have never laid a hand on one of David Drake's jars. I have never traced the contours of their making. I have never had the chance to ritualize the connection between the residue of his genius and my own self, my own body. One day, I hope to do so. But it pleases me that these sacred vessels are there. And until then, I offer this foreword and this poem as rimings, as echoes, as harmonious stretches of song.

DAVE

For Dave Drake the Potter, of Edgefield, South Carolina

Dave belongs to Mr. Miles
whir the oven bakes and the pot biles
—DAVID DRAKE, 1840

Used to be just the cost of his fingers—
a negro with some practical use.
They can grow too old to bend
to pick the cotton, but he is worth
something, has his uses, got those
fingers that can feel their way around
the muscle of clay, and turn dirt
into music—hard, lasting, lovely
thing that stays true, holds water
long, and carries on its skin poetry
inside the pottery, to make folks sigh
and say, *Yes, that is good work—a negro*
with uses, a negro with a price on his head,
not easy to let that one go, no sir.

And nothing's changed much
since they buried the old bones
of Dave Drake in the bramble
and broken crockery—Dave, the dirt-
conjuror, Dave who could fire clay just
right to make it shine like money,
man with an eye for a straight line,
keep the lip from sulking, he said—
and now, they got his name, and still
they put money on that head of his,
on those fingers he had on him.
Got white folk trading his value with smiles;
saying how that Dave had his uses,
and they paying good coin to hold
a pregnant bowl of old-time clay
in their laps for the photo, amen.

We say amen to the good hard-
working negro, cause he still has
money on his head, and that is some
magic, some roots. But them who know,
know that Dave knew roots and barks
and flowers and leaves, and saw
in dirt the dried bones of old spirits.
Most don't know that part about
old Dave. But it's not their fault.
After all, this Edgefield from whence
negroes had to flee to get a break,
where old Strum got a taste for the old
rituals of the plantation, learned
how to value flesh and dirt, put a price
on it; this place is what we call the teat
that fed every ugly hatred in this state.

So God bless the soft eye on the belly of the bowl,
God bless the song cut into the raw clay,
God bless the color hidden inside the glaze,
God bless the negro that had his uses,
God bless Mr. Miles for feeding that negro,
God bless the negro that still has his own;
for what does it mean but what it means, anyway?

NOTES

1 Hurston, "How It Feels to Be Colored Me," 215–216.
2 Hughes, "The Negro Artist and the Racial Mountain."

Acknowledgments

WE WANT TO START by thanking David Drake for his genius, wit, talent, mastery, and nobility. We know he stands among artistic giants lost to us through generations of slavery, violence, and disregard. We are your relation. To all those who passed his story on to us so that it really was never lost at all, *ashé*. Lynnette Young Overby, the modest powerhouse, brought the magic of her leadership to the collaboration that enabled this book; her community building brought and keeps this group together through performances on our first work, on Harriet E. Wilson, then on David Drake, then on the early Black Conventions movement, to the intrepid barrier breaker, journalist, and legal thinker Mary Ann Shadd Cary, and now on to the writer and activist Frances Ellen Watkins Harper. Glenis Redmond gifted first our performance and then this book with the power of her craft and spirit, with her living connection to the ancestors, and with her healing sisterhood. Jonathan Green has been a muse and oracle, a font of wisdom and patience and of energy and enthusiasm; he has been the most gracious collaborator and partner. We thank him and Richard Weedman for all the visits to and from them and for opening up their homes and hearts. We're so pleased that his wise response to curator Jill Beute Koverman's invitation to create a cover painting for the very first 1998 exhibit on David Drake with a full series of work will now be shown in its entirety. We thank Kwame Dawes and Evie Shockley for anointing this volume with their foreword and afterword. There are no more fitting inheritors of David Drake's legacy than these poet scholars, poet griots, poets of the Diaspora. David Drake must rest easier in his power knowing they have claimed him as their relation and cultural ancestor; that delight is matched only by our appreciation for their adding the opening and closing words to this volume.

We thank our long-term collaborator and composer Ralph Russell, who composed all of the pieces for the production that anchored our ongoing partnership; the scores from some of that work appear throughout this volume. We thank choreographers Vincent E. Thomas, Teresa Emmons, Gabrielle Hilliard, and Lynnette Young Overby for their pieces in the performance that inspired this volume. Vaughn

Newman and Vincent E. Thomas danced Dave and brought him to life on stage. We thank the performers who danced in Delaware, Washington, D.C., and in South Carolina, including: Audrey Wright, Megan Lamotte, Erika Brown, Dominique Oppenheimer, Tiana Sanders, Monique Bland, Aliyah Clay, Alfred Lance Jr., Andrew Widger, Blair Galiber, Kaya Simonson, Caitlin Green, Brielle Evangelista, Laura Sahd, Andrea Clendaniel, Taylor Walker, Elliot Ledford, Lauren Bonanno, Danielle Smithson, Eli Latshaw, A. T. Moffett, Rachel DeLauder, Amber Rance, Gabrielle Shubert, April Singleton, Ikira Peace, Dianna Ruberto, Ralph Russell, and Melissa Jones. We also thank conductor Duo Shen, University of Delaware Musicians, image designer Charles Marsh, and sculptors Jeannine Chapman and Kacey Boyce. Thanks also to Christina Cultural Arts Center, led by Raye Avery Jones, the University of Delaware's Community Engagement Initiative, the College of Arts and Sciences, and Center for the Study of Diversity for support of this project.

Michael A. Chaney's brilliant talk at Duke University in 2007 introduced Gabrielle Foreman to David Drake; Chaney's invitation to write about Drake's verse for *Where Is All My Relation? The Poetics of Dave the Potter* (2018) gave her an opportunity to extend her scholarship and to suggest David Drake as a subject for the artistic collaboration from which this book developed. Chaney's scholarship has been instrumental to Drake's recent reconsideration as a writer and poet. Though he may not know it, this book is an outgrowth of his work.

This book's many parts came together in large part because of Darlea Dominelli, our book coordinator. Darlea kept the editor, Gabrielle, organized and the project moving forward while Gabrielle also directed the Colored Conventions Project at University of Delaware and then launched and codirected the Center for Black Digital Research/#DigBlk. This is the second book Darlea has stewarded with Gabrielle and collaborators. Much respect and appreciation. Darlea also joined University of Delaware doctoral student Arline Wilson to work with Gabrielle to double- and triple-check the accuracy of verses that appear on David Drake's poetic vessels and to track down where they are located at the time of publication. Thanks to Arline and also to Darlea for the hours of painstaking work and correspondence that allowed us to produce the most accurate list so far of David Drake's verse. We look forward to corrections and additions. Scholar, curator, and critic of Black visual culture Tiffany Barber took time out to help with permissions. Wherever she goes, she spreads her brilliance and magic. Gabrielle also is happy to acknowledge editor Walter Biggins, now editor in chief at University of Pennsylvania Press, then with the University of Georgia Press, who in early discussions with Gabrielle about this volume convinced her that the book would be incomplete without Drake's verse—overriding her (spot-on) concern that it would take fastidious work over a long period of time to produce a collection that corrects (as best as we can) the differing versions of Drake's verse in circulation. If a close-to-definitive collection of Drake's verse appears here, it's because of Arline, Darlea, and Gabrielle's work as they took up Walter's challenge. Leonard Todd was also a key collaborator in this regard. Not only did he graciously allow us to use the list that appears in his *Carolina Clay* as a foundation to build on, but as we checked verse transcriptions, his were consistently the most trustworthy. He matched his careful transcription work with ongoing generosity, connecting us to others and cheering this volume on. We honor his request to add this here: "Leonard Todd acknowledges with deep appreciation the contributions of earlier scholars to this list of David Drake inscriptions, especially those of Cinda Baldwin and Jill Beute Koverman." We add our thanks to the Drake scholars on whose work we build.

Arline Wilson deserves special recognition for her research assistance on this volume in the summer of 2020. Her feedback and recommendations allowed Gabrielle to turn the 160-page transcription of the original interview into what appears in this book. The volume took its final shape with the expert advice and assistance of Elena Abbott of Ink Blotter Editing. Elena, it's such a pleasure to be able to thank each other in our respective acknowledgments and to have traveled together for so many years. None of this would be possible without the funding provided by the University of Delaware's College of Arts and Sciences and Penn State University's College of Liberal Arts, with additional funding from the Mellon Foundation and Delaware Humanities. Gabrielle wishes to thank UD Dean John Pelesko and PSU Dean Clarence Lang and Senior Associate Dean Scott Bennett as well as her department chairs and heads: John Ernest, Wunyabari Maloba, Mark Morrison, Cynthia Young, and Michael Kulikowski. At UD, Kaylee Olney, and at PSU, Teresa Yost, Wendy Shaffer, Tacee Sechler, and Susan Johnson were instrumental in the administrative labor that makes a collective endeavor possible.

J. Patrick Allen and Nathaniel Holly inherited this volume from Walter Biggins and we thank them and the entire team at the University of Georgia Press for their attention and expertise. We also thank University of South Carolina Press's Ehren Foley for his interest and contributions to this project. We wish we could thank the anonymous readers by name for their energy, expertise, and enthusiasm about this volume. Their thorough reviews lent ideas, and a roadmap as Gabrielle and contributors made revisions. Ellen Westkaemper of the Greenville County Museum of Art, which currently has the largest collection of David Drake pots, hosted Glenis and Gabrielle at gallery talks. We look forward to the possibility of future collaborations with GCMA. We also want to thank the Peace Center for Performing Arts for hosting the *David Drake (Dave the Potter)* and *The Three Harriets* performances attended by thousands of schoolchildren and others.

To extend the cultural genealogy that we've been honored to inherit, royalties from this book will support the Overby-Redmond-Green fund for young poets, visual artists, and performers who bring Black history to life through their work.

From Gabrielle Foreman

Most of my thank-yous are included above but I also want to thank my father, poet Kent Foreman. His death in 2010 left space to be filled with the love of language and culture that he embodied and encouraged for the entire time we inhabited this space together. Like anyone who watches her work, I am in awe of Lynnette Young Overby, a powerhouse of few words who can galvanize partnerships and energize them over time. Words can't express what a gift and balm it has been to work with her and Glenis Redmond over what is almost a decade now. Watching them both inspire young people in the arts and bring ideas to life on stage has been a great joy. Glenis, you are a sister of the spirit. I'm so blessed to dance with words with you. I first met Ralph Russell on a dissertation fellowship in St. Cloud, Minnesota, decades ago. This collaboration has kept us connected. I want to thank South Carolina, and Jonathan Green among the people who carry its spirit, for what has often felt like a welcoming home. And I give thanks to the actual home that spawned and supported me, and to my mother Lynn Foreman, who reads everything I write and everything she can about the subjects I write about; who could ask for more?

From Glenis Redmond

Thank you to Jonathan Green for guidance, leadership, and inspiration, and a major thank you to Gabrielle Foreman for her stellar research and for introducing me to my literary South Carolina forefather; he is a much-needed link personally, creatively, and spiritually. I feel overwhelming appreciation for and awe of Lynnette Young Overby for her artistic leadership for amplifying and expanding my words through collaborative dance. Thank you, Ralph Russell, for setting the tone with your wonderfully matched music. Thank you to the Peace Center's CEO, Megan Reigel, and my colleagues at the Peace Center, who made the production of *David Drake* possible. I am especially indebted to Vaughn Newman Jr. for dancing Dave and bringing him to life. I appreciate Erica Vital-Lazare for taking interest in the early versions of four of my David Drake poems and publishing them in *Red Rock Review*. Thank you to Ellen Westkaemper at the Greenville County Museum of Art for allowing me to view and touch the David Drake pots. This experience both grounded me and transported my work. Thank you to my Peace Voices Poets Starry Walker, Lena Rosemond, and Rayja Fowler, who wrote palpably about David Drake. Thank you to my brother,

Willie Redmond, who was an early reader of and listener to these poems. Ultimately, thank you to my mom, Jeanette Redmond, who shared her stories of picking cotton with me and personalized the South Carolina soil and toil, enabling me to write viscerally. Thank you most importantly to David Drake and all my ancestral relations from South Carolina. *Ashé* to all those who help me right the past. Write it.

From Lynnette Young Overby

I have been fortunate to collaborate with wonderful artists and scholars, students and community partners in creating and sharing the story of David Drake. Their names and work appear throughout this book in the writings, the photographs, the poetry, and the music we see described and displayed. I am forever grateful to be able to illuminate Dave's important story with the help of all of my friends and colleagues. A special thank you to Gabrielle Foreman, Jonathan Green, Ralph Russell, and Glenis Redmond for bringing together research, visual art, poetry, music, and movement to bring to the stage the life of a great man and to make the theatrical production and content for my chapter possible.

Introduction

His Page Was Clay

The Cultural Legacies of Dave the Poet/Potter

P. GABRIELLE FOREMAN

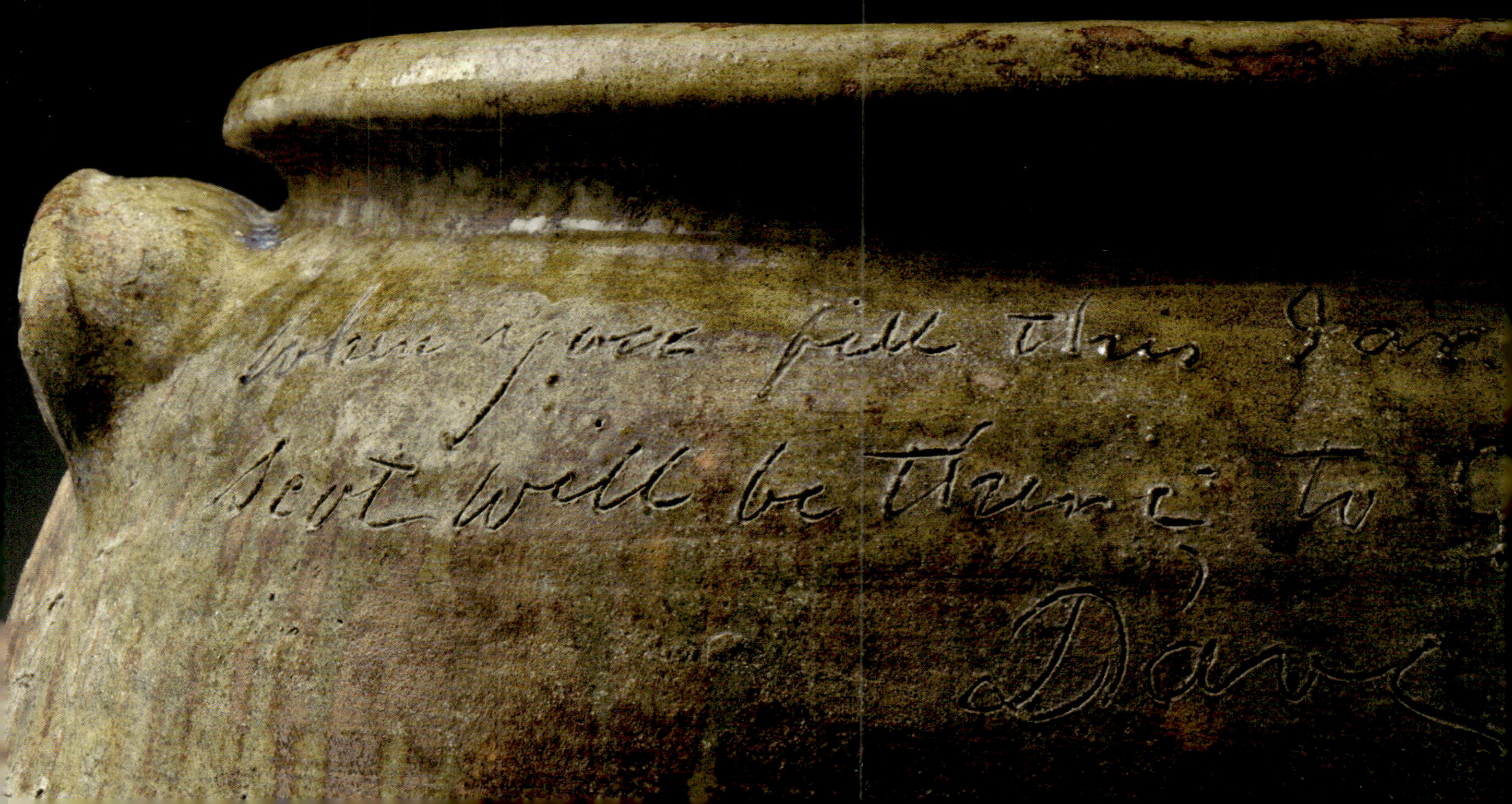

OVERLEAF: Poetic Vessel, "when you fill this Jar with pork or beef," April 21, 1858. David Drake (American, ca. 1801–1870s). Made at Stony Bluff Manufactory. The Metropolitan Museum of Art. Purchase, Ronald S. Kane Bequest, in memory of Berry B. Tracy, 2020.

What does it mean for your art to have more value than your life?

IN FEWER THAN TWO WEEKS during August 1857, "Dave," an artisan who would claim the name David Drake when freedom dawned, threw three enormous ceramic vessels, each incised with couplet verse.[1] He would make hundreds of pots in his lifetime, all while he was bound as much by the enslavers who claimed his life and labor as by South Carolina's red and white kaolin clay.

While enslaved in South Carolina, David Drake made ceramic vessels that now are revered in ways he never was. Although Drake was once considered property himself, his pots—and the verses he composed emblazoned on their sides—can be viewed today in the nation's most vaunted museums. Young people know his story because of the prize-winning children's book *Dave the Potter: Artist, Poet, Slave*. His ceramic vessels have found homes in collections all over the United States, including in cities he must have dreamed about whenever his mind turned north toward freedom. No doubt his dreams were as bold as he was. He signed his pots during an era when few enslaved people could read or write, much less advertise such outlawed skills and escape the lashes meted out as punishment. Like the jars and pots he crafted, his signature was big. Made for everyday use such as storing food, his stoneware vessels are now prized by collectors who count them among the largest and most accomplished pieces of the antebellum era.

This book is a praise song to "Dave the Potter." It is a book about how future generations recover the work of forgotten artistic ancestors and about the role of Black art, poetry, and performance in that remembering. It is a book that claims David Drake not only as one of the nineteenth century's most important ceramicists but also as a Black literary ancestor, a poet whose innovative work is just beginning to find a place among that of early Black writers of verse.[2]

A young Alice Walker once posed an essential and existential question, which echoes throughout this book: "What did it mean for a black woman to be an artist . . . in our great-grandmothers' day? It is a question with an answer cruel enough to stop the blood."[3] This is a question to ask over and again about millions upon millions of enslaved would-be artists, those of any gender, forced to find water in dry places.

David Drake is one of very few artisans and writers who produced surviving work while under enslavers' surveillance and control. He is the only enslaved author, perhaps the only African American in free or slave states and U.S. territories, to create nineteenth-century literature that did not appear in books or pamphlets or newspapers. He used his pots and jars as *pages* as well as storage vessels. This made his work popular in his own time. Still, not until the very end of the twentieth century did David Drake's work enjoy its own major exhibition.[4] The national revival—or rememory—of his work and life took off from there. Not until more than a century after his death could his artistic and cultural relations begin to fully account for the ways his make-a-way-out-of-no-way artistry and poetic innovation had been baton-passed through generations without most Black artists, scholars, or students of history even knowing his name.

Drake incised this lament onto one of his pots: "I wonder where is all my relation." To that searing question, this book answers, "We are your kin. Your legacy includes your cultural descendants as well as your ceramic vessels." Drake's historical presence and artistic mastery have inspired artists who came after him; and these artists have been central in his revival. Indeed, this book emerges from an artistic collaboration that included scholarship, performance, painting, and poetry in memory and celebration of David Drake's legacy. In 2014, Lynnette Young Overby, artistic director of Sharing Our Legacy Theater, and Gabrielle Foreman launched a work on David Drake as part of an ongoing collaboration to bring nineteenth-century Black history to the stage. They continued to work with Glenis Redmond as the project poet; the three were inspired by the work of renowned contemporary artist Jonathan Green on David Drake, a 1998 series that he called *Sir Dave*. This volume builds on the collective creation incubated in that space, bringing the words and art of Drake, Green, and Redmond to a broader public alongside the conversations this collaboration has engendered.

This volume features Green's *Sir Dave* 1998 series, including thirteen paintings and a sculpture that have never been shown or published together before. Green's paintings are saturated with the vibrant colors that enliven Sir Dave's artistic will and expressive determination. Accompanying Green's *Sir Dave* is a cycle of twenty poems by Glenis Redmond created in 2015 for the performance that led to this volume; those poems were inspired by David Drake's poetic vessels and by Green's *Sir Dave*. Sometimes the pieces in Redmond's *All My Relation* are like a poetic juba with Redmond and Drake dancing in the center of the circle. Sometimes Redmond's poetry takes to the floor with Jonathan Green's paintings to do a Charleston step.

In both Green's series and Redmond's poetry, David Drake appears with the people who make up his own community. Green paints his artistic ancestor into a world where he and his talent exist without white oversight, scrutiny, or control. Some canvases are peopled with pots or filled with cotton fields or cemeteries; when they signal loss, it is through cosmological and ceramic traditions brought to new-world shores from West Africa. Likewise, white voices narrate none of the stories Redmond tells. Still, slavery's oppressive power is everywhere. And when Redmond's verses visit Green's more somber scenes, she blankets readers in the ache and longing that bondage brought on, for centuries, as reliable as night coming.

David Drake, Jonathan Green, and Glenis Redmond all hail from South Carolina, though the work and reputations of all three have traveled well beyond their homes. South Carolina has a special claim on Americans of African ancestry in the United States. The state is one of Black America's ground zeros. Over 40 percent of those who were stolen and shipped to these shores before the Revolutionary War came through South Carolina's famous slave ports, and many more were smuggled in even after the horrors of the transatlantic slave trade came to a legal end.[5]

Drake was born in 1801 as the United States rounded the corner into a new century. Over at least four decades, he was held as property by the same number of men in a South Carolina family connected by pottery, blood, and marriage. Dave, as his name appears in early records and on the pots he signed, was loaned or leased to a member of that family, Abner Landrum, when he was in his midtwenties. Landrum had started the *Edgefield Hive*, a local paper, and was an accomplished potter himself.[6] He may himself have taught Drake to read, to write, and to turn a pot, rare skills among the four million enslaved people who had to wait for assurances of their freedom, as Drake did, until the end of the Civil War—and rare among the many millions of others who were born captive and died enslaved, and the much smaller number who liberated themselves or were formally freed before then. Despite his enslavers' regard for his talents, none seemed to think that the fame or wealth he brought them should deliver him from bondage. David Drake's creative success did not bring an effort (however unsuccessful or complex) to secure his freedom, as publication did for some other enslaved poets: Phillis Wheatley in eighteenth-century New England; George Moses Horton, the first Black poet to be published in the South and Drake's contemporary in North Carolina; and Juan Manzano, the poet and author of the only extant slave narrative composed by an enslaved Cuban. David Drake's pots were famous throughout the region in his own lifetime. Yet, when his name appeared in the Edgefield County, South Carolina, voting registry records in 1867, he had been free for just two years. When he was listed as "David Drake, Turner" (another name for a potter) in the 1870 census, the last historical record through which we can trace him, he had been free for only five of the almost seventy years of his life.

South Carolina had been the first U.S. state to outlaw teaching enslaved people to write. State authorities made it clear from as early as 1740 that they claimed the power to set limits on how elite and poor whites alike could employ Black people's chattel labor. Even if the economic benefits accrued overwhelmingly to the enslaving classes, the Black people they claimed as property were not to labor as literate clerks, printers, or managers, but only as unschooled as well as uncompensated workers.[7] Nonetheless, the man who boldly signed "Dave" on the wares he made went about the business of marrying poetry and pottery for more than thirty years, enriching his owners' families rather than his own all the while. Early in the 1800s, the extended white family who would benefit from the bounty of "Dave the Potter's" captive labor founded the Pottersville Stoneware Manufactory, named after the clay-rich district where they lived.[8] He stood out even then. Though for more than a hundred years after his death Drake was relegated to a footnote in anything more than regional craft production, his stoneware vessels were shipped across the region in his own time. As "Dave the Potter," he made a name for himself, for his work, and for those who claimed his labor, life, and creative reputation for themselves.

As an enslaved man in South Carolina, David Drake didn't always work as an artisan; enslaved people, even those who were widely recognized for their craft or expertise, did not choose what kind of work they would do. In 1857, as the South first inched, then galloped, toward war, he emerged from a several-year hiatus, a time during which he seems to have crafted no signed pots at all. Talk of politics was everywhere as he once more turned to his pots, again producing the stoneware vessels that made him famous.[9] It is hard to pinpoint why his artisan work had been put on hold. Perhaps one of the several men who forcibly claimed him, his labor, and his wares thought he had gotten above his station and needed to be reminded of his place. Perhaps a planned rebellion to secure Black freedom in nearby Augusta had local enslavers spooked—including those in whose hands Drake's day-to-day life depended. Perhaps his enslavers had lost some of the people they claimed as property to death or disease and decided that no matter his skills, he must be put to other work. In 1857, those years of unexplained artistic silence ended. Busy at the wheel, Drake began one of his most prodigious periods. He made scores of pots as the country turned to national disputes and court cases that would edge the country closer and closer toward open conflict. As he turned back to pottery and poetry, representatives from South Carolina, indeed from Dave's own Edgefield district, made clear that slavery was more important to them than the nation itself.

Since Drake's 1850s poetry and pots were produced in such a moment of heightened political fervor, we can read his work in the context of debates about Black freedom, white supremacy, and national citizenship. His most poignant words—and for that reason his most well-known verse—are found on some of the deep brown glazed pots he made in August 1857: "I wonder where is all my relation / friendship to all and every nation" he asked on one; "a pretty little Girl, on a virge / Volcaic mountain[s], how they burge," he declared on another. Slavery began with kidnapped people losing family. The history of the Atlantic slave trade and North American enslavement is saturated with that rending, with plaintive wonderings about kin and relations, with generations of grandmothers and aunties and fathers and brothers who mourned pretty little girls and boys they would never see again. During "the history of the antebellum South [that] is the history of two million slave sales," that is, during the same three decades of Drake's bondage that some now refer to as his artistic career, he lost the people he called "my relation" not once, but multiple times. They were sold away not only by the "small"-sale adjustments that enslavers so often made but also by separations en masse.[10] Though the despair and displacement of the slave trade are usually associated with the transatlantic or middle passage, almost one million Black people were transported on the roads, rivers, and railways leading from the upper South to the deeper South and Southwest after Jefferson's Louisiana Purchase in 1803 doubled the size of the United States. These forced separations make up one of the largest forced migrations in history.[11]

David Drake spent all of his recorded life in South Carolina. Why he was left behind when so many of his community were taken to Louisiana with the white Pottersville families who moved there in the 1830s, we may never know. Perhaps it was because the new South Carolina Railroad that ran through Edgefield, where Drake would live for much of his life, soon took his stoneware across the state, and a family member who stayed behind made an offer for him that was too good to turn down. Perhaps a train on that same line had recently severed one of Drake's legs and the trip was too arduous for a one-legged man to make.[12] Though scholars have yet to identify the exact relations between Drake and those with whom he had to part, a woman his age named Eliza and, later, another named Lydia, were surely among them; they may have been connected by more than the bonds of friendship and shared ownership. What we do know for certain is that in the thirty years before the Civil War, half of domestic slave sales destroyed a nuclear family and a quarter destroyed a first marriage.[13] Whether they were left behind or were sold, for enslaved people all but the rarest sale destroyed hard-won and precious family, friendships, and community.

"Dave the Potter" is often remembered or written about as an exceptional and talented, indeed transcendent, artisan who managed to escape the barbarity and limitations slavery placed on the millions it held in its thrall. It's tempting to exceptionalize him because he, himself, was so exceptional. We forget that his art didn't make him any less subject to the privilege and power of those who enslaved him. Enslaved artisans shared a great deal with those who picked cotton all over the South. Though they were skilled workers, they, their parents, friends, lovers, and biological or adopted children were too often terrorized, beaten, abused, and raped; they and their relations could be hired out or separated because of an enslaver's ad/venture or death or debt or whimsy or marriage, just as a field hand's loved ones were. Slavery was not an individual experience; people were embedded in communities. Enslaved artisans worried about their loved ones as much as those who worked in Virginia's to-bacco fields or who cleared swamps and sowed and threshed rice on South Carolina's coastal plantations, as much as those who plowed, weeded, and cut indigo in fetid and fermented plots in South Carolina and Georgia. The making and hauling of clay that an enslaved potter often did was also backbreaking labor. Despite his literacy and years at the wheel, in many ways David Drake shared the fate of so many other enslaved people who, like him, lived their lives under southern slavery. Despite how well his pots sold during his lifetime and despite their placement in lauded national and regional museums today, he had no say in the fates of those he cared about, no way to ensure their safety, education, and physical well-being. Like millions upon millions of others, he was left wondering where his relation/s might be, thinking about a pretty little girl—a sister, daughter, or young woman he loved—on the verge of a volcanic future over which he had little or no control.

Jonathan Green's *Sir Dave*

In 1998, an exhibit titled *I Made This Jar: The Life and Works of the Enslaved African American Potter, Dave* ushered Drake irrevocably from the regional to the national museum world as a master potter. Curated by Jill Beute Koverman, it debuted at the University of South Carolina's McKissick Museum the following year before traveling to Atlanta's High Museum of Art, Detroit's Charles H. Wright Museum of African American History, and Delaware's Winterthur Museum.[14] As one of the most lauded and popular southern painters of his generation, Jonathan Green was invited to contribute paintings that would accompany the exhibit of his artistic predecessor's stoneware pots and jars.

A dozen years earlier, when he first heard about David Drake, Green was already enjoying international success for his vibrant palette and subjects inspired by South Carolina Gullah culture. Art historian Carroll Greene Jr. (who had curated the 1967 exhibit *The Evolution of Afro-American Artists: 1800–1959* with Romare Bearden) had kindled Green's interest by sharing "Dave the Potter's" story. Struck by an absence of Black artistic ancestors that could make twentieth-century Black artists and artisans feel as if they had sprung from dry and shallow soil lacking both rich loam and deep roots, Green explains that "it was almost like rediscovering parts of your history" in a culturally verdant but sparse genealogical art landscape in which "I rarely discov-ered much about. . . African Americans who were artisans." Deeply embedded in his own South Carolina Gullah history, Green was drawn to Drake. So "when I was later approached by the McKissick Museum," Green commented, "I felt that Dave was such an important figure in terms of American arts and crafts that he should be presented in a full body of work."[15] Six of Green's paintings traveled with the *I Made*

This Jar exhibit. Only one was featured in the catalog. The full series, Green's thirteen paintings and the sculpture he created to honor "Sir Dave," hadn't appeared together until we began the collaboration that resulted in this book.[16]

Green's *Sir Dave* recalls the work of Black painters who precede him. With his use of color, his visual celebration of Black women, a cream to coffee range of Blackness's hues, and a commitment to documenting place and community, Green in some ways recalls Archibald Motley.[17] Yet Green's series is in conversation with no artist more than it is with the work of the painter he calls a mentor, Jacob Lawrence. Lawrence's 1938 *Toussaint L'Ouverture* paintings mark his first use of the series format that would become Lawrence's signature. It is followed closely by two additional series that relay the stories of those who also fought against slave power and won: Lawrence's now famous work on Frederick Douglass and Harriet Tubman. Green's *Sir Dave* narrative series recalls Lawrence's multipanel visual narration of the lives of enslaved rebels. Green has also memorialized Robert Smalls, who like Drake had once been enslaved in South Carolina. Smalls later was elected a U.S. congressman, after sailing himself, his wife, his children, and thirteen more to freedom by commandeering a steamer and sailing past Confederate forts and checkpoints. In Green's paintings' "historical sequence that presents a dramatic biography," to borrow from Ellen Harkins Wheat's description of Lawrence's epic narrative series, Green's *Sir Dave* work echoes Lawrence's offering of Black self-determination.[18] In its choice of subjects, Green's art has been called a committed display of love for the land and people of South Carolina.[19] Green's paintings are testimony, "each story [his work tells] is always in dialogue with the mutual experience of the community."[20] His paintings depict a community whose histories of resilience reverberate through both place and time.

Jonathan Green's *Sir Dave* is a variation on visual storytelling styles exhibited by earlier Black artists. Lawrence's thirty-two small panels on Frederick Douglass, for example, are divided into three sections: the Slave, the Fugitive, and the Free Man. Carefully numbered, they march triumphantly toward freedom. As Green depicts David Drake's life, he creates a narrative that is less linear and certain, allowing room for readers to imagine the unimaginable, its alternatives, and the im/possibilities that characterized the experience of slavery.[21] Like Lawrence's *Frederick Douglass* series, the paintings that comprise *Sir Dave* can be said to fall into three groupings—those that narrate the artisan's biography, those that showcase his communities' relation to (his) pottery, and those that are peopled only by pots or shards. Though not numbered, the works that make up *Sir Dave* suggest a loose arc: a genesis in the painting *Young Dave*, and an ending, or at least the certainty of endings, in paintings called *From Earth We Came*, *From Earth to Earth*, and *Vessels for Taking Us Home*. Green's medium, dimensions, and use of narrative serve as close cousins to Jacob Lawrence's. Green's panels speak to each other, to David Drake's work, and to history in deeply nuanced and complex ways.

Though Drake's life coincided with the United States' relentless expansion, the spread of slavery, and South Carolina's leading role as a defender of the peculiar institution, Jonathan Green's colorful outdoor scenes display an absence of whites, whips, or signs of compulsion that granted slavery its force. Green grounds his visual storytelling in Black vitality and wholeness, reminding viewers of how unnatural slavery was by situating Sir Dave in the midst of Black family and community. Green's focus is on Black joy and celebration (of family, of place, of work as creative space) that existed in spite of slavery's relentless brutalities. Expelling whites from his series performs a certain exorcising power that affirms alternative Black realities and relations between enslaved people.[22] *Sir Dave* depicts the humanity, creativity, and agency that slipped through, above, or below enslavers' domination to find expression through the Black feet that made the potter's wheel turn and the fingers that made the fiddle or the quill sing—if only, sometimes, in the moment the artist chooses to imagine. Borrowing from the oral and living histories of the South Carolina communities out of which he sprang, Green emphasizes the healing dimensions of artistic recovery.[23]

Glenis Redmond's *All My Relation*

Once introduced to David Drake's history, pottery, and poetry, South Carolina writer Glenis Redmond, like Jonathan Green, found artistic and historical connections to this cultural ancestor almost everywhere. As an award-winning poet and teaching artist, Redmond describes herself as a spiritual or imagination activist.[24] In *All My Relation: Poems for David Drake*, Redmond's poetry cycle of twenty pieces, the poems both call and respond to David Drake and Jonathan Green, whom she might call her cultural relation/s. Like the verse in her previous volumes, *What My Hand Say* (2016), *Under the Sun* (2008), and *Backbone* (2000), her David Drake poems affirm Redmond's penchant for the past, for all things old, as she puts it. She calls on readers to attend to the elders and to "listen with more than our ears," especially to those whose shattered pasts and lives offer lessons in the universality of Black survival.[25] "Where does history go when it dies?" she asks in the poem "Footnotes" from *Under the Sun*:

> When corn cribs and makeshift houses
> no longer riddle the mountain slopes
> and forty years of hands culling
> Comfrey into a healing balm
> along with Gospel Songs cease.
> This silent edge is where I live
> filled with heartache remembering history
> and where it goes without a foothold.[26]

Redmond finds the toehold crevices that artists and historians before her have carved in hard stone, and climbing, she describes the vista she sees.

In the poems in *All My Relation*, Redmond shifts her focus from the elders to the ancestors. She joins a cohort of Black poets who choose to embody once enslaved historical figures who fled or fought for their freedom. As poetry scholar Howard Rambsy points out, "the large number and wide circulation of persona and tribute poems featuring Harriet Tubman and Frederick Douglass alone suggest a tacit agreement among poets and editors of keeping the spirits of these beloved fugitive slaves on the minds of the living."[27] Rambsy's observation extends to visual artists, collectors, and curators as well.

In Redmond's *All My Relation*, as in Green's *Sir Dave*, no whites speak or appear, though the shadows and structures of the world enslavers made are everywhere apparent. Still, readers don't encounter the world this poetry paints from the point of view of those who bought, separated, violated, and extracted work from enslaved subjects. Redmond's persona poems highlight Black points of view and everyday, as well as extraordinary, Black creativity and love as forms of resistance. She sees them expressed in settings like slavery, or afterward, in "that ingrown South / where revolution never happened, / not even now."[28] Redmond understands that sometimes "the revolution / is in staying alive."[29] So she coaxes back almost dead things and all-but-forgotten stories from dry ground. Glenis Redmond makes words bloom as she brings gardens of untended history back to life in verse.

Many of the pieces in Redmond's *All My Relation* are persona poems; they share the stories and thoughts of a person, often a historical figure, embodying that figure's own voice to create a connection, even an intimacy, with readers.[30] In a persona poem, "the writer eliminates the middleman and actually becomes the subject of his or her poem. The voice is both immediate and immediately engaging," as poet Patricia Smith explains.[31] Redmond is one of a cohort of contemporary Black poets who "often employ personae to create more fully fleshed out characters, and they frequently include explorations of the past and various ties of kinship or community."[32] By adopting a persona, by jumping into another's time, mind, and skin, poets don't need to speak for their subjects because they speak *as* them.[33]

Redmond opens *All My Relation* with two persona poems inspired by Jonathan Green's painting *Young Dave*. In the opening poem, her Dave reflects on the importance of family and maternal elders, a theme that both Green and Redmond revisit regularly in their larger bodies of work. Redmond launches this first piece by weaving into words what Green puts on the canvas; both reach beyond the little—the nothing, really—that history has recorded about Dave's childhood. Both recreate what has been erased: that David Drake was once a child, and before that a newborn, that he had a mother who almost certainly held him in her arms. Redmond gives voice to other things she "knows": that before they were separated by force or death, young Dave was loved by a woman who, like countless mothers of enslaved children, endured a cutting away of kin that was so historically casual, so violently a matter of course, that it became the norm for hundreds and hundreds of years.

Redmond gives life to Drake's undocumented beginnings in this poem, and she calls it "What I Knows." As readers, we can imagine that title being voiced by either the poet or by Dave, the poem's subject. But it is the poem's speaker who says: "[my mama's] love be like butter churned," "be like feeding Guineas / and Carolina Reds. Constant. / Ise from slave cabins and shackles / but feel free when I'm held by her." Redmond references Green's *Young Dave* painting directly as she also expands its orbit. Guineas and Carolina Reds are the names of the kinds of poultry pecking happily in the painting's foreground. They are also the ground from which Drake and his mother may have sprung, Carolina's red dirt, and also "Guinea," one of the regions of Africa that slavers raided to people South Carolina and Georgia with chattel and artisan laborers.[34]

All My Relation includes poems linked to every one of Jonathan Green's *Sir Dave* paintings. Centering Jonathan Green alongside David Drake creates an artistic genealogy of inspiration and response between three Black artistic lives and three sets of work. This complexity—this added dimensionality—unsettles narrative timeframes and storytelling sequences, making them anything but linear or straightforwardly referential. With scores of pots, paintings, and poems in conversation with and through each other, these shards of information, housed in images, objects, forms, and language, reflect the unconventional historical tools and the nonlinear, multidimensional methods sometimes required to resurrect the lives of enslaved people whose existence was never meant to be recorded and remembered on any but enslavers' terms.

This book is a time-traveling, ancestral, and ekphrastic call-and-response between artists separated by centuries, as well as a tribute to the brilliance and resilience of enslaved creatives who survived when they, much like the products they produced, were likely to be auctioned and sold. In the book's title and throughout this volume, David Drake sometimes appears as "Dave," because he asserted his artistry and self-ownership by signing that name so boldly, the large and flourished letters incised into his pots in his own accomplished hand. Still, however much pride and fame may be associated with the moniker "Dave the Potter," the tradition of calling grown African Americans only by their first names has a long and insidious history; for example, another of Drake's popular names is "Dave the Slave." Naming is often a tool of racial supremacy, one that denies Black people both respect and dignity and one that also erases or denies us power, genealogy, and family connections. It is for that reason that

Jonathan Green calls his series *Sir Dave*, challenging the casual, first-name moniker used disrespectfully over generations. Green's rechristening echoes the practice of formally naming Black boys "Sir" to ensure they receive the respect they were otherwise routinely denied. Green's knighting stakes a claim to artistic royalty.

This volume also uses David Drake's full name, which first appears in historical records in 1870. That U.S. census marks the first time that Drake, alongside some four million other formerly enslaved Black Americans, was officially counted as a full citizen of the United States. We have no way of knowing when David Drake adopted that name or in what circumstances he used it. Yet, we can follow the best practices of historians of slavery and use the full names of enslaved people whose names and genealogies were so often casually ignored and historically erased. Contributors to this book try to strike a balance by honoring the cultural ancestor and innovator this volume showcases in every way we call his name.

Praise Songs emerges from a decade-long collaboration between a renowned scholar of dance education, a literary historian, and a poet, who all share a commitment to resurrecting Black history through poetry and performance. Our work on David Drake emerged when as a trio, Lynnette Young Overby, Gabrielle Foreman, and Glenis Redmond met to celebrate our first work, a now widely taught piece on the author known as the first Black woman novelist: the spirited entrepreneur Harriet E. Wilson.[35] When Lynnette asked what project we should tackle next, Gabrielle proposed the work of David Drake and suggested adding Jonathan Green and his series to the partnership. Although Glenis hadn't known about Drake, she did know Jonathan, who brought the graciousness, historical expertise, and enthusiasm to this project that marks his many collaborations with artists and scholars. Lynnette then approached Vincent Thomas of *VTDance* to join the company as Dave the Potter. Vincent was thrilled not only to learn of David Drake but also to discover that though separated by centuries, the two men lived overlapping lives in Edgefield, South Carolina; the dancer was born and raised in the very county seat where the artist he would embody lived so much of his life. Dancing Dave in later performances, Vaughn Newman Jr. infused his spirit and talent throughout the entire company in performances at the Peace Center in Greenville, South Carolina.

Working with Lynnette Young Overby's Sharing Our Legacy Dance Theater (SOL), the poet, historian, and artistic director have continued to work together. Performances about the Colored Conventions, the nineteenth-century movement for educational justice, economic equality, and voting and political rights, as well as about the intrepid Mary Ann Shadd Cary, the first Black woman newspaper editor and later the first Black woman law student in North America, followed from work on Harriet E. Wilson and on David Drake. The trio is currently embarking on work about activist Frances E. W. Harper, the prolific novelist and the most popular Black poet before

Paul Laurence Dunbar. Composer Ralph Russell joined in this ongoing collaboration starting with the score for Dave the Potter performances. Pages from his score are featured throughout the book. Under Lynnette Young Overby's direction and with the members of Sharing Our Legacy, the group has toured internationally and created educational components and a curriculum to accompany the performance. This book seeks to build on this ongoing collaboration and to reclaim David Drake as a poetic innovator as well as a master in ceramic arts. It also reaffirms the place of Black arts and culture as guardians of Black histories, which official records kept and curated by the powerful often reflect in mere slivers and shards.

Launching *Praise Songs* with a foreword is Kwame Dawes, griot of the Black Diaspora and award-winning author of more than a dozen books of poetry and nonfiction; his own poem in honor of David Drake is included as well. What follows after this introduction is the most complete and comprehensive collection of Drake's verses to date. This volume reclaims Drake's name as one that should be called alongside enslaved writers such as Phillis Wheatley and George Moses Horton. It joins work on Drake by literary critic Michael Chaney, *Where Is All My Relation? The Poetics of Dave the Potter*, and by Kevin Young, one of the leading poets and curators/cultural arts leaders of the twenty-first century, who first anthologized a selection of Drake's poetry in his magisterial *African American Poetry: 250 Years of Struggle and Song* (2020).[36] The verses included here have been rigorously checked to correct for the frequently casual transcriptions of his poetry that routinely appear in the newspaper pieces, museum websites, catalogs, and scholarly articles that mention or discuss his work. The poetry featured here builds on the impressive list of Drake's poetry recorded by Leonard Todd in *Carolina Clay: The Life and Legend of the Slave Potter Dave* (2008).[37] *Praise Songs* includes newly found poems that have been recovered since Todd's 2008 book helped build interest in Drake's life and work. And it has updated the information on where Drake's poetic pottery can be found in the wake of a renewed interest in his work by museums across the United States.

After the section including David Drake's extant poetic work, readers will find Jonathan Green's *Sir Dave* series, which appears side by side with Glenis Redmond's *All My Relation* cycle (with a one-poem cameo by Gabrielle Foreman). That work is introduced by two short pieces by Foreman, the editor, meant to allow readers to enjoy a tour of the paintings and poetry that are presented together, almost as if readers were in a museum with their own personal docent. Rounding out this section is a lively conversation about cultural and generational connections and connectedness featuring Redmond, Green, and Foreman.

The final section of *Praise Songs* includes three essays in different styles. The first is a personal essay by Redmond that complements her poems. In it, she digs deeper into the rich loam and South Carolina ancestry out of which her own artistry has grown and that ground Jonathan Green's and David Drake's work as well. Redmond's piece shares her own family and artistic journey as she meditates on the concepts of home and place and reflects on Drake and Green, her artistic interlocutors. Redmond's essay also provides more context for the collaboration out of which her poems sprang. The essay by Lynnette Young Overby narrates the student-centered, arts-based research she incorporates into performance as a way to share forgotten Black history. As an internationally renowned professor of dance education known for her arts advocacy and leadership in university community partnerships, Overby creates ongoing collaborations among scholars, composers, writers, and performers. Overby's focus is on the *engagement* that leads her productions to include a range of performers, from professional dancers (with their own companies and studios) to schoolchildren and community elders. Her goal is to create a process steeped in both research and acknowledgment of difficult social issues, one, as she puts it in this volume, "that provides audiences, contributors, and performers with the opportunity to experience place, time, and situation through their visual, auditory, and kinesthetic senses."

The volume also includes a scholarly essay by its editor, Gabrielle Foreman, who served as the David Drake performance's research director. In it, Foreman positions Black visual and performance artists as cultural historians who resurrect ancestors left for dead and kept in unmarked graves by traditional archives and art establishments. Foreman reads Green's painting *Edgefield* in relationship to the enslaved labor that fueled southern economies and to African American cultural traditions that bound Black communities to each other, on the one hand, and in conversation with Carrie Mae Weems's *Sea Island* series (1992), on the other. Alongside the editor's conversation with Green and Redmond, the essays by Redmond, Overby, and Foreman offer additional insight into contemporary artists who have chosen David Drake as their subject; into Drake's historical, cultural, and artistic contexts; and into the performance that brought them all together. Evie Shockley, one of the most accomplished poets and scholars of her generation, graces *Praise Songs* with an afterword.

David Drake is this book's subject, but the volume's spirit extends out to all of the ancestor artists whose names we do not know, those who not only practiced, but passed on, their creativity despite the extinguishing efforts to quell their power and beauty. At long last, David Drake has been recognized as one of the most important potters of the nineteenth century. As the only known African American writer to transform clay into his page and to do so at a time when literacy was outlawed for generations of Black people enslaved across time and place, David Drake is celebrated here as one of the nineteenth century's most innovative poets.

If Black artists and poets have managed to make their visions and voices heard in North America, early progenitors too often had to do so without peers or predecessors. Those who followed them had to do so without a sense of continuity that builds a genealogy of artistic belonging, without the knowledge of recognized ancestors whose existence would relay: *You can do it, I did.* Still, from the beginning, Black artists and poets have recognized each other and held up each other's accomplishments. Against all odds, Phillis Wheatley found a peer in Scipio Moorhead, a portrait painter, when they were both enslaved in Boston. Wheatley celebrated her colleague in verse and Moorhead memorialized the poet, quill in hand, in the image that graced the cover of her famous *Poems on Various Subjects* (1773). In her poem "To S. M. a young African Painter, on Seeing His Works," Wheatley grants her enslaved colleague the stature of the esteemed elite professionals and British earls to whom her poems were often dedicated. David Drake and other enslaved artisans rarely enjoyed that public elevation from their peers. How did Black people keep such creativity alive "year after year and century after century, when for most of the years black people have been in America, it was a punishable crime for a black person to read or write? And the freedom to paint, to sculpt, to expand the mind with action did not exist," as contemporary writer Alice Walker once asked.[38]

Focused on survival, and so often surveilled, David Drake and other enslaved artists and artisans rarely received public elevation from their peers in the spirit of Wheatley and Moorhead. More than fifty years later and almost a thousand miles south, David Drake started creating and signing his name on his pots around the same time that Daniel Payne, a nominally free Black South Carolinian, was being run out of Charleston for teaching young Black schoolchildren to read and write.[39] The laws that outlawed Black literacy and consigned generations of enslaved sculptors, potters, novelists, poets, and painters to the mind-numbing labor of tobacco, rice, and cotton cultivation—and then the practices that relegated Black artists to Jim Crow's kitchens, fields, and factories for a hundred years more—makes our make-a-way-out-of-no-way cultural forebearers that much more rare and precious. Centuries removed, Jonathan Green and Glenis Redmond both came of age without knowing that they were connected to such a deep genealogy of Black artistic genius in art and verse. Green and Redmond were good and grown, as the old folks say, before they knew David Drake's name. As the first fine artist of Gullah ancestry trained at the School of the Art Institute of Chicago, and as a Kennedy Center teaching artist and poet, Green and Redmond no doubt also wondered, "Where is all my relation?" As cultural kin midwifed into life without knowing about the richness of those who came before, they nonetheless built on the base their South Carolina progenitor left behind.

The art and poetry, conversation, and essays in this volume seek to gather shattered, scattered pieces of Black history and put them back together again.[40] If the history of enslaved ancestors exists mostly in shards, like broken pot pieces that are all but impossible to reconstruct, this book asks how art, culture, and performance can play a part in preserving Black narratives of the past that have been largely discarded, lost, or poorly preserved. *Praise Songs for Dave the Potter* offers a resurrectionary artistic and historical practice that helps lift just one dismissed, disregarded, and disremembered cultural ancestor from an unmarked grave. When faced with a history that has been purposely forgotten and disremembered, that is, dismembered and disrespected, this book centers the role of the arts in historical *recovery*, when that word carries not only resonances of historical reassembly but also of cultural healing.[41] In the face of David Drake's legacy as one example of often faint archival traces of Black pasts, how do artists and poets and performers take their place as historians' siblings, or at least as those close cousins who lived right up the street? Like Glenis Redmond and Jonathan Green, history's poetic griots and visual bards not only preserve the stories that make up historical memory but also weave scraps, patches, and anecdotes into the larger quilt of national consciousness. They play a role in urging museums, archives, and scholars—that is, the more recognized preservers and record keepers of cultural and national memory—to honor a fuller and more inclusive sense of the past's connections to the present we live in today. In doing so, they join others in singing praise songs to the past that keep Black history alive.

NOTES

1 See Foreman, "1857," and also her forthcoming book *The Art of DisMemory*.

2 This book is indebted to and builds on the work of Michael A. Chaney. Gabrielle Foreman was first introduced to David Drake's work during Chaney's stunning 2007 talk at a Duke University symposium of authors who would contribute to the volume *Pictures and Progress: Early Photography and the Making of African American Identity*, edited by Maurice O. Wallace and Shawn Michelle Smith. Chaney later invited Foreman to write a piece for his *Where Is All My Relation? The Poetics of Dave the Potter* (2018). With its innovative format featuring literary critics' longer essays interspersed by shorter pieces on Drake's verse, Chaney's book turned scholarly attention to David Drake's writing.

3 Walker, "In Search of Our Mother's Gardens," 402.

4 Curated by Jill Beute Koverman, after its opening at the McKissick, the exhibit traveled to the High Museum of Art (May 16–July 31, 1999), the Charles H. Wright Museum (October 9, 1999–January 2, 2000), and Winterthur (February 5–June 25, 2000). The catalog was influential and the exhibit catapulted David Drake, then commonly referred to as "Dave the Potter," beyond the notice of the regional collectors and museums who had previously known and valued his unique contributions and relaunched national interest in his work. Koverman, *I Made This Jar*.

5 In the three years that preceded the 1808 prohibition of the slave trade, enslavers rushed to deliver some forty thousand captive Africans to Charleston. Quoting Higgins, Michael Angelo Gomez reminds us that South Carolina was so central to the transatlantic trade that one out of every four ancestors in the current Black American population "passed through the colonial port of Charleston." Gomez, *Exchanging Our Country Marks*, 23. Also see Stodghill, "In Charleston, Coming to Terms with the Past."

6 While Drake worked there, the *Hive* was deeply embroiled in roiling debates about states' rights and early succession. The Library of Congress *Chronicling America* entry lists the *Hive*'s run as between 1827 and 1829 then adds that it "Began in 1827. Ceased in 1829?" In *Carolina Clay*, however, author Leonard Todd includes an image of the November 26, 1830, edition and explains that he has examined a bound set in private hands. The last column he refers to is in January 1831. Todd, *Carolina Clay*, 48 and 57.

7 From the South Carolina Act of 1740: "Whereas, the having slaves taught to write, or suffering them to be employed in writing, may be attended with great inconveniences; Be it enacted, that all and every person and persons whatsoever, who shall hereafter teach or cause any slave or slaves to be taught to write, or shall use or employ any slave as a scribe, in any manner of writing whatsoever, hereafter taught to write, every such person or persons shall, for every such offense, forfeit the sum of one hundred pounds, current money" (from the PBS website *Thirteen*). South Carolina also prohibited free Blacks from reading and writing. See, for example, Williams, *Self-Taught*, 400–401. The 1740 law was in response to the Stono rebellion, one of the largest of the colonial period.

8 Pottersville Stoneware Manufactory helped establish Edgefield as a "cultural hearth" and "core area" for the diffusion of alkaline-glazed stoneware for the entire South. "The presence of African-American [and African] slaves in Edgefield District stoneware factories was perhaps the single most important influence on stoneware production in the area." See Baldwin, *Great and Noble Jar*, 2 and 71. Todd, *Carolina Clay*, 19–23.

9 For more on David Drake's poetry, a close reading of his 1857 pots as political commentary in the context of the *Dred Scott* decision, and on Edgefield's centrality in Charles Sumner's violent beating by South Carolina congressman Preston Brooks on the Senate floor, again see Foreman, "1857."

10 Johnson, *Soul by Soul*, 17. When Drake was in his late thirties, the man who then claimed him as property left Pottersville and headed for Louisiana with a seven-family caravan that included a man who had previously enslaved Dave for almost two decades. Theirs was part of a mass movement that relocated an estimated 288,000 enslaved people from the upper South to the lower Southwest in the 1830s. See Johnson, *Soul by Soul*, 5. Williams, *Self-Taught*, 12.

11 This number reflects smaller scale sales before 1803 as well, encompassing the time between "the Constitution and the Civil War." See Johnson, *Soul by Soul*, 5.

12 See Todd, *Carolina Clay*, for comprehensive information on the Landrums, from whom (through the Lewis Miles line) Todd is a direct descendent. He and Jill Beute Koverman document the relocation to Mt. Lebanon, Louisiana. Todd, *Carolina Clay*, 74–78; Koverman, "The Ceramic Works of David Drake," 86.

13 Johnson, *Soul by Soul*, 19. Johnson is speaking "of the two thirds of a million interstate sales made by the traders in the decades before the Civil War." Drake's sale reflects these historical forced separations. He was transferred or sold to a local family member while others in his enslaved community became forced migrants.

14 See note 4 for dates at the High, the Wright Museum, and Winterthur.

15 Poutasse, "Jonathan Green's Canvases Bring Dave the Potter to Life," 13. Terry and Thelma Harris of the Thelma Harris gallery note that *Footnote*, the series's only sculpture, didn't accompany the tour. Visit with collectors, February 27, 2014. Now in museums and in private collections, *Sir Dave's* thirteen paintings and single sculptural piece have never been exhibited together.

16 Poutasse, "Jonathan Green's Canvases Bring Dave the Potter to Life." Among the six that were exhibited were *Marshland Passage*, *Sir Dave*, *Dave the Potter*, and *Dave's Market*.

17 There are differences in their work of course; Motley is celebrated for his forward-looking urban modernism, Green for his preservation of Gullah culture.

18 Wheat, *Jacob Lawrence*, 15. She is referring to the Douglass and Tubman series Lawrence painted between 1938 and 1940 and writes in the plural.

19 Conroy, foreword to *In Gullah Images*, 7.

20 Hartfield, "Gathering Light in the Gray City," 24.

21 When talking about readers' role in meaning-making in relationship to poetry, Natasha Sajé's extension of Roland Barthes and his discussion of readerly and writerly texts is useful. As she puts it, Barthes insists that "the goal of literary work (of literature as work) is to make the reader no longer a consumer, but a producer of the text" (*S/Z*, 4), as quoted in Sajé, "Dynamic Design," 149–150.

22 Green conceives of "representation in art as a proxy for their desired representation" in historical and political memory, to build on Ivy Wilson. See Wilson, *Specters of Democracy*, 7. Wilson's "project interrogates the ways in which antebellum African Americans conceived of representation in art as a proxy for their desired representation in politics."

23 Copeland and Thompson, "Perpetual Returns," 2.

24 As a teaching artist with the South Carolina Arts Commission, the Kennedy Center, the Peace Center, and the State Theater New Jersey, and also with the Lloyd agency, Redmond has traveled all over North America. See http://www.glenisredmond.com/activist/.

25 This sentence draws from Redmond's poem for her grandmother, "She, for Katie Latimore's Birthday, 101."

26 Redmond, *Under the Sun*, 83.

27 Rambsy, "Catching Holy Ghosts," 551.

28 "She, for Katie Latimore's Birthday, 101," in Redmond, *Under the Sun*. The title of this poem points us to lessons learned (in college introductory classes) as well as the wisdom of the elders, as in "Life Lessons 101."

29 "She, for Katie Latimore's Birthday, 101," in Redmond, *Under the Sun*.

30 See, for example, Hazelton, "Teaching the Persona Poem." "Persona is also a very intimate form of poetry. In a persona poem, a writer often speaks directly to readers and, in doing so, forges an almost interpersonal relationship with them. It whispers in their ears or grabs them by the shoulders."

31 Smith, "Persona Poetry," 71.

32 Dungy, "In Others' Voices," 16, as quoted in Rambsy, "Catching Holy Ghosts," 550. Some include: "Opal Palmer Adisa, Elizabeth Alexander, Alvin Aubert, Lucille Clifton, Lance Jeffers, Gayl Jones, Quraysh Ali Lansana, Naomi Long Madgett, Thylias Moss, Tim Seibles, Evie Shockley, Frank X. Walker, and Jerry W. Ward Jr.," as well as Marilyn Nelson, Tyehimba Jess, and others (553).

33 Smith, "Persona Poetry," 71.

34 Though there is an imprecise connection between what enslavers called "Guinea" (very generally) and those raided from Sierra Leone specifically, those from Sierra Leone, or larger "Guinea," were highly valued because they were very knowledgeable about rice, indigo, and cotton. Michael Angelo Gomez, *Exchanging Our Country Marks*, 103–104.

35 The video of the production is called "Contemporary Dance: Sketches (The Life of Harriet E. Wilson in Dance, Poetry, and Music)" and is easily found on YouTube at https://www.youtube.com/watch?v=RJgWgL9Zb4A. Also see the Penguin Classics edition of Wilson, *Our Nig*.

36 Poet, curator, and cultural critic Kevin Young is among the first to include Drake in a poetry anthology. Young, *African American Poetry*, 26–27. Young also discusses "Dave the Slave,"

another name Drake has been called by, in Young's *The Grey Album*, 3 and 83. Accompanying blogs and pieces on Drake as a writer have followed. See, for example, "In Pictures."

37 See Todd, *Carolina Clay*, 229–251. I thank Leonard Todd for his generosity on visits to Edgefield and for connecting me to those who have located new verses. That appreciation was augmented after months of research to check accuracy, when Arline Wilson, then an advanced graduate student at University of Delaware, worked with me to confirm that Todd's work was the best transcription not only of Drake's words but of the punctuation he inscribed on 150-year-old to almost 200-year-old pots. Todd has graciously allowed me to use his list as the foundation for what appears in this volume.

38 Walker, "In Search of Our Mother's Gardens," 402.

39 Strobert, *Daniel Alexander Payne*, 15.

40 Many readers will hear echoes of one of the most famous songs in the gospel canon, "The Potter's House," by Gospel Hall of Famer Tramaine Hawkins. It's based on Jeremiah 18:1–6. The refrain ends, "The potter wants to put you back together again."

41 For more considerations of this question, and on the term *disremembered*, see Gabrielle Foreman's forthcoming book about Black artists' role as cultural historians of slavery, *The Art of DisMemory*.

David Drake Verses

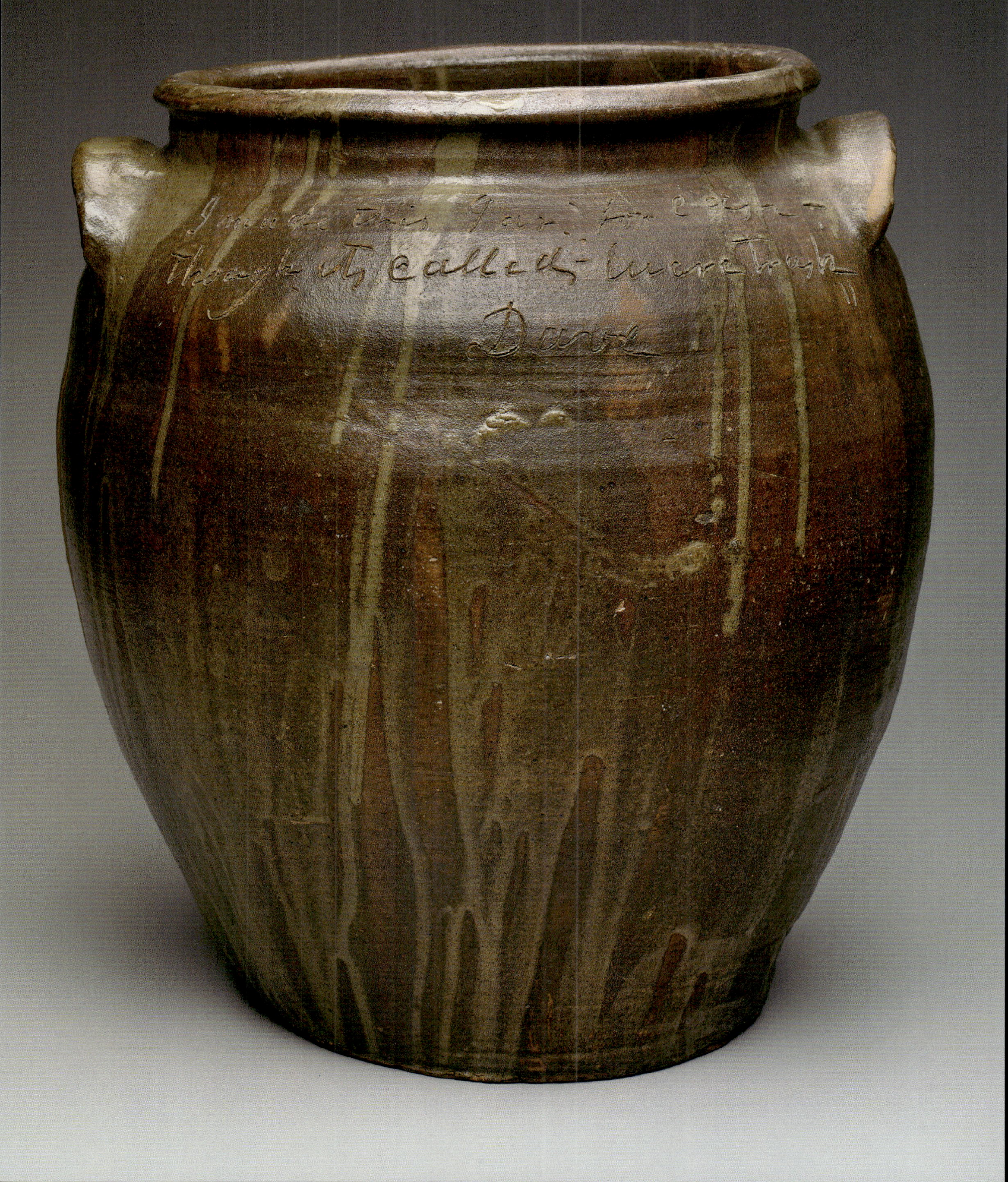

OVERLEAF: Poetic Vessel, "I made this Jar = for cash —," August 22, 1857. David Drake. Photograph © 2022 Museum of Fine Arts, Boston.

TRANSLATING DAVID DRAKE'S POETRY from clay to page is not straightforward. Because his reputation is based on his status as a master potter, those who write about him haven't always been careful about how his inscriptions appear on the page. Different versions of Drake's verse abound. Scholars, museums, and academic centers alike routinely publish casual renditions of his verse. Like the poetry of his contemporary Emily Dickinson, his verse has been silently "corrected." In catalogs and collections, in essays and online, it often appears without the dashes, slashes, capitalization, apostrophes, and other stray marks that characterize the work he incised on the vessels he made.

This section allows readers to engage more deeply with the writing of one of the most innovative early African American poets—the only Black author we know whose surviving writing never appears in print or paper. When we focus on Drake's inscriptions as poetry incised on his massive and masterful pots, rather than as decoration, readers are more attuned to his rhetorical nuances, the small things that make a difference in the potential meanings of Drake's writing. This section seeks to offer an expanded and careful accounting of David Drake's verse—a term that itself lacks clear definition.

What follows here is the most complete list of David Drake's verse to date. It builds on the thorough compilation of inscriptions Leonard Todd included in his 2008 biography *Carolina Clay: The Life and Legend of the Slave Potter Dave*. In this section, readers will also find additional works. They appear alongside emendations to poems that have appeared in other places, including word changes, about twenty punctuation changes, and several line changes, including an addition of lines to a poem previously believed to be a couplet.

The enormous recent interest in David Drake's stoneware and story has resulted in significant shifts in where his pots are located. This section on Drake's poetry also provides the most up to date listing of where his pots are currently held. Drake's vessels have been traveling and changing hands, landing in museums across the country. The Greenville County of Museum of Art in South Carolina has amassed the largest collection of Drake's work. His pots are selling for record amounts (auctioned in settings where they are described, unironically, as having "crossed the block"). In 2020, one of his earliest poetic pots—"catination"—set a new purchase-price high, topping a record figure set only six months earlier; though the auction estimate was $40,000 to $60,000, it sold for $369,000 and moved from a private collection in Florida to the de Young Fine Arts Museum of San Francisco. Just months later, in 2021, one of the largest of Drake's known poetic vessels, a twenty-five-gallon vessel that required four handles to carry it, sold for a breathtaking $1.5 million to the Crystal Bridges Museum of American Art in Bentonville, Arkansas. The vessels of this master potter and poet are now housed in museums of fine art and are regarded as national treasures.

It's worth highlighting the process of comparison and confirmation that was used to decide upon the versions of Drake's verse that are included in this volume. The first step was to compare the major compilations that include his inscriptions. Researchers Arline Wilson and Darlea Dominelli then created a spreadsheet that accounted for the many discrepancies in spelling, spacing, punctuation, wording, and markings. When we found inconsistencies, we contacted the museums, repositories, and private collections that housed the pots. We also consulted any images we could find online that might help to resolve irregularities. When the inscriptions in *Carolina Clay* displayed differences with the holders of the original vessels whom we contacted, we corrected for those rare inaccuracies. Curators helped to verify inscriptions, shared images, and consulted the pots themselves. This was a collective effort.

Though a great deal of careful research has gone into creating this updated compilation, it is important to call attention to all the aspects of Drake's innovation that are lost in the translation from pot to page. Some of Drake's verse remains hard to decipher even when examining it closely. Sometimes it's difficult to agree upon a transcription with any certainty when it is incised on alkaline glaze stoneware made before the Civil War. What is lost in every instance is that Drake carved his poetry into three-dimensional ceramic objects that here appear in standardized print in black and white. When looking at this verse in its original form on vessels made to be used (that can also be seen in the round), *readers* are simultaneously *viewers* of Drake's verse. Focusing on the poetry he incised on the pots and jars he made calls for viewers to consider spacing, size, depth, dimension, glaze, and color in ways that are flattened by print technologies. Presented in print, David Drake's verse loses much of its idiosyncratic originality in the move between the possibilities of clay and the limits of the page.

David Drake was born before the transatlantic trade in captive Africans was outlawed in 1808; he carved verse on the shoulders of brown-glazed pots at a time when enslaved people's brown bodies were branded and marked with regularity. Pottery is often spoken about in anthropomorphic terms. Its rim is called a lip; its base a foot; the slope of its convex shape curving into what is called the pot's body or shoulder or belly. Drake's poems on pots take on a depth that isn't evident when they jump to the page, where they lose much of the historical, material, and tactile associations that make his work so innovative and evocative.

Though Drake's many couplets are recognizable as verse, it's worth highlighting that there are a few inscriptions included here that many would not consider poetry. Other lines are forms of literary irony: "Cash Wanted," promulgated by an enslaved artisan whom the law outlawed from participating in a formal economy, for example. Likewise, "Lm says this handle will crack" is an assertion of expertise and dismissal; it's a proclamation of artistic mastery over Lewis Miles, the Lm on the pot, who was known as Drake's "master." Viewers of the intact pot chuckle that Drake's boast has survived the test of time. That's poetic. Other inscriptions are declarative rather than creative. "[f]or Mr. John monday" and "Rev. W. A. Lawton," alongside others, were almost certainly inscribed as part of a business rather a literary practice. These inscriptions are included in this compilation so that those interested in Drake's whole body of inscriptions, and not just his verse, can visit them in one place. Readers can and will make literary distinctions for themselves.

It is also important to note that this compilation does not include what's written on the other side (what's called "the reverse") of David Drake's pots. As a result, readers can't engage the ways in which Dave incises his large signature, the dates, and the names or initials of those who claimed his labor. Though such things are not poetry, Drake's use of his signature, for example, importantly announces his boldness and self-declaration as an author. His assertion of ownership over his artistry on the reverse of his pots resonates with discussions of early African American literature and especially with slave narratives and the pride that self-liberated writers such as Harriet Jacobs displayed when she, like others, proudly wrote that her narrative was "written by herself."

Though this is the most complete compilation of David Drake to date, the move from pot to page necessarily diminishes the very genius that characterizes Drake's signature contributions to African American poetry. There is more work to be done. All of us hope that more poems will soon be added to Drake's body of work. In the meantime, claiming so many of Drake's "inscriptions" as *poetry* places him in conversation with his literary predecessors and peers: Lucy Terry, Jupiter Hammon, Phillis Wheatley, and George Moses Horton. This allows Drake's literary descendants to draw water from his poetry and call his name to serve as both libation and legacy.

Contents

another trick is worst than this xx 28
a better thing, I never saw 27
cash wanted 29
Catination 27
Concatination 27
Dave belongs to Mr. Miles / 28
Edgefield District 28
for Mr. John monday 29
the fouth of July — is Surely come — 33
Give me silver or; either Gold = 28
Good for lard or holding - fresh meat 33
Great & noble Jar 33
H. Panzerbieter 35
here is eighteen hundred & fifty nine 32
horses mules and hogs — 27
I, made this Jar, all of cross 34
I made this for our sott 30
I made this Jar = for cash — 30
I made this out of number, & cross " 32
I Saw a leopard, & a lions face = 34
I saw a leppard, & a lions face " 31
I wonder where is all my relation 29
just a mammouth Jar 29
Ladys & gentlemens Shoes = 28
Lm says this handle 29
made at Stoney bluff 33
Making this Jar = I had all thougts 30
Mark and 32
New 35
nineteen days before Chrismas ——— Eve — 32
A noble jar 36
A noble Jar . For pork or beef — 34
not counted 29
Over noble Dr. Landrum's head 32
Ponderosity 36
a pretty little Girl, on a virge 30
put every bit all between 27
Rev. W. A. Lawton 33
the Sun moon and — Stars = 31
Think of me when 35
this is a noble churn 30
This noble Jar = will hold, 20 31
A very Large Jar = which has 4 handles = 31
whats better than kissing = 28
when you fill this Jar with pork or beef 31
. . . y my chic . . . 35

Dated Verses and Inscriptions

Concatination

JUNE 12, 1834, FOR REUBEN DRAKE AND JASPER GIBBS AT POTTERSVILLE
STORAGE JAR WITH TWO SLAB HANDLES
19.5 INCHES TALL; PRIVATE COLLECTION

put every bit all between
surely this Jar will hold 14

JULY 12, 1834, FOR REUBEN DRAKE AND JASPER GIBBS AT POTTERSVILLE
STORAGE JAR WITH TWO SLAB HANDLES
19.3 INCHES TALL; SOUTH CAROLINA STATE MUSEUM, COLUMBIA, S.C.

horses mules and hogs —
all our cows is in the bogs —
there they shall ever stay
till the buzzards take them away =

MARCH 29, 1836, PROBABLY AT POTTERSVILLE
STORAGE JAR WITH TWO SLAB HANDLES
16.1 INCHES TALL; PRIVATE COLLECTION

Catination

APRIL 12, 1836, PROBABLY AT POTTERSVILLE
STORAGE JAR WITH TWO SLAB HANDLES
14.9 INCHES TALL; DE YOUNG MUSEUM, SAN FRANCISCO, CALIF.

a better thing, I never saw
when I shot off, the lions Jaw

NOVEMBER 9, 1836, POSSIBLY FOR REV. JOHN LANDRUM AT HORSE CREEK
JUG WITH TWO LOOP HANDLES
17.5 INCHES TALL; HIGH MUSEUM OF ART, ATLANTA, GA.

Ladys & gentlemens Shoes =
sell all you can: & nothing you'll loose. x

JANUARY 29, 1840, FOR LEWIS MILES AT HORSE CREEK
JUG WITH TWO LOOP HANDLES
17.2 INCHES TALL; VIRGINIA MUSEUM OF FINE ARTS, RICHMOND, VA.

Give me silver or; either Gold =
though they are dangerous; to our Soul =

JUNE 27, 1840, FOR LEWIS MILES AT HORSE CREEK
STORAGE JAR WITH TWO SLAB HANDLES
14.5 INCHES TALL; PRIVATE COLLECTION

whats better than kissing =
while we both are at fishing

JULY 10, 1840, FOR LEWIS MILES AT HORSE CREEK
STORAGE JAR WITH TWO LUG HANDLES
15 INCHES TALL; GREENVILLE COUNTY MUSEUM OF ART, GREENVILLE, S.C.

Dave belongs to Mr. Miles /
whir the oven bakes and the pot biles ///

JULY 31, 1840, FOR LEWIS MILES AT HORSE CREEK
STORAGE JAR WITH TWO SLAB HANDLES
15.2 INCHES TALL; THE CHARLESTON MUSEUM, CHARLESTON, S.C.

Edgefield District

AUGUST 25, 1840, FOR LEWIS MILES AT HORSE CREEK
STORAGE JAR
15 INCHES TALL; GREENVILLE COUNTY MUSEUM OF ART, GREENVILLE, S.C.

another trick is worst than this xx
Dearest miss; Spare me a kiss xx

AUGUST 26, 1840, FOR LEWIS MILES AT HORSE CREEK
STORAGE JAR WITH TWO SLAB HANDLES
15.4 INCHES TALL; GREENVILLE COUNTY MUSEUM OF ART, GREENVILLE, S.C.

not counted

MAY 16, 1843, FOR LEWIS MILES AT HORSE CREEK
STORAGE JAR WITH TWO SLAB HANDLES
27.7 INCHES TALL; PRIVATE COLLECTION

just a mammouth Jar [illegible]
for I not [illegible]

OCTOBER 17, 1850, FOR LEWIS MILES AT STONY BLUFF
STORAGE JAR WITH TWO HANDLES
24 INCHES TALL; CURRENT OWNER UNKNOWN

cash wanted

MAY 17, 1852, FOR LEWIS MILES AT STONY BLUFF
PRESERVE JAR WITH TWO SLAB HANDLES
16.1 INCHES TALL; PRIVATE COLLECTION

Lm says this handle
will crack

JUNE 28, 1854, FOR LEWIS MILES AT STONY BLUFF
JUG WITH ONE LOOP HANDLE
HEIGHT UNKNOWN; PRIVATE COLLECTION

for Mr. John monday

JULY 6, 1857, FOR LEWIS MILES AT STONY BLUFF
STORAGE JAR WITH TWO SLAB HANDLES
21.7 INCHES TALL; MCKISSICK MUSEUM, COLUMBIA, S.C.

I wonder where is all my relation
friendship to all and every nation

AUGUST 16, 1857, FOR LEWIS MILES AT STONY BLUFF
STORAGE JAR WITH TWO SLAB HANDLES
19 INCHES TALL; GREENVILLE COUNTY MUSEUM OF ART, GREENVILLE, S.C.

I made this Jar = for cash —
though its called = lucre Trash //
Dave

AUGUST 22, 1857, FOR LEWIS MILES AT STONY BLUFF
STORAGE JAR WITH TWO LUG HANDLES
19 INCHES TALL; MUSEUM OF FINE ARTS, BOSTON, MASS.

a pretty little Girl, on a virge
Volcaic mountain[s], how they burge

AUGUST 24, 1857, FOR LEWIS MILES AT STONY BLUFF
STORAGE JAR WITH TWO SLAB HANDLES
19 INCHES TALL; MCKISSICK MUSEUM, COLUMBIA, S.C.

Making this Jar = I had all thougts
Lads & gentlemen = never out walks

JANUARY 30, 1858, FOR LEWIS MILES AT STONY BLUFF
STORAGE JAR WITH TWO SLAB HANDLES
20.6 INCHES TALL; CURRENT OWNER UNKNOWN

this is a noble churn
fill it up, it will never turn
Dave

MARCH 19, 1858, FOR LEWIS MILES AT STONY BLUFF
BUTTER CHURN
25.9 INCHES TALL; GREENVILLE COUNTY MUSEUM OF ART, GREENVILLE, S.C.

I made this for our sott
it will never-never, rott

MARCH 31, 1858, FOR LEWIS MILES AT STONY BLUFF
STORAGE JAR WITH TWO HANDLES
22 INCHES TALL; HIGH MUSEUM OF ART, ATLANTA, GA.

This noble Jar = will hold, 20
fill it with silver = then you'll have plenty

APRIL 8, 1858, FOR LEWIS MILES AT STONY BLUFF
STORAGE JAR WITH TWO SLAB HANDLES
16.8 INCHES TALL; CURRENT OWNER UNKNOWN

A very Large Jar = which has 4 handles =
pack it full of fresh meats — then light = candles —

APRIL 12, 1858, FOR LEWIS MILES AT STONY BLUFF
STORAGE JAR WITH FOUR SLAB HANDLES
24.5 INCHES TALL; CRYSTAL BRIDGES MUSEUM OF AMERICAN ART, BENTONVILLE, ARK.

when you fill this Jar with pork or beef
Scot will be there; to Get a peace, —

On the opposite side:

this Jar is to Mr Segler who keeps the bar in orangeburg
for Mr Edwards a Gentle man — who formly kept
Mr thos bacons horses

APRIL 21, 1858, FOR LEWIS MILES AT STONY BLUFF
STORAGE JAR WITH TWO SLAB HANDLES
22.6 INCHES TALL; THE METROPOLITAN MUSEUM OF ART, NEW YORK, N.Y.

the Sun moon and — Stars =
in the west are a plenty of — bears

JULY 23, 1858, FOR LEWIS MILES AT STONY BLUFF
STORAGE JAR WITH TWO SLAB HANDLES
20 INCHES TALL; GREENVILLE COUNTY MUSEUM OF ART, GREENVILLE, S.C.

I saw a leppard, & a lions face, "
then I felt the need of — Grace.

NOVEMBER 3, 1858, FOR LEWIS MILES AT STONY BLUFF
STORAGE JAR WITH TWO SLAB HANDLES
24.3 INCHES TALL; MUSEUM OF EARLY SOUTHERN DECORATIVE ARTS,
WINSTON-SALEM, N.C.

nineteen days before Chrismas ——— Eve —
Lots of people after its over, how they will greave . . .

DECEMBER 6, 1858, FOR LEWIS MILES AT STONY BLUFF
STORAGE JAR WITH TWO SLAB HANDLES
21 INCHES TALL; COLLECTION OF DRS. C. PHILIP AND CORBETT E. TOUSSAINT

Mark and
— Dave —

MARCH 10, 1859, FOR LEWIS MILES AT STONY BLUFF
STORAGE JAR WITH TWO LUG HANDLES
15 INCHES TALL; NATIONAL MUSEUM OF AMERICAN HISTORY, SMITHSONIAN INSTITUTION, WASHINGTON, D.C.

I made this out of number, & cross "
if you do not lisen at the bible you'll be lost —

MARCH 25, 1859, FOR LEWIS MILES AT STONY BLUFF
STORAGE JAR WITH TWO SLAB HANDLES
21 INCHES TALL; MADISON-MORGAN CULTURAL CENTER, MADISON, GA.

Over noble Dr. Landrum's head
May guardian angels visit his bed

APRIL 14, 1859, FOR LEWIS MILES AT STONY BLUFF
STORAGE JAR WITH TWO SLAB HANDLES
ABOUT 15-GALLON CAPACITY; CURRENT OWNER UNKNOWN

here is eighteen hundred & fifty nine
unto you all I fell in , cline "

APRIL 18, 1859, FOR LEWIS MILES AT STONY BLUFF
STORAGE JAR WITH TWO SLAB HANDLES
19.5 INCHES TALL; PRIVATE COLLECTION

Good for lard or holding - fresh meat,
blest we were when peter saw the folded sheet

MAY 3, 1859, FOR LEWIS MILES AT STONY BLUFF
STORAGE JAR WITH TWO SLAB HANDLES
26 INCHES TALL; PHILADELPHIA MUSEUM OF ART, PHILADELPHIA, PA.

Great & noble Jar
hold Sheep goat or bear

MAY 13, 1859, FOR LEWIS MILES AT STONY BLUFF
STORAGE JAR WITH FOUR SLAB HANDLES
25.7 INCHES TALL; THE CHARLESTON MUSEUM, CHARLESTON, S.C.

made at Stoney bluff,
for making this old gin enuff

MAY 13, 1859, FOR LEWIS MILES AT STONY BLUFF
STORAGE JAR WITH FOUR SLAB HANDLES
28.7 INCHES TALL; THE CHARLESTON MUSEUM, CHARLESTON, S.C.
* THE POT-TO-PRINT TRANSCRIPTION FOR THIS VERSE
IS PARTICULARLY CHALLENGING.

the fouth of July — is Surely come —
to blow the fife = and beat the drum //

JULY 4, 1859, FOR LEWIS MILES AT STONY BLUFF
STORAGE JAR WITH TWO SLAB HANDLES
24 INCHES TALL; ATLANTA HISTORY CENTER, ATLANTA, GA.

Rev. W. A. Lawton

JULY 19, 1859, FOR LEWIS MILES AT STONY BLUFF
JUG WITH TWO LOOP HANDLES
16.2 INCHES TALL; PRIVATE COLLECTION

I Saw a leopard, & a lions face =
then I felt, the need of Grace =

AUGUST 7, 1860, FOR LEWIS MILES AT STONY BLUFF
STORAGE JAR WITH TWO SLAB HANDLES
16.7 INCHES TALL; PRIVATE COLLECTION
* THIS IS THE ONLY EXISTING INSCRIPTION THAT IS A NEAR DUPLICATION FROM AN EARLIER POT.

A noble Jar . For pork or beef —
then carry it . A round to the indian chief //

NOVEMBER 9, 1860, FOR LEWIS MILES AT STONY BLUFF
STORAGE JAR WITH TWO SLAB HANDLES
21.5 INCHES TALL; PRIVATE COLLECTION

I, made this Jar, all of cross
If, you dont repent, you will be, lost =

MAY 3, 1862, FOR LEWIS MILES AT STONY BLUFF
STORAGE JAR WITH TWO SLAB HANDLES
20 INCHES TALL; NATIONAL MUSEUM OF AMERICAN HISTORY, SMITHSONIAN INSTITUTION, WASHINGTON, D.C.

Undated Verses and Inscriptions

New
X

UNDATED, POSSIBLY FOR REV. JOHN LANDRUM AT HORSE CREEK
JUG WITH ONE LOOP HANDLE
8.8 INCHES TALL; PRIVATE COLLECTION

Think of me when
far away Rosa D G Wever
Mr Milton Miles
Edgefield

C. 1860, PROBABLY FOR LEWIS MILES AT STONY BLUFF
STORAGE JAR WITH TWO SLAB HANDLES
15 INCHES TALL; GREENVILLE COUNTY MUSEUM OF ART, GREENVILLE, S.C.

H. Panzerbieter
Groceries

King & Columbia
Charleston
S.C.

UNDATED, PROBABLY FOR LEWIS MILES AT STONY BLUFF
STORAGE JAR WITH TWO SLAB HANDLES
12.5 INCHES TALL; THE CHARLESTON MUSEUM, CHARLESTON, S.C.

. . . y my chic . . .

UNDATED, FOR REV. JOHN LANDRUM
SHERDS; CURRENT OWNER UNKNOWN

Rumored Verses and Inscriptions

A noble jar
For lard or tar

Ponderosity

Exploring Jonathan Green's *Sir Dave* in Context

P. GABRIELLE FOREMAN

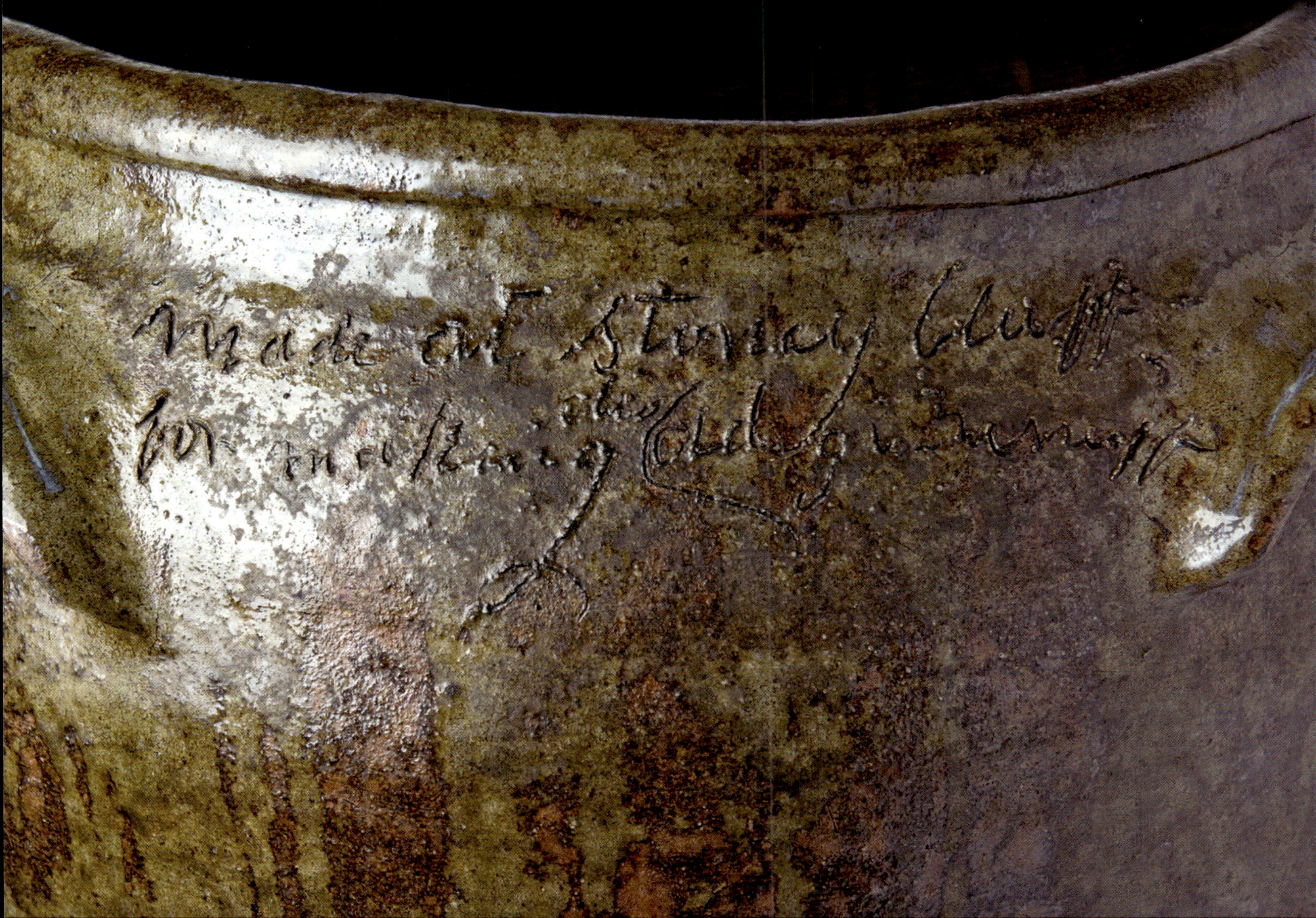

OVERLEAF: Poetic Vessel, "made at Stoney Bluff," May 13, 1859. David Drake. Courtesy of the Charleston Museum, Charleston, South Carolina.

ON JONATHAN GREEN'S CANVASES, David Drake's biography comes to life—the *Sir Dave* series showcases Drake's existence and experiences with a fullness that scarce and selective historical sources cannot reveal. David Drake's birth and childhood have been lost to researchers looking for clues in the archives. He first appears in official records as a teenager in a mortgage document from 1818 that reveals almost nothing about him or his family. Rather, it discloses information about the man who claimed him as property and was using him as collateral to secure other property. Dave appears as the guarantee on a loan some think was used to expand the Pottersville Manufactory, where he likely was already working.[1] He's listed with Eliza, a young woman just slightly older than the teenaged Dave, who was enslaved alongside him.

Securing cash by offering to sell off young, strong enslaved people if a loan went bad was not unusual across slaveholding states. Indeed, while those interested in David Drake today ponder how exceptional his life and work were, this historical document reveals how his life was intimately connected to horrors endured by millions of enslaved people. In *securing* a loan with Dave and Eliza as collateral, historical records reveal how *insecure* their relationship was to everything they knew.

Jonathan Green's *Sir Dave* series captures this reality without being restricted by it. In Green's work, viewers are granted a view of the plentitude of a vibrant life full of family, love, loss, and triumph. In *Young Dave,* David Drake is pictured with the family he was born into. In *Dave the Potter,* he appears at the height of his power, turning a pot, surrounded by others outside. He is reading in a moment of repose in *Sir Dave,* and he is seen with festive community members on their way to *Dave's Market.* In *Crossroads,* he is being cared for by three others after losing a leg in a railway accident, a loss that is speculated by some but difficult to verify.[2] Yet there is no formal beginning or end to the *Sir Dave* series. While books such as this one, with their linear format and necessary page-by-page order, will necessarily impose a sequence, *Sir Dave* is not numbered as some other series are. In this way, he departs from the sequential style of other artists, including one of Green's mentors, Jacob Lawrence, who is among the most famous painters to bring historical figures and movements to artistic life. David Drake's biography doesn't follow the familiar slavery-to-freedom, South-to-North arc traced in slave narratives. To honor the openness of Jonathan Green's *Sir Dave* series, all that's unknowable about David Drake's history, and the way that one might move around in a museum gallery as well, this discussion or "docent tour" moves around with more freedom than the imposed order in which the paintings appear in the next section.

We know that by the time Drake appears in historical documents, he had already lost what hasn't yet showed up even in traces of such records: the family of his childhood.[3] Green's *Young Dave* (p. 56) speaks imaginatively across this absence. The painting foregrounds a slender Black woman in a colorful outdoor tableau engaged in everyday work.[4] In her neat blue dress and straw hat beneath a blue sky, she's linked visually to a thicker, perhaps older, woman who also dons a white-collared blue dress and hat. Such visual cues suggest they're family; and the latter holds a swaddled child, "young Dave," in her arms. Chickens peck casually in the foreground. A cat sits nearby, cows graze in the background, and a neat home sits to one side. Together they make up an idyllic domestic scene.

Through the use of perspective and the placement of important objects in *Young Dave,* Green brings home a message about Black family and culture. The slimmer, more upright woman in blue fills up the canvas; in her A-line skirt, she is larger than life, larger than the A-frame house that sits to her right, and as big as the nearby tree. If she is meant to be Dave's mother, Green's use of dimension signals the overwhelming importance of family, how large it looms. Inserting such a prequel to Drake's known life likewise demonstrates the inadequacy of relying on the masters' tools—the masters' records—to tell the stories of those they enslaved. With implicit references to Green's own childhood growing up in his grandmother's home (symbolized by the yellow house that often appears in Green's work), this painting brings home the generative wholeness that could have been Dave's.

Pots are also an important part of this scene. The young woman in the foreground seems to churn butter in a vessel that is clearly one of the painting's focal points; another pot is showcased in the foreground. The very presence of these vessels in the painting conveys a message: despite narratives about Drake being taught by Abner Landrum, a patriarch in the white family who would claim the potter's labor for nearly all of his recorded life, Green's painting suggests that Drake's art springs from somewhere else, from Black traditions that run through his own family—even if that family has been effectively severed from what we know about Dave.

Unlike the sparse and hemmed-in cabin scenes featured in Jacob Lawrence's famous *Frederick Douglass* series, Green's *Sir Dave* series places the potter and his story entirely outdoors in a vibrant natural world. Yet, despite this colorful optimism, Green's inclusion of lost and unaccounted for figures in Drake's historical life also adds complex layers to his visual storytelling. Three of the paintings that depict "Sir Dave" as an iconic figure in his prime showcase a rare paradox in antebellum South Carolina: an enslaved master potter who could also read. In the painting *Sir Dave* (p. 65), he sits outside alone on a pot with other vessels lined up neatly in rows near him, his broad back to the viewer, reading a newspaper, low hills and blue skies in the background. *Dave the Potter* (p. 61) recalls this same scene. Though his muscular body faces the viewer, his straw hat obscures his eyes. Here, he's at work on a pot; a newspaper lies open nearby, and again he is surrounded by vessels of his own creation.

Outdoors but in different locations, both paintings casually signal how exceptional Drake is as both a potter and as an enslaved reader. In the third painting, *Dave's Market* (p. 63), the action and energy of the piece spill off of the canvas, replacing the reflective mood of self-determination the other two paintings relay. In *Dave's Market*, the painting's borders cut off the faces of the market goers and bifurcate the straw hats they wear. The effect is a bustling feeling that the painting also exudes from its colorful palette. Viewers have to look to the larger narrative Green shares in the series to apprehend the disruptions and loss Green brings to life; joy and community, not loss, are represented here.

It's not David Drake, but a girl in red, who takes center stage in *Dave's Market*, though her importance is bolstered by her proximity to him. Recalling the "pretty little Girl" in Drake's couplet, her full face is the only one available to the viewer—not only in this piece, but in any of the paintings in *Sir Dave*. Placed in the foreground, she looks slightly up, mouth parted in song perhaps. Her plaited hair tells us she's young; two white ribbons are in place where today's barrettes would be. She walks next to Dave, simultaneously leading the crowd and cradled under his protective arm, as he carries his jar easily on a broad shoulder, the brim of his hat cut off by the canvas's edge.

It's worth noticing the jug the celebrated potter carries. His able hand and strong arm link the girl to his handiwork. Green's artistry is on display in this detailed tableau; in-person viewers can see the brushwork and note how the painter calls attention to the casual strength the potter uses to steady his work on his shoulder. It's as if the detail and attention point viewers' gaze to both the girl and the pot. In this way, the girl in Green's painting could be linked to the pretty little girl *on* the jug, the one memorialized in Drake's pot and couplet:

a pretty little Girl, on a virge
Volcaic mountain[s], how they burge

Her importance is particularly notable because almost all the other figures' arms and hands are noticeably absent, blocked by the press of the crowd. Dave's strong arm and the upturned face of the pretty little girl in red serve as symbols of individuality in this festive but faceless crowd, more wagons coming in the background, more figures to each side.[5]

The girl in red provides a link between two of *Sir Dave*'s biographical paintings.[6] Now older, she seems to appear again in *Dave the Potter*, where he is pictured turning a pot outside. Placed in the background in this painting, she no longer has braided hair and instead is graced with a figure of abundance that tells of the growth and maturity that often threaten Black women who are enslaved. He expresses this as "Volcaic mountain[s]" "burging" or erupting. This woman in red is carrying a covered platter or basket on her head—Dave's midday meal perhaps—with grace and seeming ease that signal her comfort and connection to him. The two paintings are linked by their size as well; at 60 × 48 inches, both of the paintings featuring the pretty girl in red are the largest of the three sizes Green created for this series.

Three additional figural paintings extend Green's exploration to include the larger Black community. In these paintings, pots, not David Drake, are central. *Three Vessels* (p. 86) points to ceramic pots' many uses. Here, two Black men travel in knee-deep sky-blue water that stretches into the horizon, carrying three large vessels on a pole between them. Viewers can assume the pots have traveled from land-bound Edgefield at the western edge of the state where Drake made them to the rice-growing region of coastal South Carolina or Georgia, the Gullah communities where Jonathan Green was born. In *From Earth We Came* (p. 81), shards of pots blanket the ground as cones of light illuminate the nighttime wooded scene. A path leads somewhere, but there's little clue as to where, and the only figure in the painting isn't standing on it. Instead, head down, her face fully obscured by her straw hat, her hands folded in front of her, she seems suspended in one of the columns of light.[7]

In a series where day-time skies provide the background for every other person whom Green paints, *From Earth We Came*, the darkest image, is a mystical and mournful scene that signals death and loss. Its title connects it to the cemetery scene in another work, *Earth to Earth* (p. 78), where shards of pots also appear as part of Black funerary traditions. In *From Earth We Came*, no figures appear in the other columns of light. Without other visual cues viewers can piece together, they are left with a woman alone and asked to contend with the heft of her solitude. Perhaps she's meant to stand in for a woman we only know as Ann, who when enslaved and working alongside David Drake in Benjamin Franklin Landrum's pottery works, lost hope, patience, and who can imagine what else, and hanged herself. Since viewers aren't likely to know that story, she stands in for other unnamed and faceless enslaved women, literally millions whose children or parents, whose siblings, friends, or husbands, were stolen and sold away.

From Earth We Came can be grouped with two paintings that explore death (*Earth to Earth* and *Vessels for Taking Us Home*); but it also closely resonates with

Marshland Passage (p. 44), which explores how African cosmologies are woven into Green's rendition of the potter's life story. Also set on the coast, *Marshland Passage* is a majestic piece. In it, a man stands, bare back to the viewers, looking out onto the ocean water, a staff in hand. Green's iconic marshland grasses reach almost to the man's waist, leaving just the top of his blue slacks and matching suspenders showing.[8] This could be Dave, but neither location nor body type tie him directly to the other renditions, leaving viewers with an ambiguity that helps complicate the piece. This man carries a large clay vessel on his shoulders. It is perched in such a way that it blocks—or actually becomes—his head. When viewers realize that the painting offers them an image of both a man *toting* a pot and a man who *is* part pot, *Marshland Passage* begins to suggest an Egyptian divinity, a therianthropic god. In this case, the deity figure isn't part human and part beast or falcon, as are so many Egyptian gods. Rather, he's a hybrid of man and regal pot. Seen through this lens, the staff recalls the one carried by Ra, the god of the sky, earth, and underworld, often pictured with a potlike orb atop his head. It also recalls the staff carried by the Egyptian god Set, lord of the red land.

Marshland Passage, the title of this painting, closely mirrors "Middle Passage." And the ocean in the background affirms the title's resonance. The title's suggestive echoes prime viewers to look for signs of African cosmologies that millions of sold and captured people carried with them from their homelands and passed on to their descendants in South Carolina. In this context, the large birds in the background symbolically point to the famous stories of flying Africans who crossed the waters, returning to Africa, rather than being enslaved.

In five of Green's *Sir Dave* paintings, people are present only as hauntings. In these works, ceramics, cotton, or cemetery scenes take center stage. Joining *From Earth We Came,* where colored pottery shards decorate the forested floor, is *Potter's Fragments* (p. 75), where fallen leaves and ceramic pieces carpet the ground in a close-up reminder of clay's connection to the earth and its cycles. Two other pieces are peopled almost entirely with pots. In *Vessels of Sir Dave* (p. 88), more than a dozen claim the canvas, announcing their grandness in size and scope, so big that there's only space for a sliver of sunset sky and a still smaller slice of green pasture to serve as backdrop to the pots themselves. *Vessels for Taking Us Home* (p. 90), a larger painting, echoes but also departs from *Vessels of Sir Dave*—like fraternal twins that on first glance you might mistake for identical. Though the two paintings mirror each other in composition and color, *Vessels for Taking Us Home* features not a dozen but a colony of pots. They stand proud, tall, and erect in the foreground and are ever smaller in size in subsequent rows as they grow in number.

Green chose the word *vessels* for this title, a term used for ships as well as pots. Here they lead to water and otherworldly orange clouds, into which colossal birds

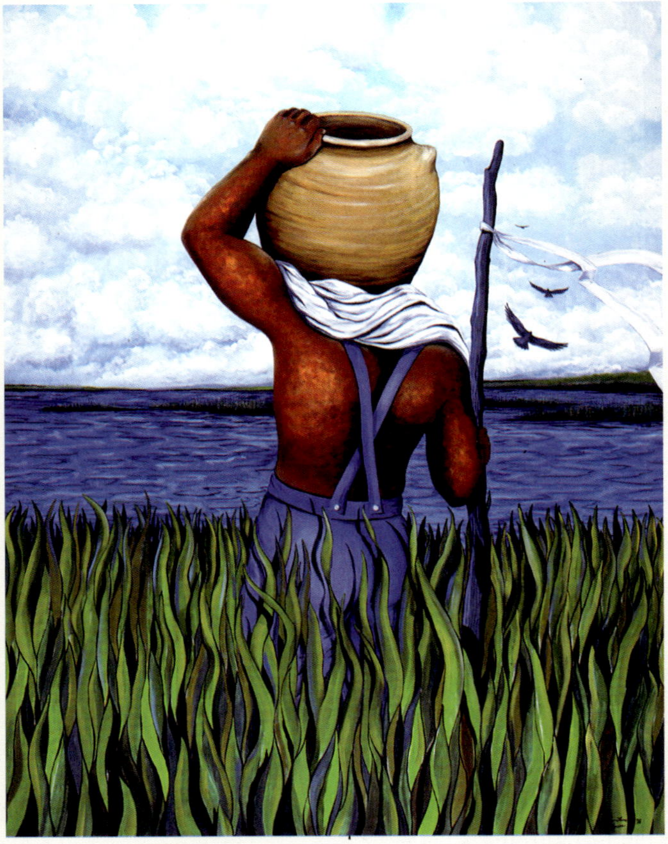

Marshland Passage, 1998. Jonathan Green (American, b. 1955). Oil on canvas, 60 × 48 inches. Courtesy of Jonathan Green Studios. © Jonathan Green.

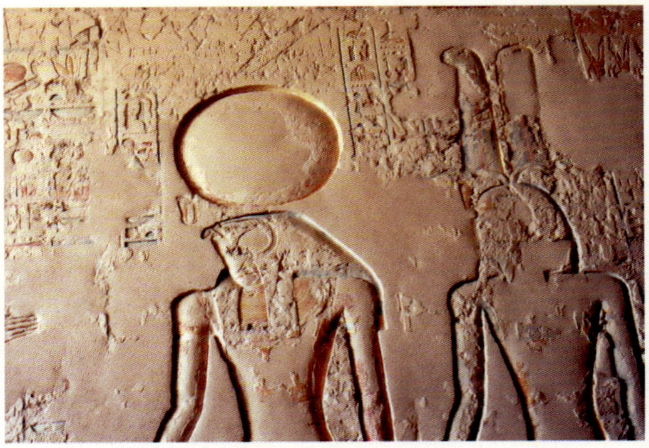

Relief of the god Ra, First Courtyard of Ramses II, Temple of Luxor, Dynasty XIX (1320–1200 BCE), New Empire. This image appears in the tomb of Ramses IV.

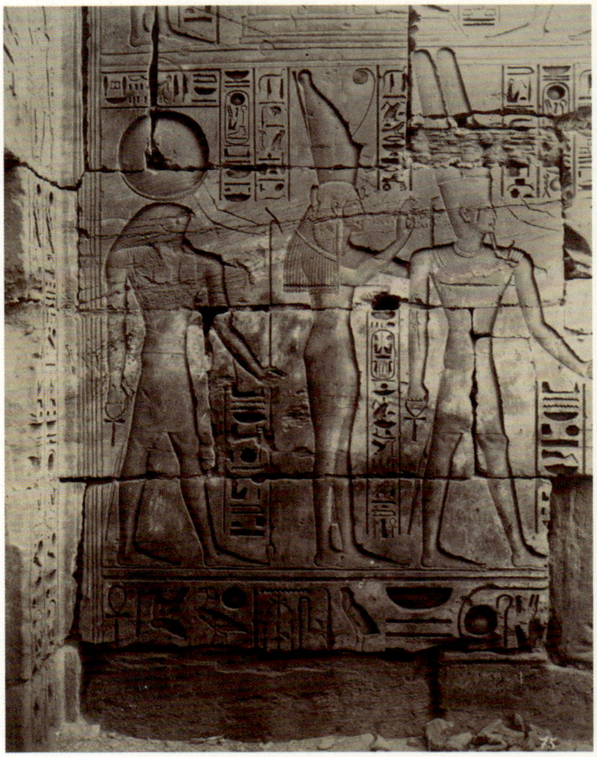

Relief of the god Ra with staff. From The New York Public Library. https://digitalcollections.nypl.org/items/510d47d9-6078-a3d9-e040-e00a18064a99.

are in flight away from the coastline, huge wings spread wide, headed back to Africa, as oral tradition has it, "taking us home."[9] The painting's name, its oversize birds, and the ocean all point viewers toward a famous story passed on in oral tradition: that of Ibo Landing, which is examined in more depth in Gabrielle Foreman's long essay in this collection. There, a group of captives stolen and shipped from Ibo land mutinied in 1803 on St. Simons Island, off coastal Georgia. Some stories say they walked into the water, preferring collective suicide to slavery. In the painting, the most distant row of pots leans toward the water on the horizon, a close view reveals, as if they are a holding place for the ancestors' spirits.[10]

But Green's *Vessels for Taking Us Home* also draws on another version of the story; instead of drowning, these captives sprouted wings and flew home. Tales of these flying Africans appear in WPA interviews of those who were once enslaved. They also appear in children's books by Julius Lester, Jerry Pinkney, and Virginia Hamilton and are motifs in novels such as Toni Morrison's *Song of Solomon* and movies such as Julie Dash's *Daughters of the Dust*. These cultural memories, what Jonathan Green calls "visual memory, hear/say memory," have been transmitted and "incubated," as he puts it, from one generation to the next.[11] In *Sir Dave*, these references to flying Africans appear in both the suggestively titled *Marshland Passage*, with its overt nod to the Middle Passage, as well as in *Vessels for Taking Us Home*.

In *Vessels for Taking Us Home*, Jonathan Green links David Drake's legacy to African culture and ancestors and to a larger collective in multiple ways. Although no human figure is present in this image, Green embeds his subject textually rather than figuratively in this painting. Though it is not visible in reproductions, Green has signed the name Dave above the left handle on the green pot in the painting's foreground, adding the potter's signature alongside Green's own, which appears in the right foreground, where painters so often sign their own paintings. In so doing, Green connects them as artistic kin, situating them as cocreators from a shared cultural genealogy who are linked by ancestral and artistic continuity.

While David Drake's own life and vessels are Jonathan Green's most obvious focus in this series, Green trains his gaze on Sir Dave's cultural and historical community as well. Since many in the potter's community spent their sunup to sundown in fieldwork, not ceramic work, Green's *Edgefield* (p. 54) includes scenes of their labor. Cotton is so central to the South's economic history that painters from both African American and white plantation traditions often revisit it. Titling the painting *Edgefield*, Green points both to fieldwork and to the name of the South Carolina district where David Drake plied his craft for others' gain, just like those who worked in the fields for their enslavers' profit. Green riffs on the popular southern tradition of the plantation panorama, which is often painted so that the landscape draws the viewer's attention to the planter's grand mansion in the background. In paintings that function to affirm white wealth and to obscure the barbarity that produced it, viewers are invited to survey and appreciate the patriarchal institution's impressive and masterful accumulations. When white southern painters working in Drake's era faced the challenge of portraying "the beauty of nature and the brutality of forced captive labor," they often left enslaved workers "out of the picture."[12] When captive Blacks appear in such works, they do so without whips or scales to weigh the day's yield, a beating often coming if a field hand came up short. These images excise that brutality, depicting the fields as if picking cotton were a pleasant and picturesque way to spend a summer day.

People and buildings make no appearance in Green's painting, even as he subtly counters the belief system that suffuses such cotton plantation paintings by and for the racial elite. In Green's work, open bolls reach as far as the eye can see, occupying all the land until they run into the low hills in the distant horizon. *Edgefield* depicts the branches, bolls, and thorns that tore and pricked the hands that picked, dragged, and carried millions of pounds of the fiber that made the region rich. The further the viewers' eyes travel, the more intense the cotton becomes; it crowds out the brown earth it springs from in the foreground, stems disappearing, converging middle ground into a field of beautiful white bolls picked up in and mirroring a swath of blue-white clouds in a turquoise sky, separated only by a thin line of hills.

However pastoral the scene may seem, what there is in Green's *Edgefield* is cotton, endless cotton, cotton now and cotton forever, cotton that calls viewers to imagine and engage the way it, and the people enslaved to cultivate it, were treated and represented for hundreds of years. Empty of the many captive workers necessary to cultivate a cash crop that reached across geography and generations, Green's painting beckons viewers to walk in the rows and occupy the spaces its figural absences invite. When Green's *Edgefield* and Redmond's poetry were used as the backdrop for a choreo-performance in a Dave suite that Lynnette Young Overby discusses in this volume, the ensemble piece acted as a response to the call to people in Green's painting and to give voice to those who ghost those fields. When Green painted the pieces in the *Sir Dave* series, they were unnumbered and without any set order, but *Edgefield* is so evocative that when paired with Glenis Redmond's poetry, it is the first to appear in the poetry inspired by Green's work.

After the Thirteenth Amendment granted David Drake his postwar freedom and the ability to legally claim that name, records of his work and life largely trail away—no descendants or family that we know of, no grave marker other than the ones later poets and artists provide. Nor did Drake ever migrate onto the page the words he wrote on his pots; he didn't join the many, if lesser known, postbellum authors who narrated their enslaved experiences.[13] *Sir Dave*'s original lack of a fixed, sequential order reflects the scattered archival remnants and fragmented records of David Drake's recorded life. Indeed, as Jonathan Green's paintings show, for all the violent erasures that slavery enacted, it also creates a space for, and calls on, creative artists to join historians in the work of recovery and remembrance.[14]

NOTES

1 See Baldwin, *Great and Noble Jar*, 2; Todd, *Carolina Clay*, 19–23.

2 Leonard Todd bases the loss of Dave's leg on interviews taken in 1930 by researchers from the Charleston Museum, one of whom, a German man born in 1862, did not know Dave but had heard about the "one-legged negro named Dave. He was said to have been mighty good." The other, also an Edgefield pottery worker, named Carey Dickson, says, "They say he got drunk and layed [*sic*] on the railway track." In other words, the evidence pointing to the how and why Dave lost his leg is based on oral histories by people far removed from the incident and may or may not be true. See Todd, *Carolina Clay*, 68–69, 266n3.

3 Eliza, unlike Dave, the mortgage reveals, had been born overseas, that is, at hardly twenty, she had been transported, sold, and collateralized at least once before.

4 Thanks to Curtis Small, who provided the wording that appears in this sentence.

5 Thanks to Denise Burgher, who accompanied me on a visit to view the painting in the original and for her ideas as we viewed the piece together. Thanks also to collector Gloria Williams, Oakland, California, February 26, 2014.

6 Note that in the *Winterthur Magazine* piece, *Dave's Market* and *Dave the Potter* are printed side by side, which highlights the relationship between Dave and the woman/women in red. Poutasse, "Jonathan Green's Canvases Bring Dave the Potter to Life," 2000.

7 Thanks to Bill Boyd, the owner of this painting, who shared photographic close ups and responded to my queries, June 29, 2018.

8 *Marshland Passage* traveled with the original 1998 *I Made This Jar: The Life and Works of the Enslaved African American Potter, Dave* exhibit, alongside *Dave's Market*, *Sir Dave*, and *Dave the Potter*.

9 Buzzards appear in African American folktales—including those about the flying Africans of Ibo Landing.

10 Such pots' spiritual lives appear in the WPA slave narratives over and again. George Rawick notes that "a graphic example of how West African meanings reemerged in North America in totally different contexts with some of the original behavior lost and new behavior added is . . . slaves using an iron kettle or pot in order 'to deaden' the sound during the nighttime prayer meetings and sings. The stories of hundreds of ex-slaves not in contact with each other tell similar stories about the iron pot" (Rawick, *From Sunup to Sundown*, 39). The cultural lives of pots the size and scale that Dave made included communal and religious uses. These pots' interiors were seen as protected and protecting spaces, where Black secret and sacred communication could be lodged and housed and could pass unheard and unseen. For more on this see Foreman, *The Art of DisMemory*.

11 Jonathan Green, unpublished interview.

12 Vlach, "Perpetuating the Past," 16.

13 William L. Andrews's work on postbellum slave narratives is foundational for almost all of the work that has followed. See his many articles on this subject cited here in "Slave Narratives, 1865–1900." Andrews is at work on a full volume on postbellum narratives to accompany his *Slavery and Class in the American South*.

14 As Natasha Sajé points out in her discussion of poetry, Roland Barthes equates this with what he calls the bliss of making meaning in the face of text that reflects a state of loss that "discomforts," that "unsettles the reader's historical, cultural, psychological assumptions . . . [and] brings to a crisis his relation with language" (Barthes, *The Pleasure of the Text,* 14). She equates this with Barthes's concept of writerly texts, extended here to writerly art or collective meaning making in the face not only of loss but of erasure. Sajé, "Dynamic Design," 150.

All My Relation Poetry with *Sir Dave* Paintings

JONATHAN GREEN AND GLENIS REDMOND

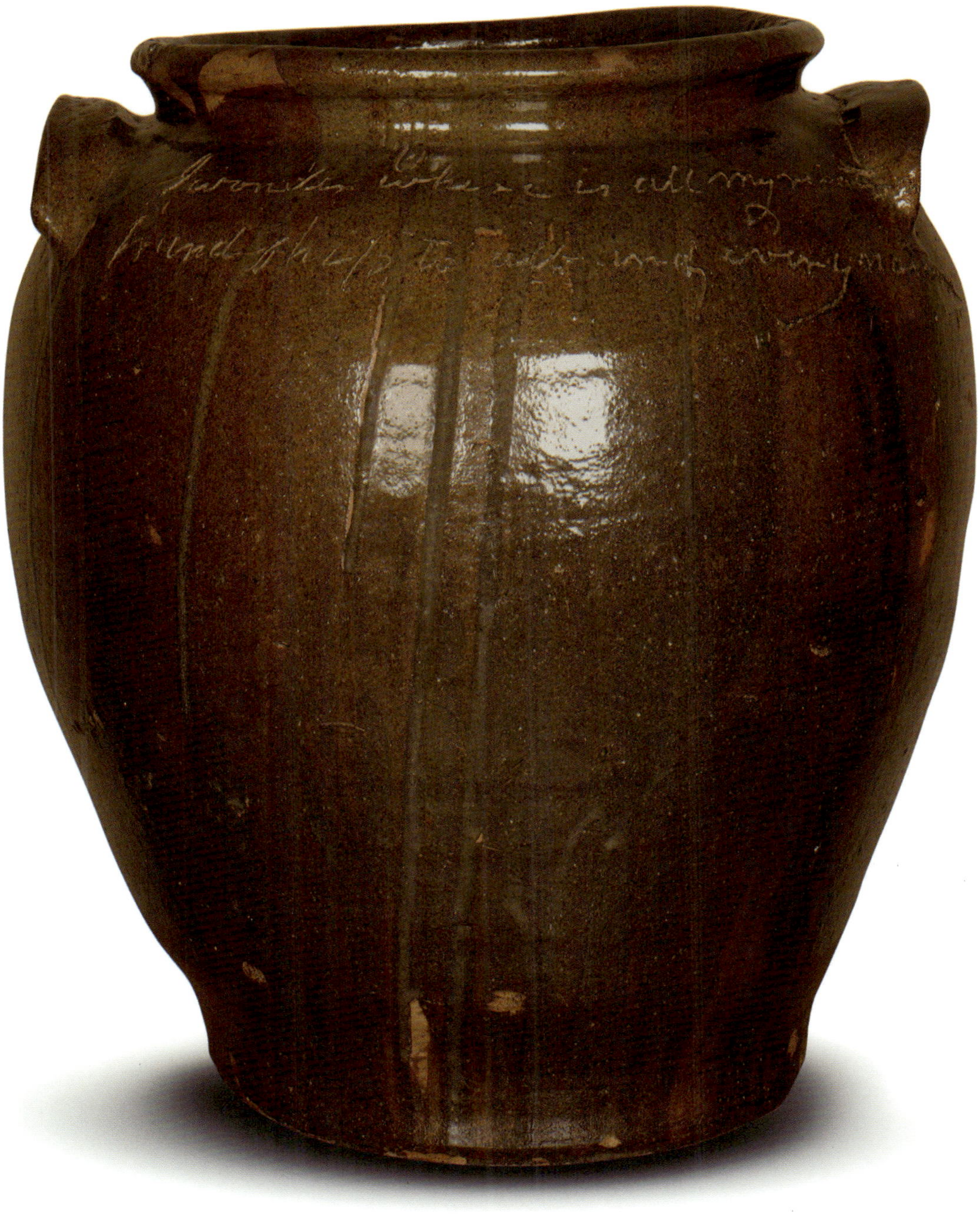

OVERLEAF: Poetic Vessel, "I wonder where is all my relation," 1857. David Drake. Greenville County Museum of Art.

Contents

All My Relation Poetry with Sir Dave Paintings. Poems by Glenis Redmond. Paintings by Jonathan Green.

PAINTINGS	POEMS
	Forefather
Edgefield	Field Cotton
Young Dave	What I Knows
	What I Don't Know
Dave the Potter	I, Master
Dave's Market	Market
Sir Dave	Read
	Brickmaking: Recipe for Writing
	Praise Dave
Crossroads	How I Walk
	Irony
	Jarring
Potter's Fragments	Slavery's Slippery Touch (Gabrielle Foreman)
	Remains
Earth to Earth	Deepest Pot
From Earth We Came	Grave
Marshland Passage	Tributaries
Three Vessels	Heaven-Human-Earth: A Found Poem
Vessels of Sir Dave	Embodied
Vessels for Taking Us Home	Carry Us
	Notes in the Margin (an Ancestral Ars Poetica)

FOREFATHER

When the landscape appears barren
of black blooms,

I reached my long arms
back to find the flare

he left, a trail of blessings
pots with two-line lessons,

"This is a noble churn
fill it up, it will never turn."

From my childhood home he stood,
a mere 73 ragged miles away

from Piedmont to Edgefield,
albeit 150 years before.

With no benefit of daguerreotypes
I made him out

through the muck
and the fog of pale deceit.

He appears a stoic visage,
a South Carolina son,

my literary forefather
turning both verse and vessel.

I spy his only portrait
In fingerprints on pots.

Walk along the loops
and ridges of his whorls.

Press ear to the hum
coming from hardened clay.

Listen to his stories singing
ringing from his handiwork.

I witness how he limbos
tight spaces—writing anyhow.

He offers me his hand.
I step forward.

We dance in this in between.

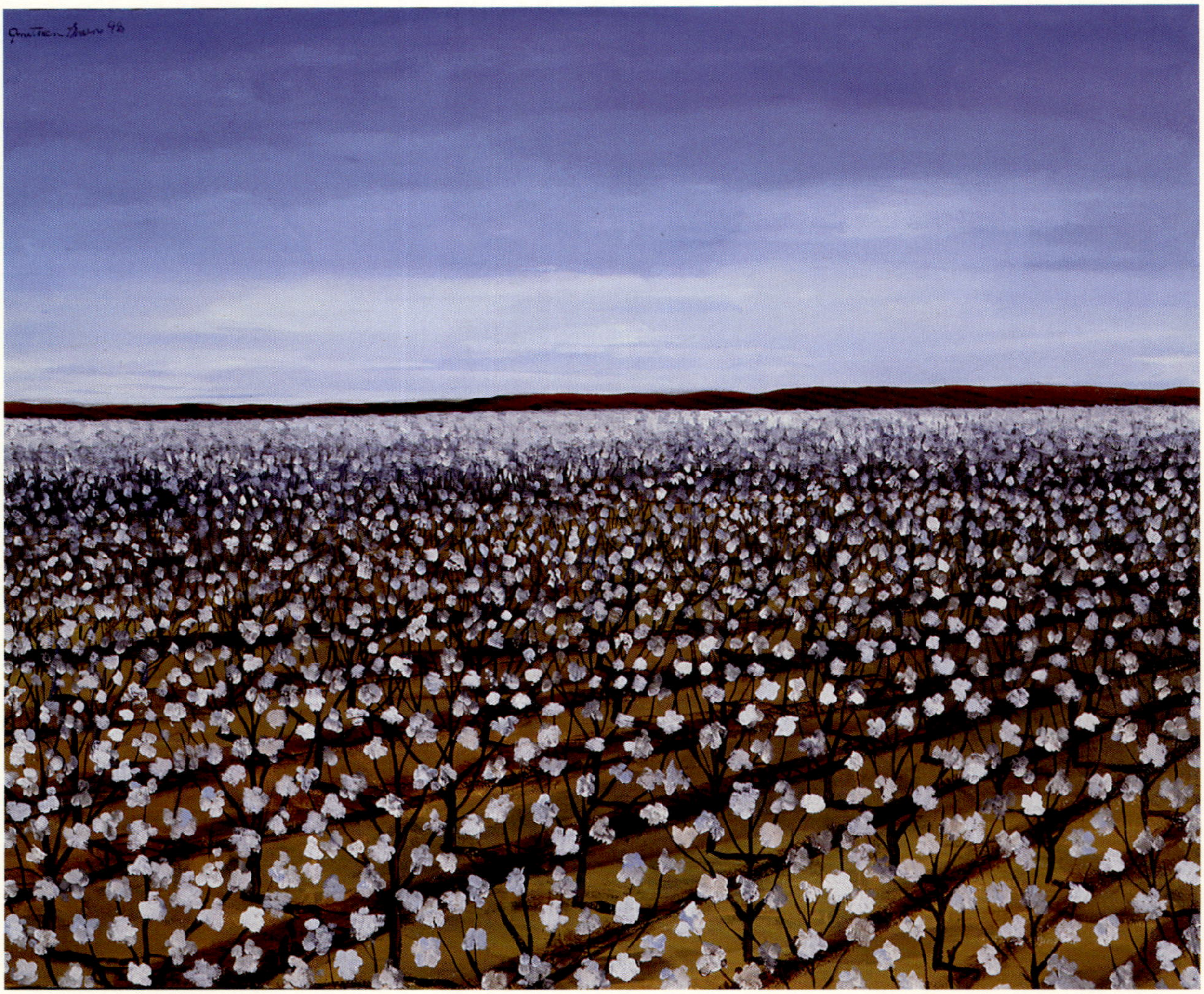

Edgefield from the *Sir Dave* series, 1998. Jonathan Green (American, b. 1955). Oil on canvas, 16 × 20 inches. Courtesy of Jonathan Green Studios. © Jonathan Green.

FIELD COTTON

We stand not on the edge, but in the middle of the field
in between this white blaze that God made.

Our minds not fixed on the North Star, but grounded
to the weight in our bones as we pick, prick and bleed.

Drag from what seems like Genesis to Revelation.
We are bred and wed to this cotton spur hold.

We sing hymns like "Steal Away," but we know these songs
be the only thing we'll ever know of wings.

How can something so comely turn so ugly?
When greed wraps its hand around the land,

cotton becomes a field of lies acting like the truth.
This cotton crop got too many mouths

works us *from can't see to can't see*
with two cotton sacks strapped across our backs.

We forget how we once dreamed
to be turned up like sunflowers in praise

or how we once prayed to be woven to a greater whole
linked by the right hand of fellowship singing,

How do you do sir? How do you do sir?

We know nuthin bout freedom in this heat.
We got a blind eye and a deaf ear to everything,

'cept to what's at hand. Cotton running in straight rows.
The only train we was ever meant to ride.

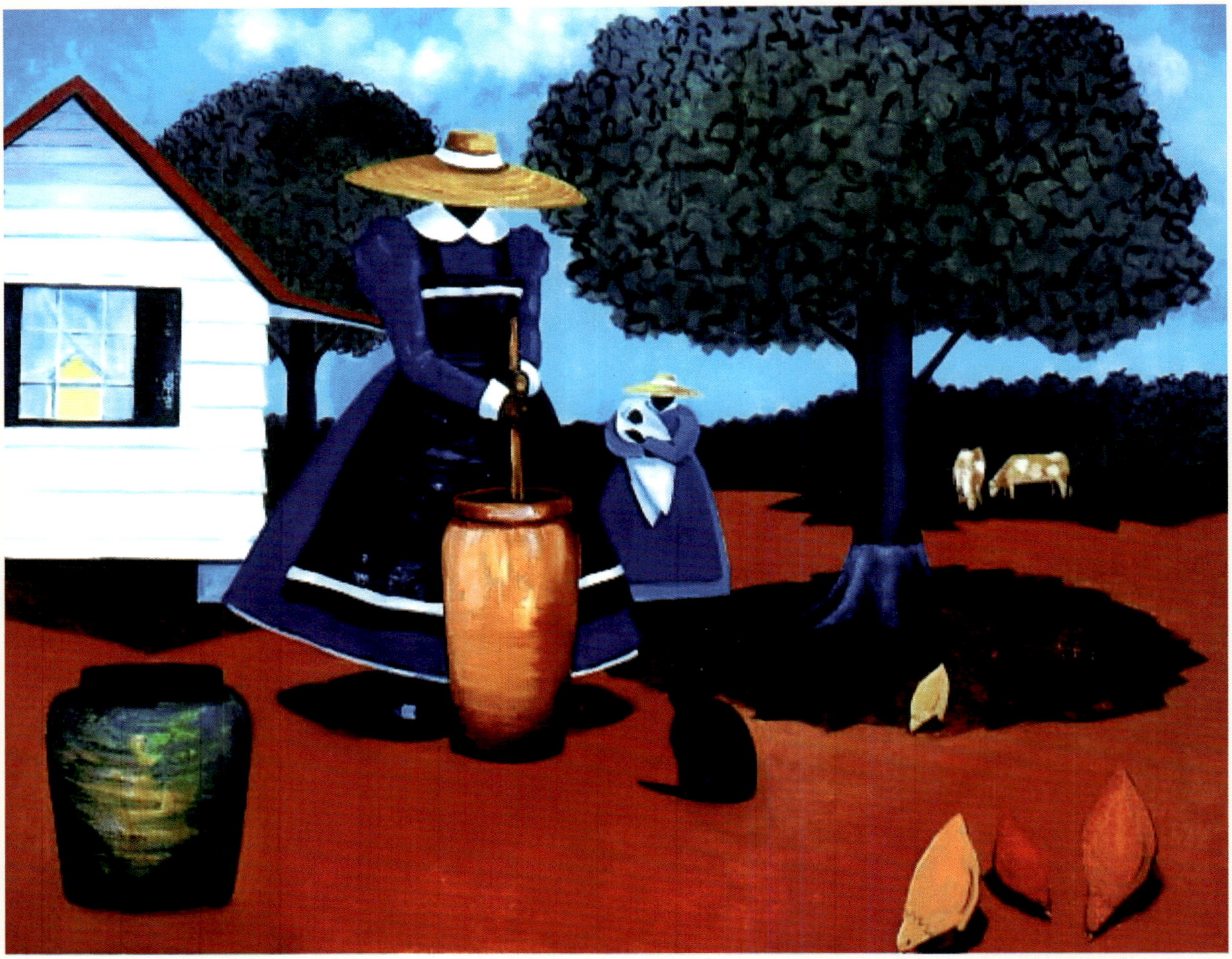

Young Dave from the *Sir Dave* series, 1998. Jonathan Green (American, b. 1955). Oil on canvas, 18 × 24 inches. Courtesy of Jonathan Green Studios. © Jonathan Green.

WHAT I KNOWS

I don't knows much,
but I knows dat

my mama's hands be rough,
but de tenderest brown.

I knows her arms be
de first world I ever knew.

Her love be like butter churned,
a doing thang,

be like feeding Guineas
and Carolina Reds. Constant.

Ise from slave cabins and shackles
but feel free when I'm held by her.

Dey says Ise Country Born,
but I specs mama ain't,

she full of de old ways:
Know roots and herbs

soothe an ache
and make a fever break.

So I gotta lotta Africa
flowin in me.

She makin ways,
where der ain't none.

Where you think
I gets fire to make pots?

Dey calls me Dave, but I believe
my mama call me by another name.

Sound like *freedom*.
Sound like *run*.

Dere are many ways to be free.

I reads when de laws say don't.
I write when de laws say don't.

I'm from a whole mess of dont's,
but I do anyways.

Like my pots I stand firm.
Pots dat hold my destiny.

Dey in me, like I in dem
no matter which way I turn

I hold onto the Almighty's unchanging hand
I always finds my center.

WHAT I DON'T KNOW

I'm from what I knows
and most of what I don't.

What I knows about my beginning
is like an empty field before seed

no crop—
no good and plenty.

Ise on de look out for how I came to be,
but I has mostly nothin at hand

cept what de lawd done showed.
I knows Ise my daddy's seed,

but who ain't?
Question is: which crop?

I look at my hands and wonder
whose hands match dese.

Dere's so much not to know.
I do know I'm from work—

every which way dat word turns
like spade and trowel—

like my people who sweat and sing
as dey pick and pull.

Ise from greed of de coin,
both sides of dat thang be evil.

Ain't nothin good in slavery.
No good in it or of it.

Ain't nothin a massa can do for me,
but free me. I've had five of em.

Dats what about dat.

Dey calls me Dave
my pots bear my name

signed by my own hand.
Dat act can get me treed,

but writing be like runnin,
in my mind

when my people needs a word or two.
I turn words like I turn pots.

From Edgefield where dey'd cut a nigga
just as soon look at one,

but I figures a way
to dance on dat blade.

I write not fully a slave,
not fully free neither.

Dis edge be where I live

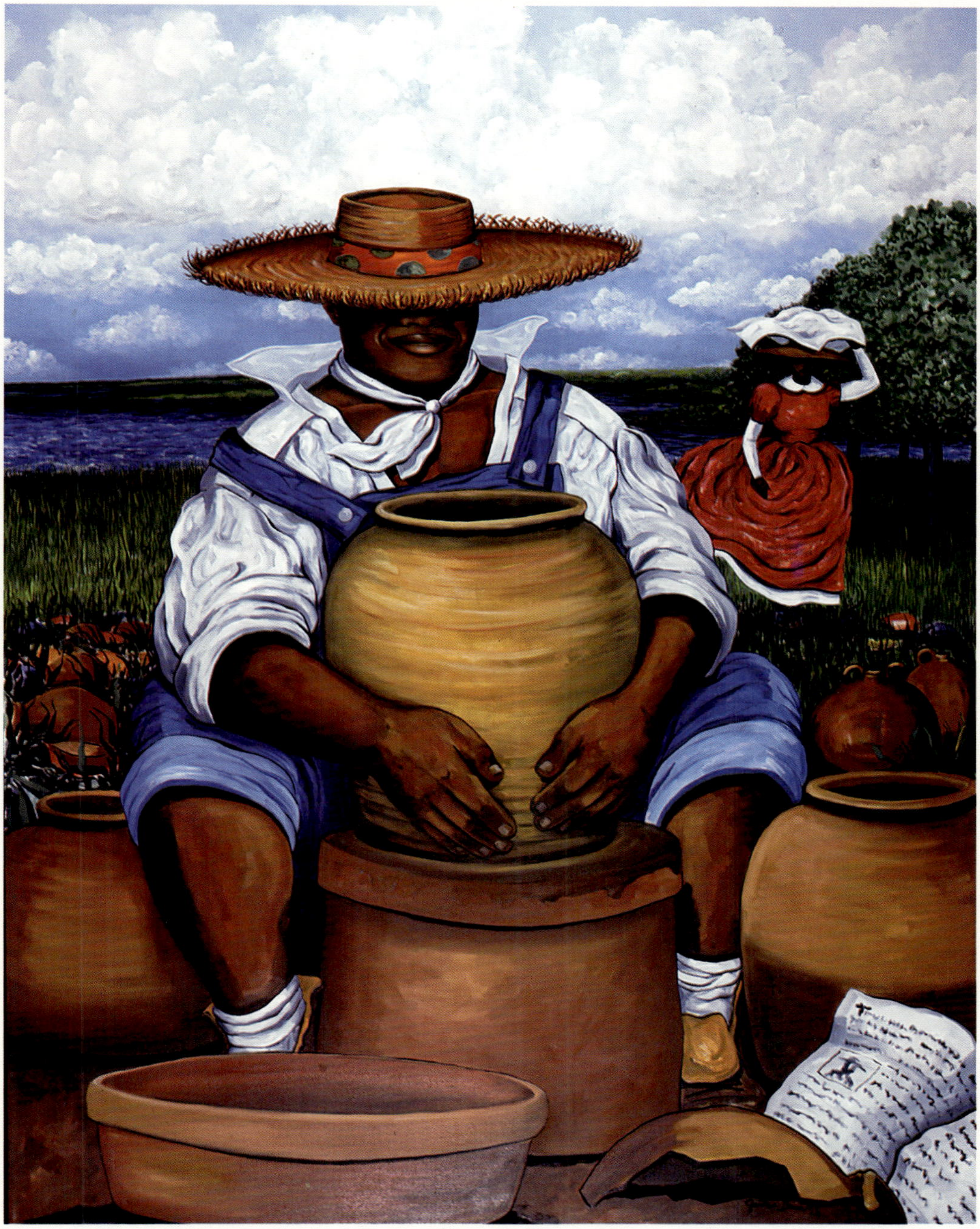

Dave the Potter from the *Sir Dave* series, 1998. Jonathan Green (American, b. 1955). Oil on canvas, 60 × 48 inches. Courtesy of Jonathan Green Studios. © Jonathan Green.

I, MASTER

Who drives de whip
be at de helm *Work harder, boy,*

don't nobody have to tell me.
Back into dis clay, I shoulder de grind.

See my pots and you'll know Ise yoked
not by lash, but by every chamber of my heart.

What my mouth don't say my hands do
my pots be what most people ain't: whole.

Head down Ise lifted up higher
dan de one tryin his best to beat me down.

Into each mound I pulls a body into being.
With dese hands a fire burns dat can't be doused.

Sometimes I get puffed up wild turkey like.
I do my best to smooth my feathers down.

Bend myself around prayer, but here I stand
closes to de Lawd, my one true master.

He turns de world; I spin dis wheel.
I breathe life into dese lumps.

I too from mud make miracles.

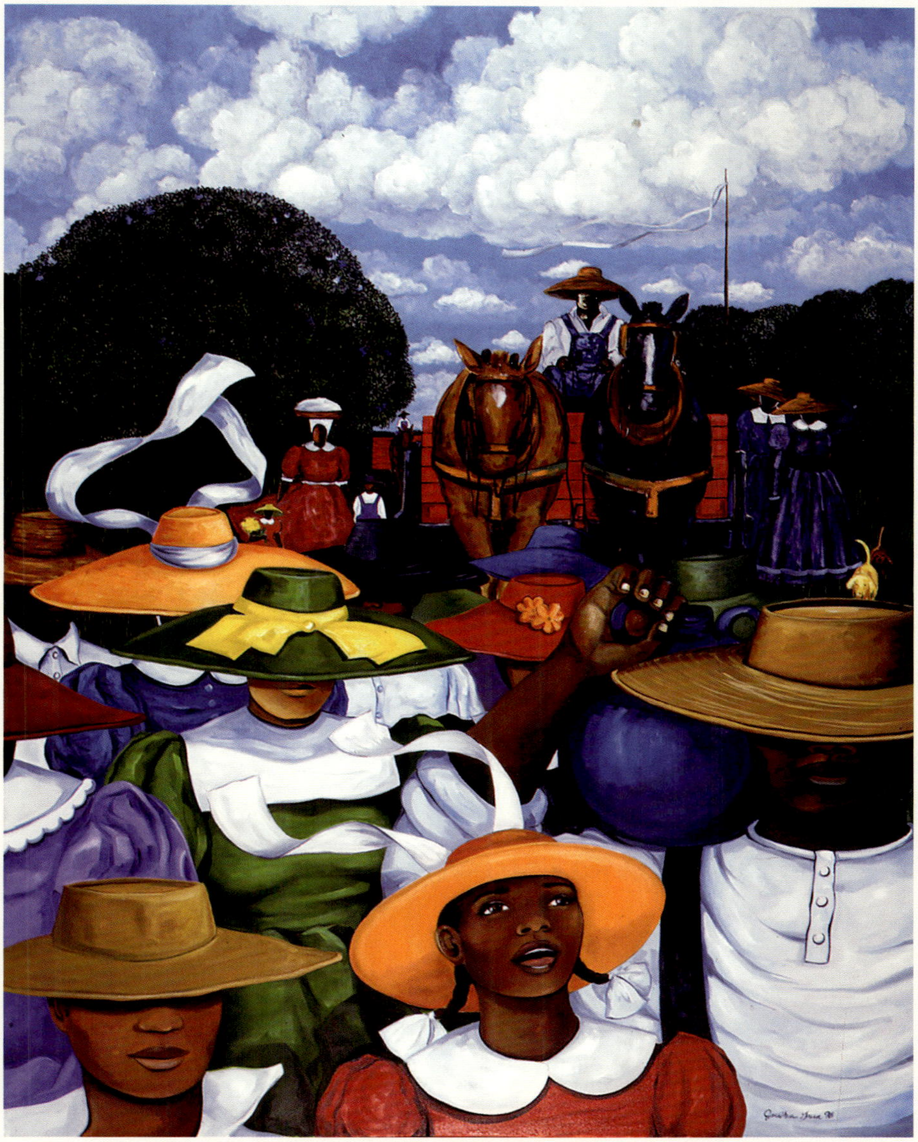

Dave's Market from the *Sir Dave* series, 1998. Jonathan Green (American, b. 1955). Oil on canvas, 60 × 48 inches. Courtesy of Jonathan Green Studios. © Jonathan Green.

MARKET

I pulls people like I pulls pots
from miles around dey come

to see what I got on spin.
Pots and plenty of talk.

I knows what to be saying.
I gots de gift of de gab.

I open hearts, wallets, and purses.
I do what I do and does it well.

Plenty of sun in my words
to keep smiles on all de faces.

Dey say Ise potter, but my work
Got many layers for de Lawd,

Dey say all dat glitter ain't gold.
Know Ise glitter and Ise golden.

I Write: *Give me silver or; either Gold =*
though they are dangerous; to our Soul =

Ise not lost. I, potter, poet and preacher.
Shout, *If you don't lisen at the bible you'll be lost* —

Dey comes to buy, but what I really got,
can't be bought or sold. Gots to be believed.

Can I get a witness? Can I get an Amen?
Step right up ladies and gentlemen.

Look at all of de pots and dis potter.
See what de Lawd done turned.

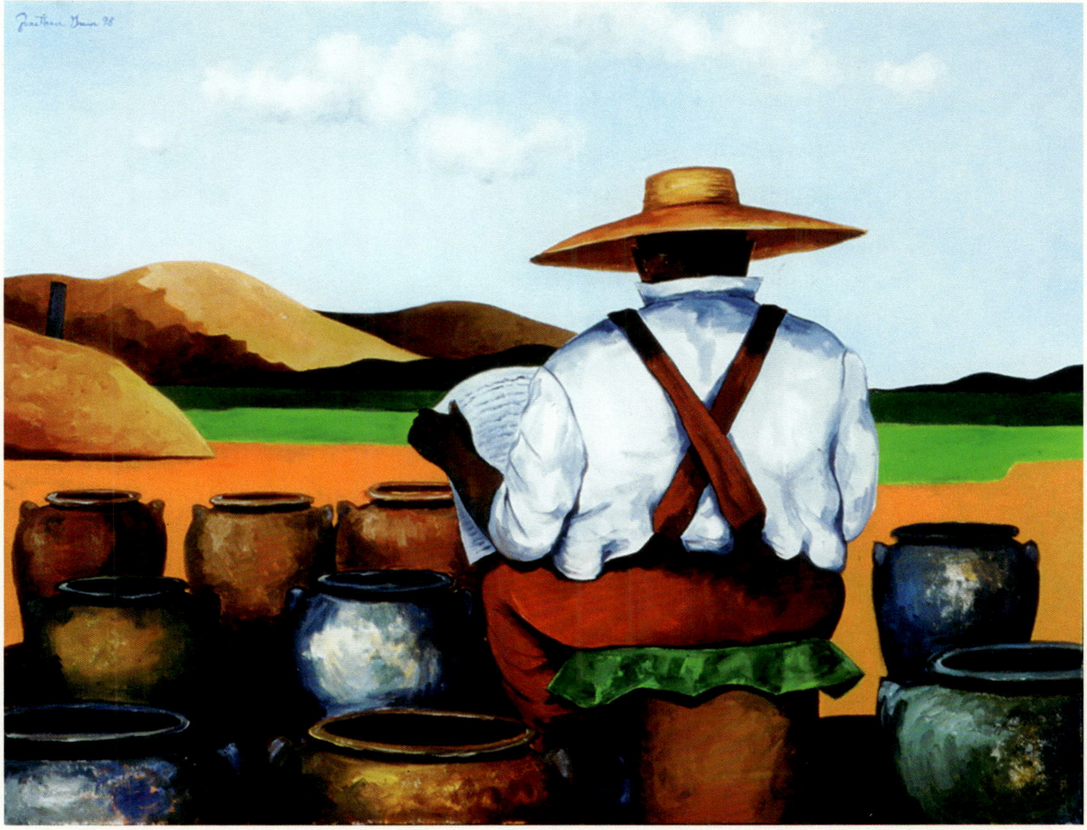

Sir Dave from the *Sir Dave* series, 1998. Jonathan Green (American, b. 1955). Oil on canvas, 18 × 24 inches. Courtesy of Jonathan Green Studios. © Jonathan Green.

READ

To sit tall in dese words,
I travel more dan miles:

from chains
to potter to poet.

Nobody knows all my doings.
I quiet when I piece dem together.

Ise a quick field study.
Sees it once, I got it.

When nobody
lurking over my shoulder,

ABC be like clay on de wheel.
I make letters into words.

I turn em
till dey come round.

I knows every thangs a living thang—
every living thang speaks.

If you got an eye and ear
to see and hear it.

Field shout: barren or ripe
Mountain show: winter or spring

Sky say: rain or sun.
I read what de Almighty wrote.

I knows it like,
I knows myself.

Genesis preach: *in de beginning was de word*
and de word was God.

In my words
be my beginning.

Everywhere I look,
I see God:

In my words, in de world
in me.

God ordered my life
like lines:

first land, next pots,
den clay page.

BRICKMAKING: RECIPE FOR WRITING

I mix mortar to make bricks:

> 1 part water
> 2 parts grit
> a whole mess of sweat off my brow

Stir
Stir

Turn my mouth just so.
Make de whole lot set right.

Before dey dry, levels dem.
Den go to school on em.

No paper, just wet slate.
No pen. Stick.

Writes: D-A-V-E.
Writes it over and over again.

Ain't easy, but wid dese letters,
I learns to steady my hand.

Den I stack dem bricks even like
—one on top of de other.

Know for miles around
de houses where white people live,

where dey lay dey heads
de walls speak my name.

PRAISE DAVE

First time I see a jar rise up,
I be midwifed into life.

Understood how these pots and I be kin
—dismissed to what's underfoot.

I learned to turn and turn—
people the world with pots.

I pour my need into the knead
until forty thousand around me crowd,

but everything I love, I lose
so I want what I mold to hold.

Even my empty pots
be full. One say:

I wonder where is all my relation
friendship to all and every nation.

There are lanterns in my words—
every story got another story.

Some call me Dave the slave, if that's all they got,
I say leave the rhymes to me.

When people look at me, a slave be
the first excuse they use not to see me.

I say praise me. It won't fall on deaf ears.
I catch praise like most people catch naps.

I am a 6-foot vessel of anything, but ordinary
a one of a kind with a Carolina shine.

I stepped out of the rows of cotton
to master the potter's wheel.

I take the wind out of can't.
With my mark, I make a mark.

I sign my name Dave.
I don't write slave.

See if my pots and me spin history.
See if we   hold   hold   hold.

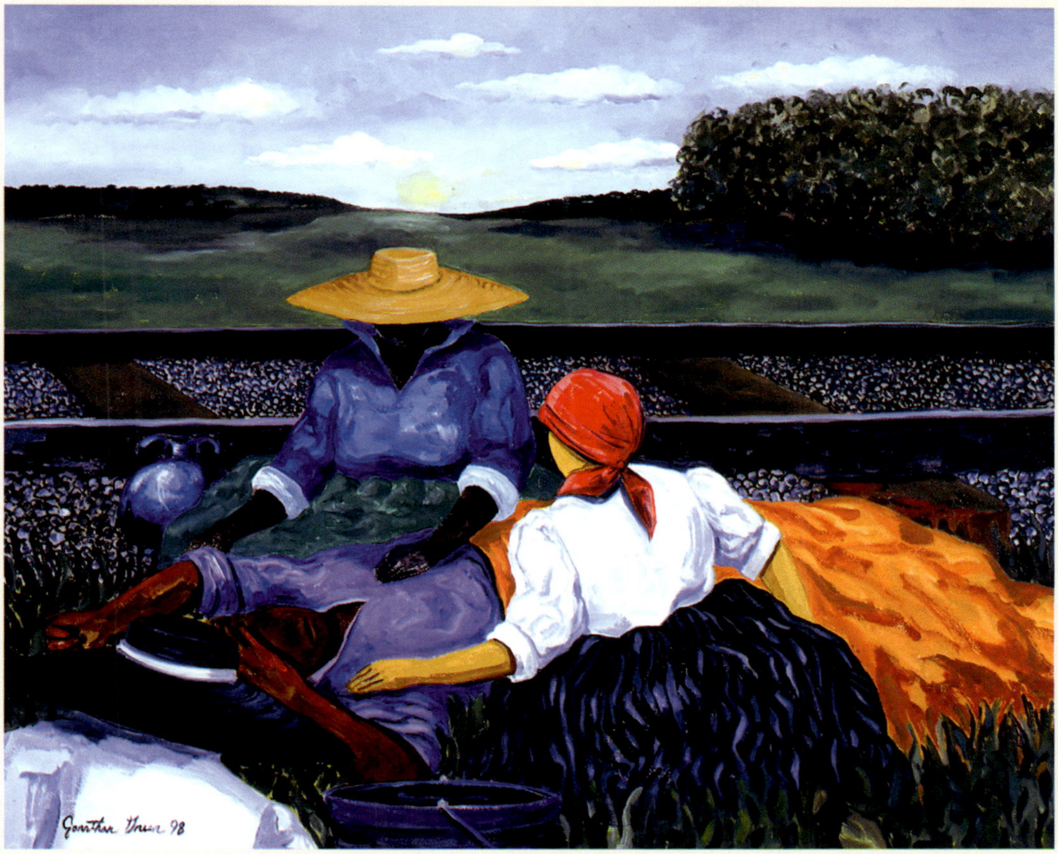

Crossroads from the *Sir Dave* series, 1998. Jonathan Green (American, b. 1955). Oil on canvas, 16 × 20 inches. Courtesy of Jonathan Green Studios. © Jonathan Green.

HOW I WALK

Dis leg gone feel de same way it always do
no matter how I walk something inside missing.

Dis one leg gone feel like I always feel
not having a say, when I gets to come and go—

about my kin being bought and sold.
What of my one leg?

Ise gotta pain I can't tote,
a toothache in my heart.

I know I be de potter dat fires de bottle
but I also be de bottle dat can't hold its fire.

I barter pots for a lil taste of de moon
in my mind dat be an even trade,

but I be out of my mind sometimes
be xactly where's I aim to go.

In dis light, I tells myself, life ain't dat bad,
but flapping mouths speak contrary.

Say I drinks too much.
Dey might be right I drinks a little.

Dere's two kinds of moonshine:
skied and bottled.

I drinks both in.
Love how dey both burn.

IRONY

A one-legged man
who writes in twos.

JARRING

He of one leg
spins pots in chains.
Writes dope deuces like
Give me silver or either Gold
though dangerous to our Soul
On the twenty seventh of July
One-thousand and eighteen forty
a man stuck in red clay—never
a run-away except in his mind.
In Carolina he gave his jars
plenty of lip. They still run
they mouths every
which way for
Dave.

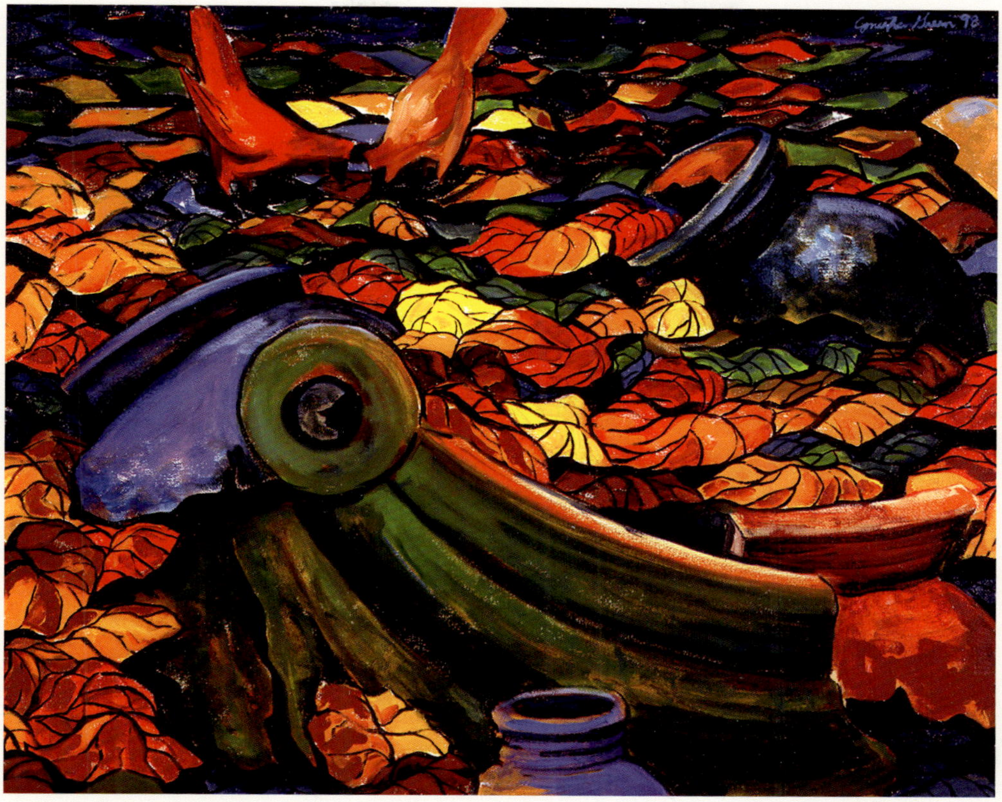

Potter's Fragments from the *Sir Dave* series, 1998.
Jonathan Green (American, b. 1955). Oil on canvas,
16 × 20 inches. Courtesy of Jonathan Green Studios.
© Jonathan Green.

Slavery's Slippery Touch

by Gabrielle Foreman

I shattered knowing hands
would search for shards, demand

you see the perfect and the marred
dig in clay and sift through dust flung-far for pieces lost in dung-ash-earth an ocean's scar

and dead-eyed glaze of thirst in recent sea—a precious little girl is gone to me.
I wonder ware to turn and turn and turn a loss I cannot flee. Conceive

that river's gaping mouth, ferocious flow, no stay, no route to track or trace
or trade the echo's sound erased along this way like empty space

within these pots' clay walls history
shatters begins again forestalled

Slavery's slippery touch, its slippery, slippery, touch . . .

REMAINS

Every broken thang speaks
in jagged edges

some shattered
some lost pieces

urging all
to re-mem-ber

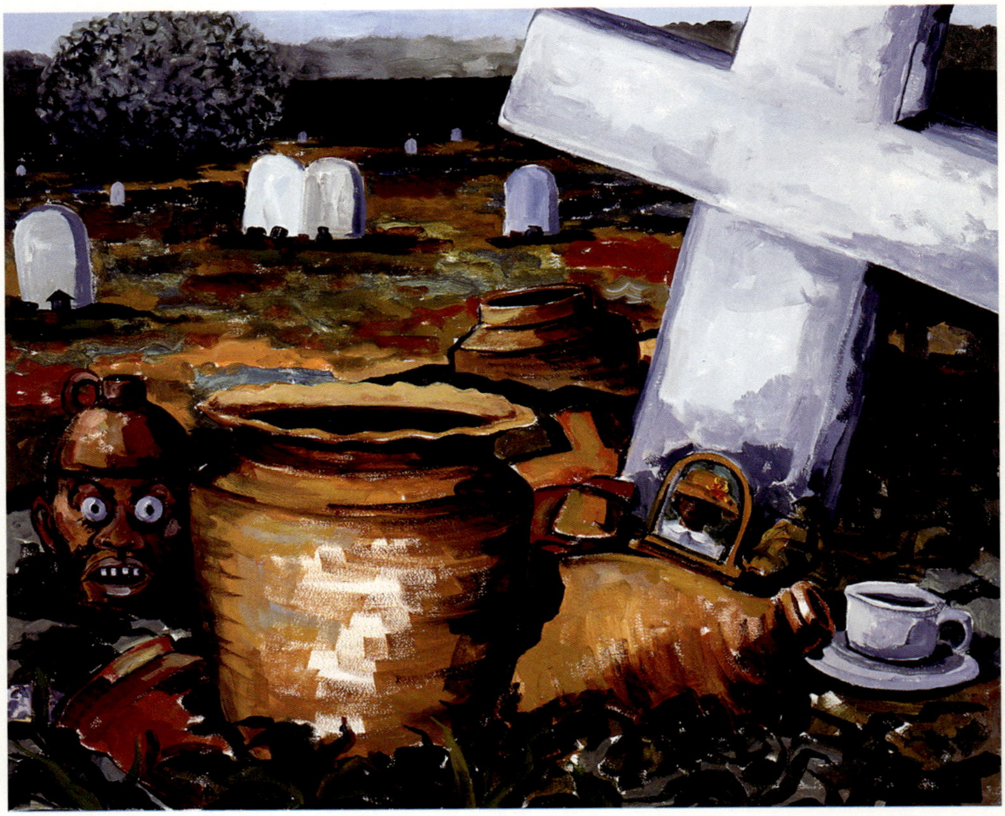

Earth to Earth from the *Sir Dave* series, 1998. Jonathan Green (American, b. 1955). Oil on canvas, 16 × 20 inches. Courtesy of Jonathan Green Studios. © Jonathan Green.

DEEPEST POT

Ise a maker of pots,
bricks and poetry,

but I don't know what to make of dis,
'cause you never dead to me.

Dis ground don't know you.
Dis grave can't hold you like I do.

Stone and cross marks yo spot,
but dey can't speak.

Can't say your name
wid de heat of my lips.

Dese thangs heah:
teacup dat yo lips touched,

pots my hand molded, just be tokens
of de love we done built.

Death be liar and a thief,
but can't steal what I be carryin for you.

Ise be yo marker, cause Ise be de one
you mark yo time wid.

Earth be a circle and my minds always
comin back round to you.

Ise yo witness and yo amen.
I be de deepest pot holdin you.

Dis good-bye ain't gone
cause as long as I'm takin in air—

yo memory
got plenty of breath.

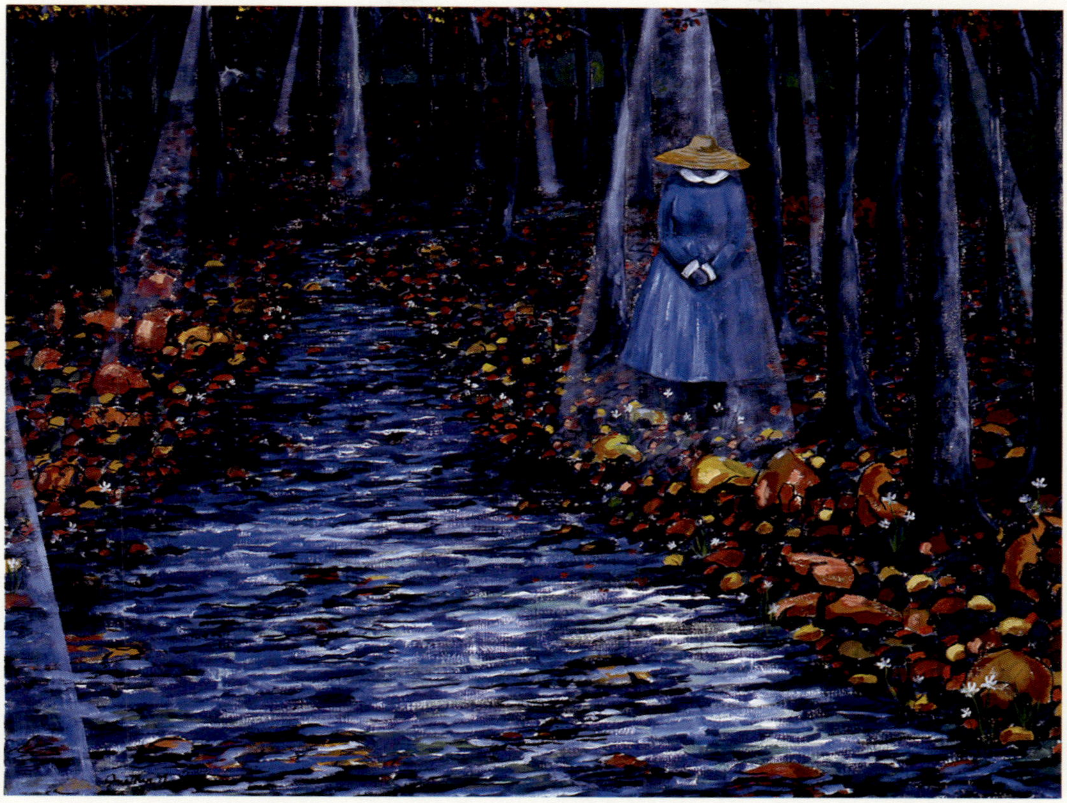

From Earth We Came from the *Sir Dave* series, 1998. Jonathan Green (American, b. 1955). Oil on canvas, 18 × 24 inches. Courtesy of Jonathan Green Studios. © Jonathan Green.

GRAVE

Even in death
we can't escape.

You in dis ragged patch
passed off as a so-called grave.

Me a-steal-away at night
'cause I ain't daylight free.

Gots to come
when de land don't call:

between washin clothes
and wringin chicken necks.

Sunday be dat day
no plow touch de ground.

I get here den, but Lawd knows
your memory calls on me every day.

Reminds me how I know myself
from my name coming out your mouth:

freedom and home
in one breath.

I was a well-held cup in your hands
I won't feel that whole again.

When your fingers danced on my skin
I grieves you all de time,

but I don't let a drop of dis river
spill from my eye

I tamp down what wails.
I 21 nails and pine box myself shut.

I come to dis place where you buried
to mark my misery—

no tombstone no name etched
—just me

From de earth we came
and to it we shall return Bible says.

I guess it be a blessing
for you,

I prays you at rest
on de other side of Jordan,

but I can't sing, *Hallelujah Anyhow.*
Dis be de heaviest work I ever done

carrying on
carrying you

living
inside my chest.

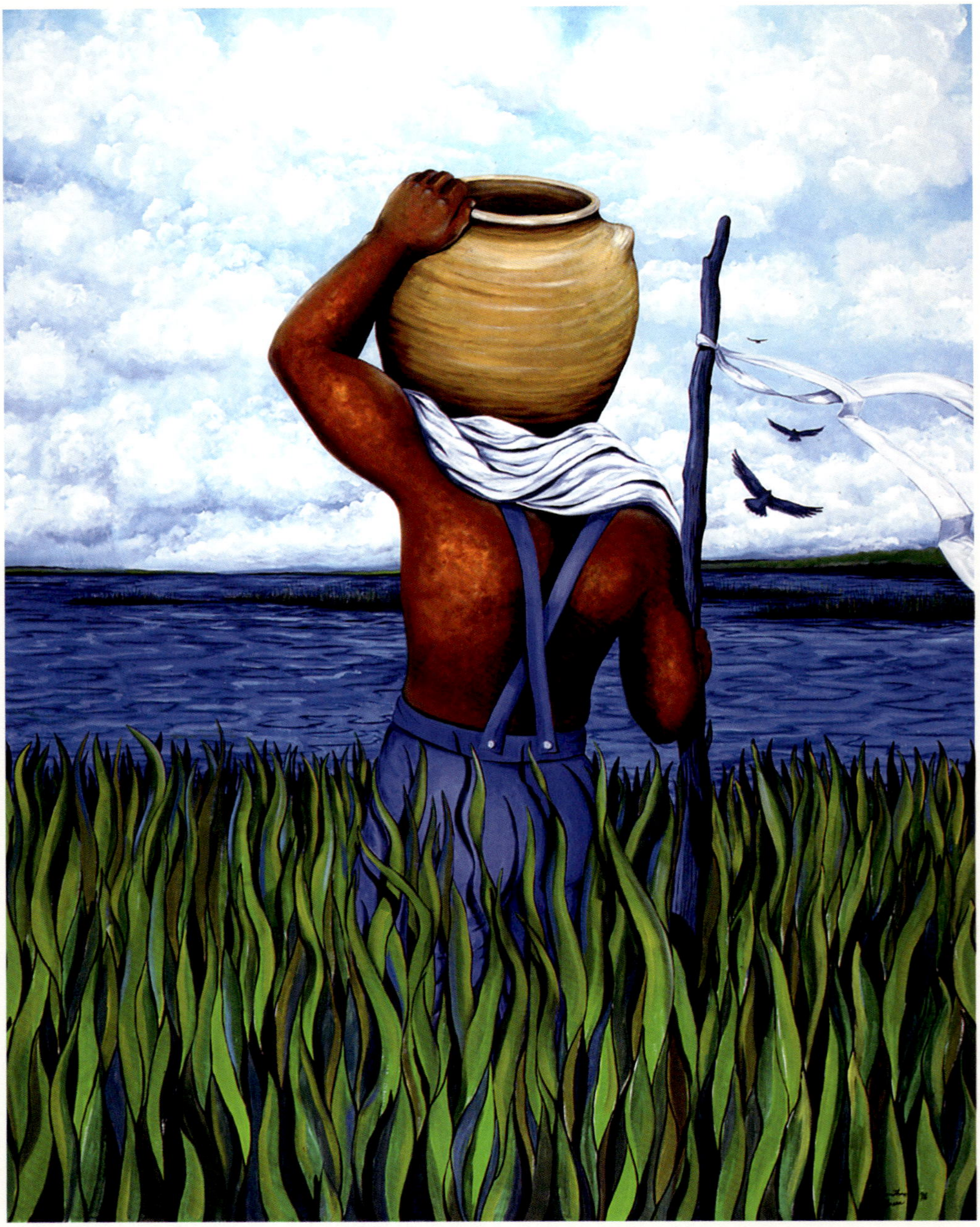

Marshland Passage from the *Sir Dave* series, 1998. Jonathan Green (American, b. 1955). Oil on canvas, 60 × 48 inches. Courtesy of Jonathan Green Studios. © Jonathan Green.

TRIBUTARIES

Travel,
if not by foot,

by water
or by land.

My pots go
where dey called

to hold meat, rice,
lard, beans, and corn.

My prayers go
where my pots go.

So, across oceans
across fields. I go.

Pots I made to carry me places
I'd never see, but I dream.

I pour into dem
and into me dey pour.

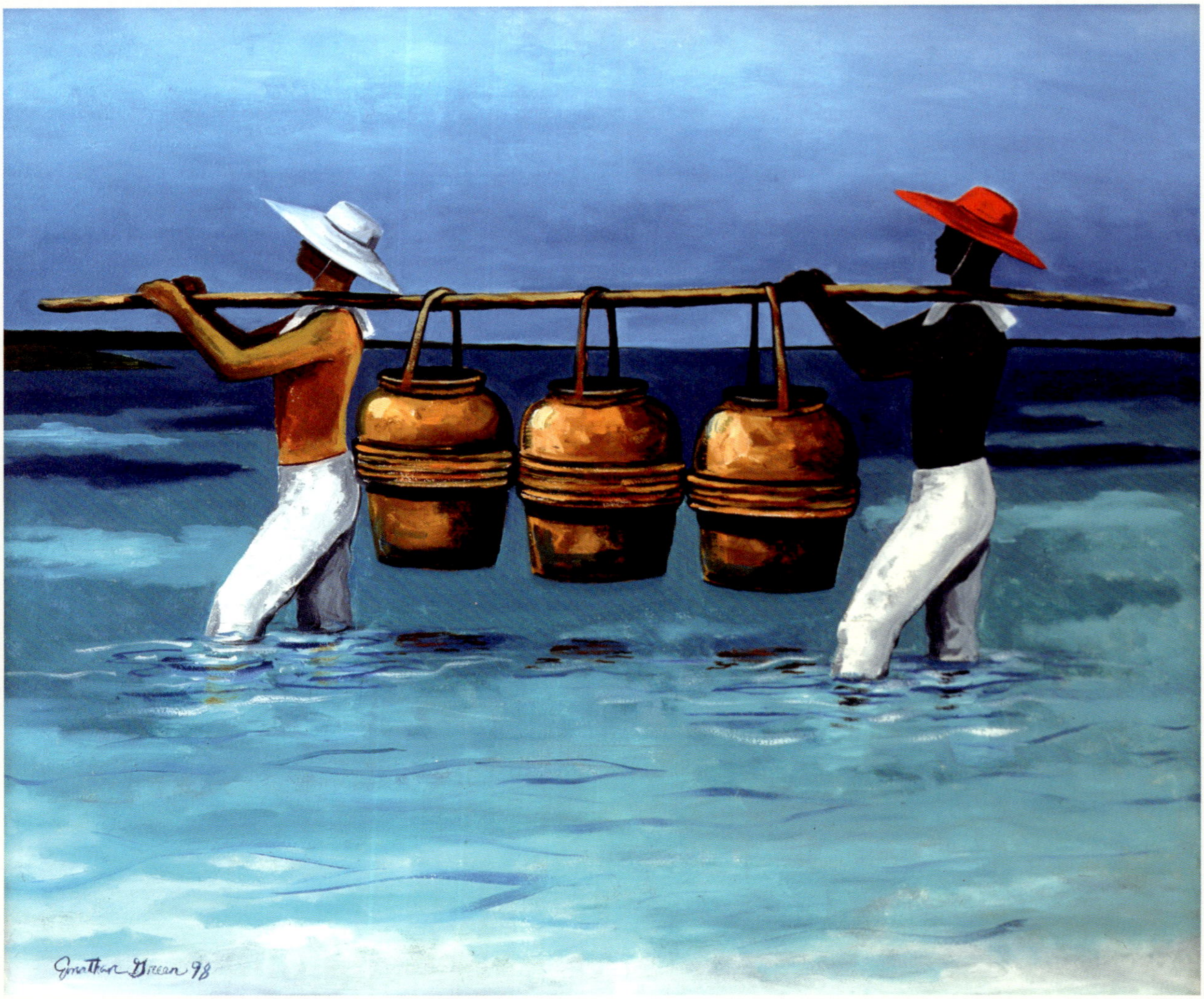

Three Vessels from the *Sir Dave* series, 1998. Jonathan Green (American, b. 1955). Oil on canvas, 16 × 20 inches. Courtesy of Jonathan Green Studios. © Jonathan Green.

HEAVEN-HUMAN-EARTH: A FOUND POEM

Numerology by Joanne Walmsley—SACRED SCRIBES

Number 3 resonates with the energies of optimism and joy,
inspiration and creativity, speech, and communication,
good taste, imagination and intelligence, sociability, and society,

friendliness, kindness, and compassion. also relates to art, humor,
energy, growth, expansion, and the principles
of increase, spontaneity, broad-minded thinking, synthesis, triad,

heaven-human-earth, past-present-future, thought-word-action,
demonstrates love through creative imagination, comprehensive,
fulfillment, encouragement, assistance,

talent and skills, culture, wit, a love of fun
and pleasure, freedom-seeking, adventure, exuberance,
brilliance, free-form, being brave, non-confrontational,

rhythm, passion, surprise, sensitivity, self-expression, affability,
enthusiasm, youthfulness, enlivenment, psychic ability, and manifestation:
David Drake via Jonathan Green and Glenis Redmond

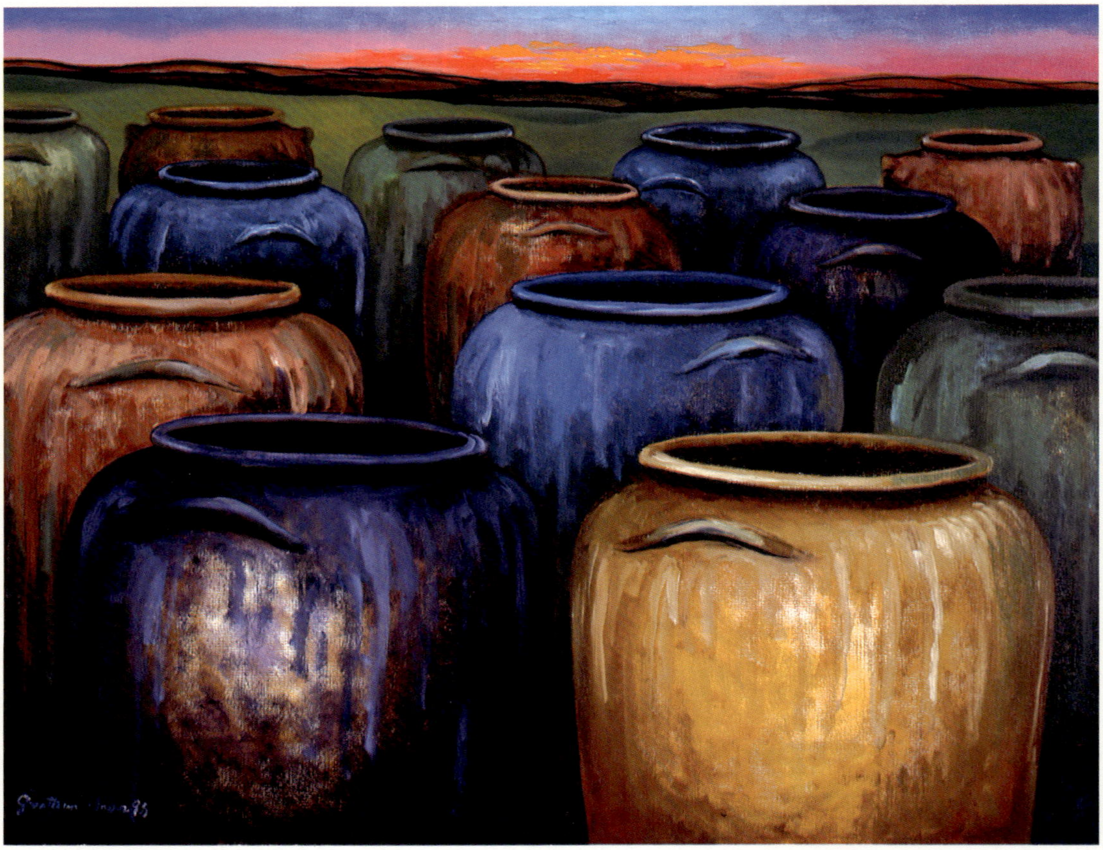

Vessels of Sir Dave from the *Sir Dave* series, 1998. Jonathan Green (American, b. 1955). Oil on canvas, 18 × 24 inches. Courtesy of Jonathan Green Studios. © Jonathan Green.

EMBODIED

Wise women have always been portals
on Sankofa wings they fly us to the past

show us how to re-mem-ber who we were.
Women unafraid to gather strength in numbers

clad in sunset and ocean colors
ready to do battle in love and in struggle.

Shoulder to shoulder village proud they stand:
our mamas, sisters, grandmas, and aunties

full-bodied, feet solid, full-lipped
mouths singing:

Lay your burdens down
what you can't bear, we were made to carry.

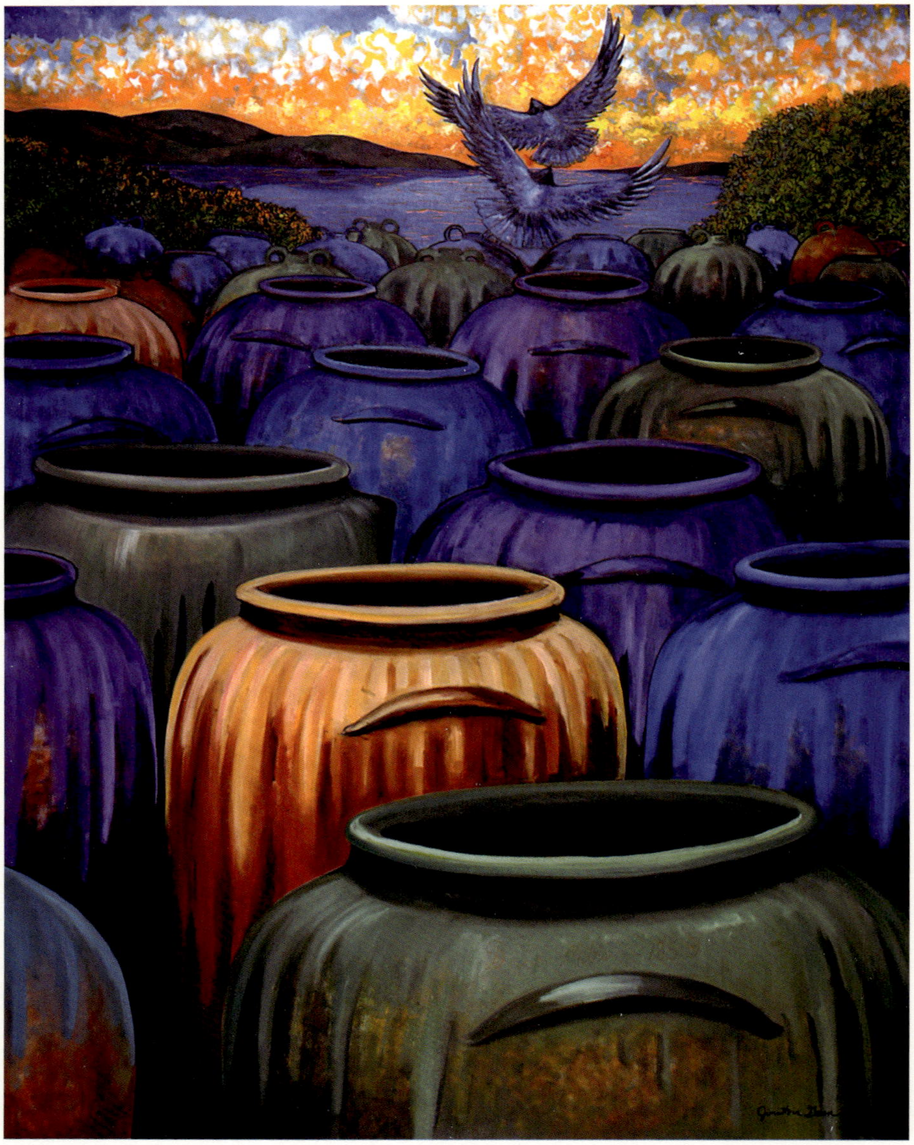

Vessels for Taking Us Home from the *Sir Dave* series, 1998. Jonathan Green (American, b. 1955). Oil on canvas, 18 × 24 inches. Courtesy of Jonathan Green Studios. © Jonathan Green.

CARRY US

I wonder where is all my relation
etched by your hand
Calls to us Sankofa-like
from torn skies

Carries us home
On this side of history
we still wonder where are all our relations?

Africa always appears in pieces
off the coast of South Carolina
on the corner of Market and Meeting Street
a woman sits with a soul as old as weaving
with blades she braids
not just sweetgrass baskets
but us back into being

Down yonder in somebody's kitchen
on the back eye of a stove
a stew of oxtails, okra, rice, and peas thicken
a stew meant to fortify us
like *the language we cry in*
the music of Gullah on tongues
passed from daughter to daughter
Mende lives in the low country
in this song that can't be unsung

Ah wakuh muh monuh kambay yah lee luh lay tambay
Ah wakuh muh monuh kambay . . .

everyone come together, let us work hard;
the grave is not yet finished; let his heart be perfectly at peace

our prayers chanted in pots
the djembe and the dundun drum
can't be undone

Africa always appears in pieces
She's in shards, but we continent stitch
we eye it and ear it
then resurrect it
we remember what's been dismembered

in drum, songs, basket weave
and our food in our dishes and trance dance

Out of this no name lineage
they tried to erase us
but you rise like one of your noble pots

Up from Edgefield you come like you never left.
Your name signed large.
Your pots world-wide travelers now
holding ground that we've been searching for
we will bear the weight of your story
the sorrow and joys held like those women
in Africa with straight backs
carrying pots like it was no burden
spines set with dignity

You carry us Sankofa-like
We carry you
walk to extend our ancestral roots
if not, what we all stepping for?
Other than bid these stories whole
the wonder spinning in your words
you in us—us in you—we your relations

We marvel at your back curved
over the potter's wheel
hand curled around a pointed stick
poised over wet clay—messages pressed into us
keep turning this struggle
keep turning
this struggle
keep turning
this struggle
carry us home

NOTES IN THE MARGIN (AN ANCESTRAL ARS POETICA)

To find our Black history,
search libraries and courthouses.

There, relegated to slave records
to property ledgers. Note:

just below animals: mules, horses, and cows.
Beneath objects: farm equipment and household goods.

Witness even in this tight space
how we are not fastened to the page.

Understand our ancestors' feet did the talking.
We're lost in these vast erased spaces.

Listen.
Hear silenced voices and lives.

Consult the field.
Hear it say: *I got more rest than they did.*

Blood cries out, so listen to the lynching tree.
Ask why does it lean? Let the whipping post tell it.

It speaks in tongues of slash and deep gash.
Smell the wounds turned to puss. Don't turn your head.

See Black backs calligraphed with grief and anger.
Measure the distance between cabin and big house,

but feel the canyon in between.
See daytime and nighttime through cabin slats.

Know cold and heat intimately. Hear bellies growl.
See chains or no chains but kept anyhow.

What of their names? You get a price. Numbers. Profit.
You might get a cook, a seamstress, a blacksmith, or a field hand.

With a little luck and a little grace, you are blessed
to find a relic to press your dream memory upon.

Conjure like a griot. Stir the pot.
Keep it hot.

Say *enslaved* not *slave*. What was done,
was done unto us: shackle and chain.

African proverb: *until the lion writes*
every story will glorify the hunter.

Grow teeth and claw. Prey with Pen.
Write in this vein: In this terror.

In this glory.

Reading Glenis Redmond's *All My Relation* More Closely

P. GABRIELLE FOREMAN

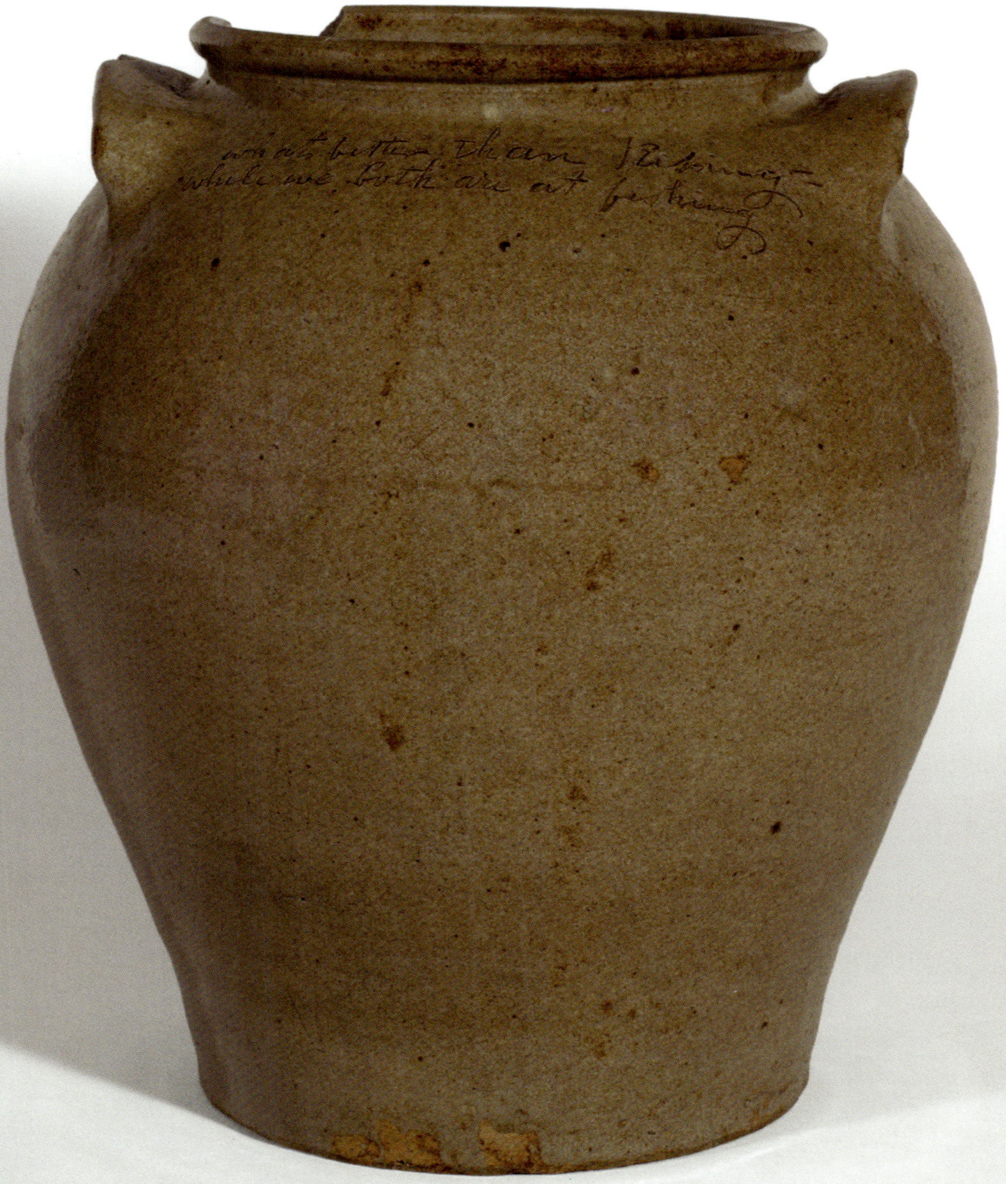

OVERLEAF: Poetic Vessel, "whats better than kissing =," July 10, 1840. David Drake. Greenville County Museum of Art.

IN THE CONVERSATION BETWEEN Jonathan Green, Glenis Redmond, and Gabrielle Foreman included in this volume, Foreman asks what scholarship on their work means to each of them. In response, Redmond mused, "When someone pays that close attention, I'm not used to being heard on that level. Who's used to being listened to on that level?" "When someone . . . takes time to take their gaze—to actually pay attention," she continued, "that is a great honor because that also elevates the work too, in a very different way. It extends the work. It introduces it to another audience."

Drake incised this lament onto one of his pots: "I wonder where is all my relation?" To that searing question, this book answers, "We are your kin. Your legacy includes your cultural descendants as well as your ceramic vessels."

What follows here is a reflection on Redmond's cycle of poems *All My Relation*, her response not only to the poetry and pottery of David Drake, a cultural ancestor from South Carolina, whom she met, as it were, late in life, but also to renowned South Carolina painter Jonathan Green, who was a beloved figure, but whose series on David Drake, *Sir Dave*, Redmond had never heard about and didn't know before this project began. Her poems speak for and to David Drake as they speak with and to Green's vibrant paintings about Drake's life. In doing so, she raises questions about Black historical treasures that have been hidden and stolen, and about Black cultural legacies that are buried and those we resurrect. Redmond's poetry asks, "How do we remember and memorialize what we know? How do we make space for what we don't?"

The beginnings of a book, or cycle, of poetry and the gestures and strategies authors use to welcome readers into their worlds "reveal a great deal about what will follow," as poet Natasha Sajé points out.[1] In Redmond's *All My Relation*, two of the early poems are paired with Green's painting *Young Dave*. Called "What I Knows" and "What I Don't Know," they are about Drake's first years and about historical memory. As persona pieces told in the potter's voice, these poems assert a legacy of Black being and remembrance that survived, when it could, by taking root in history's rocky crevices. "What I knows about my beginning / is like an empty field before seed," declares the speaker in the opening stanza of "What I Don't Know." Told in Drake's voice, this line resonates with the opening of none other than Frederick

Douglass's *Narrative of the Life* (1845). In the first paragraph of the most famous of all narratives of enslaved experience, Douglass laments: "I have no accurate knowledge of my age, never having seen any authentic record containing it." Douglass explains,

> I do not remember to have ever met a slave who could tell of his birthday. They seldom come nearer to it than planting-time, harvest-time, cherry-time, spring-time, or fall-time. A want of information concerning my own was a source of unhappiness to me even during childhood. The white children could tell their ages. I could not tell why I ought to be deprived of the same privilege. I was not allowed to make any inquiries of my master concerning it. He deemed all such inquiries on the part of a slave improper and impertinent, and evidence of a restless spirit.[2]

Redmond molds this familiar uncertainty into one poem's opening lines: "I'm from what I knows / and most of what I don't." Both of her "Young Dave" poems announce the tension between self-knowledge and self-possession under slavery. They follow the strong, competing currents of the known and unknown that flow through and underneath these paired poems' surfaces. As the speaker in each, David Drake represents the many millions of enslaved children and adults who were forced to live without claim to the most basic and intimate details of their own personal histories. These poems call attention to the self-possession and confidence Drake squirreled away despite slavery's greedy, whites-only claims to humanity. They also highlight the loss of identity and family ties that force the speaker to live on the edge. The speaker skates on the blade of white constraints that constantly cut away at his self-possession and exists "on the rim" of his pots, enjoying the sometimes ability to turn a phrase or a pot, while "not fully free neither."[3]

Spoken in the potter's voice, "What I Knows" is the first of the two poems to respond directly, ekphrastically, to *Young Dave*. The poem speaks to the known and unknown worlds of racial bondage our ancestors endured, and to the known and unknown worlds encountered by those who take on the responsibility of keeping their memory and history alive.[4] Much as slavery transmogrified so many of the features of childhood that those who grew up treated as property would never know, Redmond invokes poetic form as she also fractures and transforms it.[5]

The poem falls into three thematic sections that flow into and from each other without formal stanza breaks. The first gives voice to details from the painting that inspired it. The second showcases Redmond's attention to the research and records scholars also draw from. It begins, "Dey says Ise Country Born / but I specs mama ain't, / she full of de old ways." "Dey says Ise Country Born" references the mortgage document that ushered a teenaged Drake into the historical record for the first time—the record of his being used as collateral against the loan his enslaver took, a record that reveals that he was "country born." This historical document tells us as much as we know about David Drake's beginnings: that they began in the United States, unlike at least a quarter of the captive Africans in South Carolina in the decade in which both he was born and the transatlantic slave trade was outlawed.[6] The poem's second section extends the South Carolina landscape scene painted by Jonathan Green in *Young Dave*, evoking sound as well as sight as it ends proclaiming: "Dey calls me Dave, but I believe / my mama call me by another name. / Sound like *freedom*. / Sound like *run*."

In the last section of this poem, David Drake is mature and center stage, but his mother is nowhere to be found. This is as it was in his life, from at least his teenage years. Still, in the world Redmond creates, he builds on what his mother has taught him. "Dere are many ways to be free," he declares. As the poem's speaker, he challenges slavery's limits and proclaims his own authority: "I reads when de laws say don't. / I write when de laws say don't." "Like my pots I stand firm," the poem goes on; "no matter which way I turn / I hold onto the Almighty's unchanging hand / I always finds my center." Grounded in his work and in his place in history, Dave testifies to the certainty of his mother's love, the "what I knows" that is this poem's foundation, and links it to his own self-declared creative power.

The poem that precedes these two in Redmond's *All My Relation*, "Field Cotton," is a poetic response not only to *Edgefield*, the Jonathan Green painting that inspired it, but to cotton's hungry mouths and enslavers' ravenous avarice.[7] Redmond grounds her verse in the labor that cotton's bursting bolls required, cotton sacks dragging on like the work itself, "from what seems like Genesis to Revelation." The greedy crops crowd out children and love as "we are bred and wed to this cotton spur hold." Redmond puts her readers into those fields, lets us shoulder just a sliver of history, acknowledging how its exploitation sucked vitality from those who gave it life, using them up like cotton's sister crop, slave sugar from the cane, spitting out the leftover dry fibers. Because this is the canvas on which so many Black stories are painted, "Field Cotton" and its paired painting, *Edgefield*, open the poems that tie Redmond's poetry directly to Green's paintings.

"Field Cotton" is told from the perspective of those who ghost the fields that Green paints. Here the collective speaks directly, in one voice:

> We stand not on the edge, but in the middle of the field
> in between this white blaze that God made.
>
> Our minds not fixed on the North Star, but grounded
> to the weight in our bones as we pick, prick and bleed
>
> Drag from what seems like Genesis to Revelation.
> We are bred and wed to this cotton spur hold.

With its separated, first-line reference to the title of Green's painting, *Edgefield*, this poem gives voice to those who picked cotton in the South Carolina district where David Drake lived, to those in his extended community who shared his world. In this poem, those who must feed a "cotton crop [that] got too many mouths" converge into one nameless persona that speaks directly to the reader with a plaintive immediacy and intimacy that delivers an unsentimental message with expressive power. Providing a counter to stories of Ibo Landing, which Green's paintings and Redmond's poems each reference, the poet writes: "We sing hymns like 'Steal Away,' but we know these songs / be the only thing we'll ever know of wings."

If Green's painting is an unpeopled invitation for viewers to imagine the hauntings of the millions of Black captives who worked those fields, Redmond's enslaved cotton pickers fill up its rows and speak. These voices, steeped in resignation, offer reflection and analysis, strong and dark, before turning back to what's at hand: endless, inescapable fields of labor. This poem is told in what are called running couplets that continue from one stanza to the next, like work that went on for centuries. These short stanzas stand out on the paper, looking for all the world like rows, like lines of cotton the poem's speakers must follow, filling up their cotton sacks, spurred to move along each line by the threat of the whip if they don't make weight. With no formal rhyme scheme or defined meter, this poem sports none of the iambic pentameter that make poems easy to repeat as they trot along—any heroism to be had under slavery wilts in the relentless heat of field cotton.[8] This poem winds through each verse without end or stop, without offering relief or resolution. This poem gives voice to those who did not escape, those who are reduced from dreamers and singers, from eye and ear, to hands, which is the word used to count workers under the system of plantation slavery. Its speakers are those whose work didn't make it into museum galleries years later, those whose names we do not know—just as it was planned.

Many of the poems that make up *All My Relation* embody the voice of a particular person/a who voices their thoughts and stories, and David Drake's perspective often takes center stage. In the closing five poems, Redmond pans back to reflect on history, to reflect on the poet's and readers' relationship to archives of slavery (in what poets might call an *ars archivum*), and to address David Drake poet to poet. Before that, she shares this cultural ancestor's story in his own strong voice. Fully two-thirds of the first fifteen pieces are persona poems; of those, Redmond's Dave speaks directly to the reader in nine. Mirroring Drake's own penchant for writing couplets, many of Redmond's poems in this cycle are written in couplets too.[9] She also incorporates African literary/oral forms, such as the Praise Poem, which across the continent is often used to celebrate and document the achievements of chiefs and kings.[10]

The hybrid persona/praise piece, "Praise Dave," turns to his transformation into, or his resurrection as, a master potter: "First time I see a jar rise up / I be midwifed into life," it begins. "Understood how these pots and I be kin / —dismissed to what's underfoot." The poem moves from his understanding of white dismissal to an assertion of what can't be dismissed—his self-worth. In the vein of Nikki Giovanni's "Ego Tripping (there may be a reason why)," he proclaims, "Even my empty pots / be full."

> Some call me Dave the Slave, if that's all they got
> I say leave the rhymes to me.

And, as the poem progresses:

> I sign my name Dave.
> I don't write slave.

In "Praise Dave," Redmond extends an African-centered honorific to the knighting that Jonathan Green bestows thru *Sir Dave*. If, collectively, "a series of praises makes up a national biography," then in inserting him as a praiseworthy subject in the place of the unseen and once owned "Dave the Slave," Redmond also elevates David Drake to the national prominence he deserves.[11] "See if my pots and me spin history," announces the poem's closing couplet as he challenges those who can't see his power and artistry. "See if we   hold   hold   hold."

Though most of *All My Relation*'s persona poems are told in David Drake's voice, others join in a poetic cantata that dramatizes the enslaved community's labor, loves, and losses. "Field Cotton" shares the collective story of those in Drake's community who never found a way to freedom, "Our minds not fixed on the North Star, but grounded / to the weight in our bones as we pick, prick and bleed." Paired with Green's painting *Earth to Earth*, the poem "Deepest Pot" is an elegy to an unnamed love the potter may have lost. Likewise, the poem "Grave" paired with Green's *From Earth We Came* is an elegy to David Drake. These lonely lamentations are perhaps the most intimate pieces in the series and the most personally and historically poignant. Just as the titles of the paintings (*Earth to Earth, From Earth We Came, Vessels for Taking Us Home*) that inspire these poems bring pieces of the larger series together, Redmond's pairing and placement link them, couple them. In each poem, lovers speak to each other through the veil of death—each pronouncing their loss from the other side. Poetic images link them together too. In the first, "Deepest Pot," standing at his beloved's grave, the potter highlights the objects placed about it:

> Dese thangs heah:
> teacup dat yo lips touched,
>
> pots my hand molded, just be tokens
> of de love we done built.

The speaker's remembrances in "Grave" mirrors such longing:

I get here den, but Lawd knows
your memory calls on me every day.

Reminds me how I know myself.
From my name coming out your mouth:

freedom and home
in one breath.

I was a well-held cup in your hands
I won't feel that whole again.

These paired poems' closeness, shared imagery, and tone all suggest that the beloveds in this couple are speaking to each other. Logic upends the emotional parallels Redmond creates by linking the pieces in poetic time, one falling right after the other. The woman Redmond's Dave speaks to and the one he mourns have to be different loves, different losses, from different moments in his life. At least, if we take the poems more literally, they can't both address each other if both are on the other side. Unmoored from time even in these poems, these are wives or beloveds whose names history has discarded, like the "ragged patch / passed off as a so-called grave" marked, at best, with what time will erase.[12] Witnessing this grief, we're reminded of slavery's unrelenting erasures, of how even the most "favored" and famous of those who were enslaved were tied by love and loss to the memories of those whose names we now know, and those we don't. Listeners are asked to weigh and witness the losses ignored by those who too often caused them—in the words of the speaker who shared the potter's life and love, how

Dis be de heaviest work I ever done

carrying on
carrying you

living
inside my chest.

All My Relation is in large part a narrative that tells David Drake's story in his own voice and in the voices of those around him. Like in Green's *Sir Dave* series, Drake's story doesn't end precisely in Redmond's work; rather, it transitions. That is, the past of his life gives way to the present. His first-person voice opens the first section of the cycle; and the poet's first-person voice closes it. Redmond uses many poetic forms. In addition to using persona poems, there's a double rondeau, a found poem, two shape poems, as well as all those told in the couplets that Dave the poet preferred.

"Jarring," which takes on the shape of a pot or jar, is told in the third person with a point of view grounded in the reader's era, not Drake's. Its title and opening point to the glaring ironies of this artisan's enslaved life: a potter who may have had one leg in an age when two were needed to turn a potter's wheel, the paradox of the most accomplished artisan of Pottersville—a town named after the prized skill—spinning pots in chains, the improbability of a Black master potter also being a writer of dope-deuce couplets—who is kept enslaved. The meaning of "Jarring" is underscored not only through its title's double entendre but also by the materiality of the pot shape it takes. Its base is the word "Dave." Its lid is the poem's unsettling title. And its "lip," which is a name for a pot's rimmed top opening, here appears in the line that links the poem's two timeframes: Drake's and our own. As the poem ends, that line also announces the poem's—and the pot's—talking-back, its refusal to be silenced, its triumph over time: "In Carolina he gave his jars / plenty of lip. They still run / they mouths every / which way for / Dave."

JARRING

He of one leg
spins pots in chains.
Writes dope deuces like
Give me silver or either Gold
though dangerous to our Soul
On the twenty seventh of July,
One-thousand and eighteen forty
a man stuck in red clay—never
a run-away except in his mind.
In Carolina he gave his jars
plenty of lip. They still run
they mouths every
which way for
Dave.

The stanzas in *All My Relation*'s second shape poem, "Carry Us," recollect broken wings and recall Ibo Landing. Unlike "Jarring," it is also one of Redmond's ekphrastic works; paired with Jonathan Green's *Vessels for Taking Us Home*, it likewise recalls the story of the flying Africans. In the poem as in the paintings, the pots seem to be vessels for lost spirits' souls, which call "to us Sankofa-like / from torn skies" and carry us home. Here, the potter merges with sacred pots, merges into a winged bird that goes back to fetch it, to gather strength from the ancestors whose wings we fly on and whose stories we also pick up and shoulder.

Out of this no name lineage
they tried to erase us
but you rise like one of your noble pots

Up from Edgefield you come like you never left.
Your name signed large.
Your pots worldwide travelers now
holding ground that we've been searching for
we will bear the weight of your story
the sorrow and joys like those women
in Africa with straight backs
carrying pots like it was no burden
spines set with dignity

The imagery in Redmond's "Carry Us" is not only tied to the painting *Vessels for Taking Us Home* but also to the poem "Embodied." She pairs "Embodied" with Green's *Vessels of Sir Dave,* which like *Vessels for Taking Us Home,* is peopled with majestic pots.[13] In this poem, these vessels again are sacred spaces: part womb, part wing. In "Embodied," as in Green's *Young Dave* and the poems that go with it, women are comfort and home for the enslaved artist and for all he creates and represents: "Wise women have always been portals / on Sankofa wings they fly us to the past." In this poem, the painting's pots crowding the canvas become women, "unafraid to gather strength in numbers / clad in sunset and ocean colors." Again twined to the idea of the dynamic tension between carrying the past and laying it down, these pots, these women as a collective force, these ancestors, serve as intermediaries: "Shoulder to shoulder village proud they stand: / our mamas, sisters, grandmas, and aunties / full-bodied, feet solid, full-lipped / mouths singing: / *Lay your burdens down / What you can't bear, we were made to carry*." The theme in this poem—six couplets that marry individual resignation to the ability to carry on collectively—communicates that this Sankofa message of community strength and sacred objects is something readers can count on; it is a message worth repeating over history. It is one *All My Relation* returns to again and again.

Though they're not all discussed here, every one of Jonathan Green's *Sir Dave* paintings are linked to poems in *All My Relation*. As Redmond centers Jonathan Green alongside David Drake, she resurrects and rejoices in the artistic genealogy of inspiration and response between these three Black artists, their work, and their cultural connections. This complexity of double ekphrasis, or of responding to both Drake and Green (or Drake through Green), adds temporal and spiritual dimensionality. It unsettles narrative timeframes and storytelling sequences, making them anything but linear or straightforwardly referential.

Though necessarily printed in order, Redmond's poems don't need to be read in a conventional linear sequence, as they are paired with Green's unnumbered work. With three artists and scores of pots, paintings, and poems in conversation with and through each other, these shards of images, objects, forms, and information reflect the unconventional historical tools and the nonlinear, multidimensional methods sometimes required to resurrect the lives of enslaved people whose existence was never meant to be recorded and remembered in their own words, on their own terms, or in their own artistic expression.

NOTES

1 Sajé, "Dynamic Design," 149–162. The same could be said for shorter forms such as the chapbook.

2 Douglass, *Narrative of the Life*, chapter 1, paragraph 1.

3 Penultimate line, Redmond, "What I Don't Know."

4 Redmond's titles address the concerns poet and critic Natasha Sajé raises in her scholarship about persona poetry: "Ethical difficulty arises when poets write about subjects superficially. Poets must know their subjects better than their best readers. They must know what they don't know" (Sajé, "Poetry and Ethics").

5 Redmond is adapting what is called a double rondeau, one of whose fifteen-line variants is made up of a five-line quintet, a quatrain, and then a six-line sestet, doubled either in its entirely or parts. In "What I Knows," the poem's three sections are divided into two nine-line sections followed by a double sestet with no rhyme scheme and no conventional rentrement or refrain. The form that emerges from the place where poetry and music intersect is often used for emotional subjects. It was used for melancholy subjects; its meditations on loss and pain often turn in the last lines.

6 Michael Gomez cites Robert Fogel and Stanley Engerman's data when asserting that around 22 percent of enslaved Blacks in North America between 1790 and 1810 were African born. See chart 2.2 in *Exchanging Our Country Marks*, 20, African Importation into North America. That rate would have been higher near active port centers such as Charleston.

7 "Field Cotton" and "Praise Dave" were published in Redmond, *What My Hand Say*. "Field Cotton" also appeared along with "Grave," "I, Master," and "Jarring," in *Red Rock Review*.

8 Here I'm referring to heroic couplets, which signal resolution through rhyme. Internal rhyme replaces end rhyme here—as if whatever resolution this community will enjoy will come from within.

9 Six of the poems adopt the couplet form and three of these are told in Dave's own voice. "Praise Dave" was first published in the journal *Drunken Boat* on December 19, 2014. It also appears in Redmond, *What My Hand Say*.

10 There are countless scholarly essays on praise poetry across the African continent and in Medieval Europe. As the website Africanpoetry.net puts it: "Praise-Poems exist in many different parts of Africa. In Yoruba they are called *Oriki*, in Zulu *Izibongo*, in Tswana *Maboko*—the list of examples would be a very long one" ("Introduction to Praise-Poetry").

11 "Introduction to Praise-Poetry."

12 Redmond, "Grave," lines 1–3.

13 "Embodied" falls in the middle of the cycle, the eighth poem, before "Jarring." "Carry Us" falls near the very end, and at one point, Redmond had planned to end with it.

Black Belonging and Collaborative History Making

A Conversation with Jonathan Green, Glenis Redmond, and P. Gabrielle Foreman

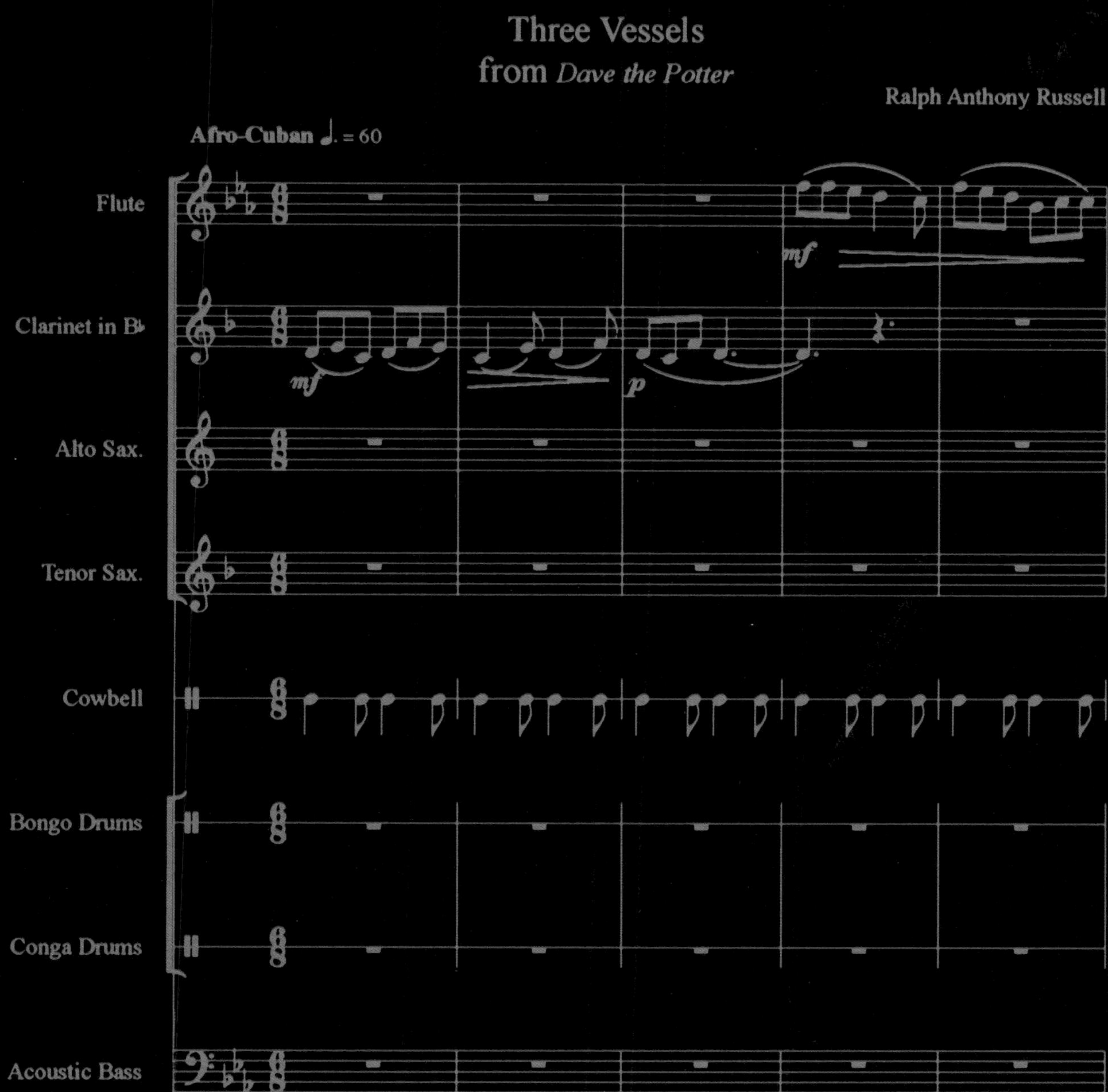

OVERLEAF: Score from "Three Vessels." Courtesy of composer, Ralph Anthony Russell.

THE COLLABORATION THAT RESULTED IN THIS BOOK developed when creative partners Gabrielle Foreman, Glenis Redmond, and Lynnette Young Overby visited Jonathan Green in 2013 at the Daniel Island, South Carolina, home of Jonathan and his partner, Richard Weedman. This began a partnership that included research trips to South Carolina, visiting lectures, museum gallery appearances, and the debut and tour of a David Drake performance. On a warm January day in 2018, Gabrielle and Glenis visited again with Jonathan in his new home in downtown Charleston. During this visit, the three spent an afternoon in a wide-ranging discussion about their joint work, which appears in condensed form below. Jonathan and Glenis reflected on place, artistic collaborations, and the importance of community, as well as their own roles in preserving David Drake's life and legacy. This conversation has been edited for length and clarity.

GABRIELLE: Let's start with *Sir Dave*, the title Jonathan uses in his series to elevate David Drake's stature and to ensure that we use his name with respect and reverence. Could you each share how you learned about Drake and talk about what his presence means to you as an artistic ancestor and an enslaved artisan?

GLENIS: [To Jonathan] You found him first.

JONATHAN: [To Glenis] But the poet . . .

GLENIS: I found David Drake through you, Gabrielle. We were working together on poetry and performance about the early Black writer Harriet E. Wilson. When I was writing the Wilson poems you said, "You know what? You need to write about Dave." And I'm like, "I'm entrenched in Harriet." And from that moment on everywhere I went somebody would say, "Do you know David Drake?" I was out in the Birmingham Museum of Art doing a poetry reading and the curator said, "I want to show you something." She just pulled me out of a group and showed me a David Drake pot. And I said, "Oh, wow. That is really beautiful. I have a colleague who talked to me about David Drake." Then I went to a school for a poetry workshop and the media specialist said, "On your break, could you come to the library?" And she pulled out a David Drake book and I said, "Okay." Then that happened a third time and I said, "Okay Dave. I will start writing."

JONATHAN: Although the subject really starts with South Carolina, I was in Florida at the time I learned about Dave. When I would come here to South Carolina, because I'm a narrative painter, people are always giving me stories. People don't realize it takes years for an artist to complete a series, and I only work in series. I don't work singly—a couple times, yes, but I really don't do that. And I think I was really fascinated with the fact that someone who once was illiterate was also a storyteller and a poet and a theologian and that he was inscribing verse on pots. I was just fascinated with the pot. And then I learned about the size of the pots and then I found out about their utilitarian value.

GLENIS: It was the Tupperware of the day.

JONATHAN: Yes, but valuable stuff. Aside from his inscriptions, the size of his pots made them valuable commodities. In folklore, the pots were large enough to put a human body in. You know, there's a culture in Africa that buries the dead in pots. And interestingly enough, when I was living in Chicago, as a student at the Art Institute, I did a very detailed ink drawing about an African man who looked like he could be in a pot. And I never really thought about that until I started to learn more about Dave. My information about Dave really came from historians, archivists, curators, and people in the museum world. They were able to share so much detail. I just became fascinated. My fascination about things is always about what our people don't know. And art is a true medium to communicate the unknown. So, I look at art as a language, as a written text. Because that's really the oldest form of communication, through visual imagery, back to cave drawings and paintings. And artists are also shamans, certainly in African culture. And I just thought it was a privilege not only to be an artist, a painter, but to have access to information, and to be able to do something with that information.

You know, a lot of us have access to information but we don't, or we can't, transform it into something that others can see and learn from. I had been talking with the poet Nikky [Finney] about rice and our project to elevate knowledge about it as a staple of South Carolina slavery that is rarely mentioned compared to cotton. And so, all these things were just coming together, and before I knew it, I was so inundated with southern culture and the lack of visual imagery of Black southern history. We have talked about this many times. If you don't have it, you have nothing. And that's what Europeans have used to control us—for hundreds of years. We need visual imagery, because we didn't always have access to written forms of text. With the artistry of writing, you have to be learned. But you don't have to be learned to look at an image and decipher what it is. When they started printing Bibles, the world was largely illiterate. And they hired or engaged these artists to create lithographs and silk screens and paintings. So, all of the great masters—Rembrandt, Renoir, Gauguin—have some relationship to the Bible in terms of what they had painted. And I think every literate artist has to deal with subject matter from the Bible. Sir Dave certainly had that connection to biblical texts.

GABRIELLE: People so often talk about "Dave the Potter" and so infrequently talk about him as a poet. Even when museums exhibit his pots, they show them as art pieces. At the National Museum of African American History and Culture, for example, their Drake pot is set too far back to see what's written on the pot! This happens in museums all of the time. Because he's known, down to what people continue to call him today, as a potter, people rarely ask about his place as an early and supremely innovative Black poet. What does he mean to you as an antecedent and as an ancestor poet?

GLENIS: I think my introduction to Dave, seven, eight years ago, came at a time when I was primed to receive Dave. But I wish I would have known about him as a youngster. Students need to see and encounter Dave. They assume all enslaved people were illiterate. We don't know how he learned to write. But he made that leap from not only writing but to creating poetry. And those couplets are amazing. "I wonder where is all my relation / friendship to all and every nation"—that, to me, is a call to us. As a poet from South Carolina, only fifty miles away from where he lived, not knowing about him makes me very angry. There's a certain rage that comes from being in school in South Carolina and not having access to David Drake. When I went to college, I had to go across those cotton fields to get there. Why didn't I ever know? So, to unearth him is personal. It is also societal. It's Dave reaching out saying, "Here I am." We've got window texts and we have mirror texts. Window text is all I ever knew growing up. It's like I was always looking out on somebody else's culture. So, I'm looking out and I'm always seeing someone else. And then, Dave comes into view. Here's a mirror.

JONATHAN: Oh, beautiful. I love that.

GLENIS: I didn't create that. Actually, my first mirror text was Jackie Earley, the poet. I heard her in the fifth grade. You know that poem "1968 Winters"? "Got up this morning feeling good and Black. Thinking Black thoughts. Did Black things. Put on all my Black clothes. Minded my own Black business. And walked out my Black door and Lawd have mercy. . ."

IN UNISON: "White snow." *[Laughter.]*

GLENIS: I was a fifth grader when I heard that poem and I sat up in my seat. Everybody else was laughing, because it is funny, because you have that repetition: Black, Black, Black. Black, Black, Black, Black, Black, white. But it wasn't until twenty years later that I found out the title. I was working with a group called Poetry Alive and they said, "Well, you're going to have to memorize 150 poems." And I said, "Good. I'm a geek about it." And then, this poem was the first poem I opened the book to. That's when I realized it was called "1968 Winters." It was about the civil rights movement. As a fifth grader, I knew it, but I also did not know it.

JONATHAN: *[Sigh.]* Let me inject one thing. When I first met Glenis, she was with her husband and her twins and we had a nice rapport. I asked you if you were a poet . . .

GLENIS: You did. I told you I was a counselor, because I was not a poet at that time.

JONATHAN: That was one of the few times I can remember feeling clairvoyant.

GLENIS: You looked at me and you said, "Why are you counseling?" And I said, "Uh, that's what my degree is in" or something. I was being very academic. And you said, "No, no, no, no." It was that shamanistic thing that you were talking about. Your presence is very much like my mother's and my grandmother's, who have these blue-ringed eyes and when they look at you and tell you something, it is like whoosh, the oracle has spoken.

I was trying to take everything I could from you. People say, "She is a South Carolinian poet," but I am a military brat. We moved back here when I was thirteen. So, I didn't understand the culture. I didn't understand racism. I mean, I knew it through my parents. But we lived in Italy. We lived in New Jersey. We lived in Washington State. I'm definitely South Carolinian, but by proxy. So when I met you, I was already on that cultural search. I also had recently been diagnosed with fibromyalgia. So, when you said, "You're a poet," I was just coming to terms with having a lifelong chronic illness. I knew I needed to do something that I adore, something that brings me life.

I had just encountered Lucille Clifton's poem,

won't you celebrate with me
what i have shaped into
a kind of life? i had no model.
born in babylon
both nonwhite and woman
what did i see to be except myself?
i made it up
here on this bridge between
starshine and clay,
my one hand holding tight
my other hand; come celebrate
with me that everyday
something has tried to kill me
and has failed.

That's when you entered my world. I was looking for ways to celebrate my life while this illness was trying to kill me. At that time, I was also in a PhD program at VCU in Richmond, Virginia. I literally was driving on Monument Avenue [and past its imposing Confederate monuments]. And a small voice said, "You are on the wrong road, literally and metaphorically." And I left and we moved to South Carolina.

GABRIELLE: South Carolina grounds so much of your and Jonathan's and David Drake's work and lives. I suggest in the introduction that your writing is sometimes a poetic juba with you and Drake in the center of the circle, and sometimes you take to the floor with Jonathan Green, and your poetry and paintings dance a Charleston step. The poetry featured in this book dances both with David Drake and with Jonathan Green's *Sir Dave* series.

JONATHAN: And the David Drake performance you all created with Lynnette Overby as well.

GABRIELLE: Yes! Can you talk a little bit about what Jonathan's presence as a vibrant young elder has meant to you in relationship to your work?

GLENIS: Well, number one he had already seen me as a poet before I was ready, while I was just practicing. He had already given me my charging orders. I practiced a long time with people saying, "Well she is a slam poet." But I really was just writing from the west African singing tradition. I fit into the slam world because there is an orality to my work. You were saying, Jonathan, "I'm a narrative painter." I am a narrative writer. And so your pictures called to me.

GABRIELLE: Glenis, you said you believe in multiple temporalities. That we can exist in different times simultaneously. You also brought this image to us of doors that open to different times. Some of those doors adorned with mirrors—and you speak of mirror texts. Does your work mirror both Jonathan and Dave the Potter?

And Jonathan, I wonder about how you are in relationship to that continuity of time and also the way you jump-start time. You're the first artist to actually reflect on David Drake's story. There are people who come after you. But it's that moment of the 1998 traveling exhibit that includes some of your art that really reintroduces David Drake as his work is seen in South Carolina, and then at Atlanta's High Museum, Detroit's Charles H. Wright Museum of African American History, and then the Winterthur Museum in Delaware. You're also the person who insists on an elevated place for him that "Sir" communicates so he doesn't return to the art world and late twentieth-century as "Dave the Potter." Can you talk a little bit about this?

JONATHAN: There was a young lady who was working on her PhD at the University of South Carolina and she was doing this incredible work on Sir Dave.

GABRIELLE: Jill Koverman.

JONATHAN: You know she has passed? She was the person who really got me onto a Dave Drake journey because she wanted me to create visual imagery of Dave. When I take on such an assignment, it's up to me to do my own research and studying. So, Richard, my partner, and I do the research together. Jill didn't understand what goes into creating a series of work. So, after the series was done—which took me like two, almost three years to complete, she only wanted one painting for the cover. So, when people heard about our collaboration—

GLENIS: They thought there was going to be more of you.

JONATHAN: Multiple images in her catalog.

GABRIELLE: So this will be the first time that the full series ever appears in a book.

JONATHAN: She was afraid that the paintings might override all the years of her work on Drake himself.

GLENIS: She was thinking academically. And we were thinking more expansively because what we do is a spiritual journey as well. There's Sankofa there.

JONATHAN: You know what it was? She had a window, but she didn't have a mirror.

GLENIS: And so what that meant is that you, Jonathan, you were the pioneer. You went there way before any of us were even thinking about David Drake.

GABRIELLE: What does it mean to you that the paintings are appearing in the volume for the first time, now, more than twenty years later?

JONATHAN: You know the mind can't go there, not that it was twenty years ago, but the work that goes into creating a series, the healthiest thing you can do is let it go.

GABRIELLE: Now we are coming full circle and finally the public will be able to see the full series here. You gave me the contact information of almost all the collectors who own the pieces that make up the *Sir Dave* series. I went on a journey for two years. I've seen maybe ten of the fourteen, from Oakland to Hilton Head. I needed to see them for a longer book I'm writing, as well as for this volume. To me, to have them all in one place matters so deeply because of the ways in which your work precedes other work and because some of those paintings, although not all of them, did go on that original tour. And that is the moment that relaunched David Drake as a master potter. Your art was part of that moment.

Let's talk about your *Sir Dave* as a narrative series. It always puts me in mind of Jacob Lawrence.

JONATHAN: My mentor.

GABRIELLE: Yes! Like him, you work in narrative scenes. But his paintings about Toussaint L'Ouverture, Harriet Tubman, Frederick Douglass, like the migration series, are numbered. And I love how the unnumbered nature of your series invites us to make meaning out of a life that was erased in so many ways. What we have in your work are pieces of his life and his objects that we can't quite put in order, that we can't puzzle together linearly.

JONATHAN: And *Potter's Fragment* is one of the titles of a painting in my *Sir Dave* series. When I work, I, the artist, I'm in the middle. So, there are no dimensions of control when I work. I try to imagine from a three-dimensional perspective what it was like in that world, from the perspective of Jonathan Green at the center. I'm not trying to be a literal painter, painting things exactly the way they were. I'm trying to be more luminous and imaginative and more folklorist in dealing with the paintings.

Many of my peers are people much older than I am: Dr. Richard Law, Maya Angelou. And they would not so much tell me stories, but they would talk. And as a young person having access to them, I knew, because I was raised by my grandmother, my role was to listen. And that's all I did. I just listened to people. So, when these projects come on, I just feel that I have to envelop myself in the story in such a way that I get lost in it. Not that you say, "Oh, this is what happened. This is one, and then two happened, and three happened." No, you're just immersed in all of it at the same time. I found over the years that when that is a part of your behavioral pattern and artistic process, you really get lost.

GABRIELLE: That brings us back to different ways to think about time, about the difference between time as a sequence of events and time as immersive simultaneity of events and experiences between the past and present.

JONATHAN: Yes, and I was just so engrossed in potter Dave as a person to have survived. I think I go into a trance.

GLENIS: It's almost as if David is speaking directly to you and through you, Jonathan. What I'm drawn to is your use of color and the paintings' rootedness to South Carolina. Because South Carolina, for good or bad, now's got David Drake—this favorite son. You know, now we have this son who's risen, you know? And in some ways, he comes through you.

JONATHAN: You know what I find fascinating? I find it fascinating that here I've already done this work and you and I had already met and I've deemed that you are a poet, and look what we're doing right now.

GLENIS: This is so full circle.

JONATHAN: That's channeling. So that's my answer to when you asked me about a series of work.

GABRIELLE: It's not a linear series but a channeled circle?

GLENIS: Well, who knows why people meet at a certain point in time or why artists are introduced to figures who inspire work at a certain time. It's like a chain reaction, a spark. I don't know if you remember, Jonathan, you called me one day and you said, "Glenis, I'm doing a calendar. I need twenty-one lines for low-income housing." I wrote a horrible twenty-one lines. But it was after I failed in that poem that I wrote my signature poem "Mama's Magic." I woke up in tears the next day and I realized that I grew up in a ramshackled house in Lawrence, South Carolina, and I just hadn't remembered. I woke up in tears and in gratitude for my mother, so I see you as a grounding rod. You were the ground. By asking for those twenty-one lines you were like, "Come back to your roots." *[Laughter.]* What is that movie, is it *Sankofa* [by Haile Gerima]? It's an independent film and the woman's modeling [on the Ghanian coast without any sense of history] and there was a shaman who appears and orders her: "Go back to your roots!" Jonathan, you be like: "You go back to your roots!"

I wasn't disconnected in an irreverent way. I was just a military kid. I had not remembered. I had been dismembered. I feel like that's the work that I'm doing. I'm remembering what's been dismembered. "Mama's Magic" was when I finally got it. That poem is not about someone or something out there. "You grew up in poverty. This is what your mama did for you. This is what your grandmother did for you." In college no professor had ever said, "Go back to what you know." Not one of them. It was all academic. It was all disconnected. I had been writing for nine years but once I was told to go back, I realized, "I know who I am now."

JONATHAN: But don't you think that for the work that you're to do, it's very important to have academic exposure? In my case of being an artist, I'm known as having taken more classes in drawing than any student in the history of the Art Institute of Chicago. I didn't know quite what I was doing, but I knew I had to do something.

All of that prepared me for now. One of my professors, Emilio Cruz, whose wife was the director of the Studio Museum in Harlem, he said to me on my first day at the Art Institute in his painting class: "Until you have drawn one thousand figures, you can't paint." You know how crushing that was? But I took him seriously. There are people who say—I hear this from artists all the time—"I can just pick up the brush and do this right now" *[snaps fingers]*.

GLENIS: You have to practice.

JONATHAN: You've got to pay your dues.

GLENIS: You do, and—yes, I was working at my craft. I was doing that. But it wasn't until I got to a place of understanding *what* I needed to write that I started going back to the source. Then I was grounded and rooted and ready to move forward in a different way.

GABRIELLE: You talk a little bit about growing up in a "ramshackle" house. And I have heard you, Jonathan, talk about the *Young Dave* painting in the series. You once told me that the house that's featured is your own grandmother's house. For each of you, your grandmothers play such an important role in your work.

Can you share how this informs the *Sir Dave* series and your poetry, Glenis? The importance of women in each of your work allows you to insert women back into Dave's story. Can you share how these maternal genealogies connect you to your roots?

JONATHAN: It's a fair question, but the honest to God answer is that I'm sixty-three, so I'm probably the last, or close to the last, of generations of southern African American children who were all raised by our grandparents.

GLENIS: *[Laughter.]*

JONATHAN: I mean, our parents were like our siblings, older brothers and older sisters. So, that's the world we come from. Because I mean—I never called—even to this day, I don't call my mother "Mom" or "Mother."

GABRIELLE: My grandmother is "Mama." That's what we all call her.

JONATHAN: That's a direct connection back to our African culture. Children are raised by the elders and the extended community.

GLENIS: I look at your world, and as an air force kid, I didn't have that rootedness, that community aspect. I was born in Sumter, South Carolina, and then my immediate family moved. So, I didn't really remeet my grandmother again until I was twelve, and she was a curiosity to me. Number one, I couldn't understand what she was saying. Because she was speaking Gullah and no one had prepared me. Now, my parents were from South Carolina. My father was enlisted. They had left sharecropping to go out into the world. So, when it was time for us to come back, they didn't say, "We're going to preview you. And this is what's going to happen when you go south—" No. They were going home. *[Laughter.]*

And I was not ready for home. I did not understand what home meant. Home meant a series—I lived in twelve, thirteen, different homes by the time I was twelve. And so, I had the southern experience because my father was a jazz-blues-gospel piano player. My mother cooked by hand and scratch. She sewed. So, I always identified as southern, but I didn't even know what *kin* meant. When I went to my high school and they said, "we kin," I went home and asked, "Mama, what is kin?" So, I was piecing things together. I had a great experience at college, but I also knew there was something I was not getting there. And it was turning back and looking at my mother and my grandmother; they were the wisest people that I knew. They were the smartest people that I knew. They were just expressing their intelligence in a very different way. And once I got that—my grandmother had a third-grade education, but every time she opened her mouth—

JONATHAN: Wisdom.

GLENIS: She was imparting something. And her thing was—her thing was love. Love everybody.

At this point, as the conversation turned from the importance of family and place, the discussion turned to Dave, the ancestors, and spiritual cosmologies of the African Diaspora.

GABRIELLE: Respecting the elders, the women in our lives, their contributions and wisdom, allows us to hold space for women who don't appear in the records that are used to preserve and tell men's stories. Dave's story could have been told that way, but both of you really do insert women as speakers into his story.

GLENIS: Well, you know it's so funny because I never looked at it like that. I got tired of hearing things about slaves. What does that mean that a person is enslaved? You know, so when I'm encountering Dave, it's like he's a person. With needs and wants and desires just like any other person.

JONATHAN: Hence, "Sir Dave."

GLENIS: Sir Dave. And to make him . . .

JONATHAN: Larger than life. Magical. Ancestrally important. DNA information crafted.

GLENIS: We're also talking about Christianity and we're talking about Africa. Because Dave is so biblical, right? Like you said, Jonathan, he's a theologian. And I think he's a performance poet. I think he's our first performance poet because he's shopping his wares. He's an entertainer. He's a preacher. He's all of these things. Which Orisha is he? I'm always looking ancestrally because we've got our feet in two worlds. When I look at you, Jonathan, I see you're expansive. I had never met anyone like you. That's why I was big-eyed and going, "Oh my gosh. There's someone in South Carolina, spiritually; here's someone not just telling our story, but also vibrating and radiating at such a level that I have not seen on the landscape anywhere." You had the benefit of mentors. I just couldn't find anyone who was speaking to us. I'm sure countless people have that experience. But there was a quickening that happened when I looked at your work. It was like, "Oh, okay, so I can be in a lot of worlds at once." And I hadn't seen that; I hadn't gotten that permission anywhere.

JONATHAN: Wow.

GABRIELLE: So which Orisha do you think Dave was?

GLENIS: I don't know. That's hard to answer. I mean, there's a part of me that feels like I was looking at Harriet Tubman and I definitely feel like she's . . .

JONATHAN: Shango

GLENIS: You think it's Shango?

GABRIELLE: You want to say a little bit about that?

JONATHAN: The reason I'm saying it is because as you were talking about "Sir Dave," my mind went to André Pierre, the famous Haitian artist. Picasso said he was the most important artist in the universe. Pierre took care of his people in a compound. And they had all of the gods, the Orishas, in this compound; when I was there he took me through them. But he just refused to look at me. I was with mostly white people and he was looking at all of them and talking to them, but he would not look at me. So I felt kind of rejected. But his interpreter later explained to me it was my spirit that he wasn't ready to accept. And so, as some people commissioned works, I commissioned him to do a work for me. He did beautiful paintings of Haiti-influenced stuff. For me, he did Elegba.

GLENIS: Crossroads.

JONATHAN: When he painted Elegba for me, I felt it because I was born with a veil. I was covered with a placenta membrane at birth, and I've been told all my life who I am. But it was the first time that, from an African Diaspora perspective, I saw a mirror. As African Americans, again, we are looking through a window. So, when I think of Potter Dave, Harriet Tubman, Robert Smalls, Sojourner Truth, all these people, they are gods.

GLENIS: They are. You know, I always think of Harriet Tubman as the trickster Orisha because she was able to shift. She was shape-shifting—there's no other way to explain those kinds of happenings. I think art has that spirit; it stands at the crossroads.

GABRIELLE: Tubman led whole families through treacherous territories, elders and children, those who rarely ran, without being recaptured. Without the trickster, Elegba, the magician disrupter and sorcerer, you're saying how could she do the impossible and do it over and over again?

GLENIS: When I'm writing poetry, something more enters and I don't always know what it is, but I know it exists and it comes through and it has a lot to say. And I think when I'm in the classroom with these young people and you start introducing Dave and you start talking to them. Then they wake up and they want to know Dave's story.

JONATHAN: It's a powerful story.

GLENIS: It's a powerful story and many students tell you: "I don't like reading. I can't read." It breaks my heart. So, if you hear about Dave, this storyline to me is urgent and immediate. That's been one of my critiques of my work: that everything's so immediate, everything's so urgent. Well, if you've been thirsty a long time—when you start drinking water, you say, "I can live. I can stay on the planet." And that's what I want to give to young people. It's like: "You need this. This is bread. This is water. This is sustenance. This is not an aside. This is not art out here. This is art in here."

JONATHAN: Art for the soul.

GLENIS: We talk about our young people being disenfranchised. Well, a lot of times they're disenfranchised because they're not connected. I was disconnected in a very different way. I was always into the arts. I was always into books. But not to place. Then South Carolina started to operate like a person in my life. Charleston started to operate like a person.

JONATHAN: A sense of belonging.

GLENIS: Place started speaking to me. "This is what belonging is. This is what having an experience with the land, with the people, with God, with the past, means." And my life started to make meaning—I started to have meaning.

GABRIELLE: And Dave is part of that belonging? You're addressing this but I want to ask it in a different way and see if it brings up a different response. How does history resonate for you poetically and how is poetry necessary to the preservation of Black history?

GLENIS: History is one of the most powerful subjects, especially in school. But I was taught on a timeline. "What does this mean?" I had no idea. What a step would it have been for the teacher to say, "Here's this story." Because when I learn history through a story, especially when that story has to do with the place that I belong to or the people I belong to, then all of a sudden I start to lean in and I'm engaged.

GABRIELLE: And poetry is a part of that storytelling.

GLENIS: Poetry is to me, archaeological; it's a creed of archaeology. I'm digging. I'm always digging. And like you said, Jonathan, you were listening. I was the kid in the room when my mom said, "Get out of here and stop looking at grown folks' mouth." *[Laughter.]* But I was absorbing. I was trying to take in everything they had to give. That's why I write the way my grandmother speaks. But when I started to purposefully engage history, I started hearing voices that led me to ask: "what would my great-grandfather say?" He wouldn't speak in mainstream standard English.

History to me has to do with the land because I think the past is present. So when I went to Edenton, North Carolina, it was the first time I was always surrounded by cotton fields. Now, I had seen cotton fields all my life, but I had never been just surrounded.

JONATHAN: It goes on forever.

GLENIS: Forever. I know people thought I was crazy. I pulled my car over and I just stood out there just looking.

GABRIELLE: I think we've all done that. *[Laughter.]*

GLENIS: There were four plantations. I didn't have a cell phone. I didn't have any internet. And I started hearing my great-grandfather speak, and that's where "What My Hand Say" comes from.

> My hand say, *Pick, plow, push and pull,*
> 'cause it learned to curl itself around every tool

of work. The muscles say, *bend yourself like the sky,*
coil yourself blue around both sun and moon.

Listen, my back be lit by both. My hand
got its own eyes and can pick a field of cotton
in its sleep. Don't mind the rough bumps—
the callused touch. I work this ground

like it was my religion and my hands
never stop praying. Some folk got a green thumb,
look at my crop and you'll testify my whole hand
be covered.

He just started to resonate. I felt strange. I was like, "What is that?" when I wrote that poem.

JONATHAN: It's the same thing in painting.

GLENIS: I was just writing, and it was automatic. I was working on my master's degree at the time. I was so ashamed of that poem that I did not show it to my advisor. It took me three months. And she said, "That poem is fully formed."

JONATHAN: So, we are channeling.

GABRIELLE: What is the role of the artistic channeler in recovering what's been lost? When we talk about the history of enslaved people and communities, we are speaking about fragments of historical records. Rarely can we recover their voices in surviving documents, rarely is what they made preserved. Do we need channelers?

GLENIS: It's through stepping into the space of the unknown that we can put our hands on what can't be found in a book. It's not there. Their names are not there. There are some names but—

JONATHAN: I love your analogy. So, our job is to get them to look in the mirror and not out the window. Most academics are looking through the window.

GLENIS: Which is needed, I mean, let's get all that we can. We need that. Let's see if there is any additional evidence. But there's another place in which we live. And we as Africans have always lived in that other place. So, to say that this world can hold everything of who we are is not true. Now, it's a travesty that there's so much loss. But it's speaking to us all the time, I think, through the ethers. Like in Charleston, just being here, there's an incredible vibration that speaks.

The conversation turned at this point to a discussion of how history and archives have informed each artist's work.

GABRIELLE: Both of you are engaged in research-based artistic production. I know how deeply you engage sources. From the African Diasporic history of South

Carolina rice to the bold South Carolina Civil War hero Robert Smalls, to David Drake, I have seen you engage in this work, Jonathan. I have photos of you, Glenis, looking through my endless files on Harriet Wilson records. When you talk about both historical and artistic archaeology and the dynamic relationship between what is lost but also passed down to us, what keeps you rooted in this work? How do the arts, the visual arts, the poetic arts, work with the archive? Can you flesh out that relationship?

GLENIS: Well, reading you, reading other people who have come before, this work is fastidious, it's meticulous. You're doing that intellectual work. But it's also what's in between that speaks to me; it's not always "the facts." The facts are there and I need the facts, but that's already been done.

JONATHAN: So, the facts are like the guide?

GLENIS: The guide, yes. I ask what does the voice sound like when you get to the end of the research? What happens? We're speculating. We're personifying. When I'm writing in persona, it's not me but it is me. I'm not interested in telling the literal truth. I'm interested in a resonant truth. If you resonate with something that is true, people feel it. Just because you share facts, people are not necessarily going to say, "Yes, yes." But if you resonate with something, people will say: "When you are speaking, you sounded like my grandfather." I'm using your work as a researcher as a jumping-off platform to get what I need answered, and a lot of times, it does that. It's Dave through the lens of Glenis and Jonathan. It's just so many lenses and then there's also—

JONATHAN: —lots of room for others. So, we're not closing the window. I think we're expanding it.

GLENIS: I think Dave is having his say. *[Laughter.]* I think that's really powerful. I have a Dave poem called, "I, Master" because he becomes the master.

JONATHAN: Well, let's hear a verse.

GLENIS: That poem is in this book. I play with that term. Because in his whole world, he becomes the one who becomes known. And the other thing before I read the poem, I want to say, Jonathan, how revolutionary, how rebellious, how badass is it to have Dave seated reading the newspaper in your paintings. How iconic.

JONATHAN: *[Laughter.]* The people that housed him first—notice I didn't say owned—they owned a newspaper. Dave was likely a typesetter. So, he knew letters and he knew words because that was his job. That's why the newspaper was important.

GLENIS: When I look at that image, it never gets old. It's like a turn in a poem. Like every time I see that, I was like *[claps]*. "There it is. That's it."

GABRIELLE: He's sitting on a pot outside, and much of your work in this series is situated in the open, linked to land. The other thing that I love about the fabulous qualities of your work is that white folks are nowhere to be found in this series. Because he is in a world that you imagine in a way that gives him expansive community.

JONATHAN: Now, what I do is I might share a multitude of variations on skin tone. Even to the point of being questionable. But then that's who we are.

GABRIELLE: Charcoal to chalk.

GLENIS: Every time I see your title painting *Sir Dave*, that speaks to every reason why we are attracted to Dave.

JONATHAN: And I always kind of think of Glenis as a collaborator *[laughter]* in the project Dave. So let's hear that poem.

Glenis recites "I, Master," reproduced in full on page 62.

GABRIELLE: I just love the way that Dave actually masters his masters. He does it in the way he signs his name, proudly, deeply, often in huge bold letters while his enslaver, Lewis Miles, ends up with just his initials on Dave's pot. He minimizes Miles's ownership of him, of his pots, by writing his "master's" name in the diminutive. He takes the people who claimed him as property and turns them into footnotes to his own story.

JONATHAN: That's right.

GLENIS: On the plantation, and now, people talk about how to manage your boss. Dave is the ultimate at figuring out how to navigate his space to become so wonderful at his craft. And when you reach a certain level of your craft, there's jealousy. So how do you master that and still continue to put couplets on your pots and jokes and advertisements?

GABRIELLE: When literacy is outlawed to enslaved people no less!

GLENIS: Yes! So, he's doing the limbo. He's navigating those narrow spaces in the ways that we do as descendants of Africa. We make this margin walking look good—and that is powerful. That's why I give him so much respect. He's got so much hubris to announce, "I did this thing. I did this."

GABRIELLE: Jonathan, you personified jugs in your series too. There are paintings that are peopled only by the jugs. Two are very similar, but one features birds flying away. I was wondering if you could talk a little bit about the importance of birds in your work and in the series?

JONATHAN: Well, every time my elders spoke of birds, and they were usually buzzards, they spoke of the birds from the perspective of someone watching over us. Someone guiding us. So, the visual imagery of birds, for me, is navigational. And it's divine. They're another dimension on the greatness of life. You know, something that can fly up in the sky. And look down at you and you have a personal relationship with it, and it sees and encompasses everything. So, I use the birds as a way of channeling that three-dimensional belief. It's larger than us. It's just not here; it's way out there. And in that painting, the jugs, I wanted to speak to vessels carrying us home. You can die and carry a situation here in this space, but that does not mean you can't go home. So those birds are going home to Africa.

GLENIS: It's so interesting. My mother has a relationship with birds. It's passed down generationally. It is not something we ever discussed, but it's just there. I take cues from nature as well, and I also wonder, if you were enslaved, what is your relationship to the land? Nature is very healing and very powerful, but at the same time if you're forced to work or you're lynched or you witness lynching and violence and trauma, what does that do to your relationship? I always wondered about that dual nature.

There are certain fears we have because the land does speak of what's happened. I had a professor—she said write a pastoral poem, from that poetic tradition where you only see beauty in the land. Which is great. I mean, I want to see beauty. I see beauty all the time. I love the trees, but at the same time the trees are telling more than one story. We are always walking around with double-consciousness vision. To me, those are a lot of different worlds to live in.

GABRIELLE: Dave teaches us how to claim beauty and mastery and craft alongside loss and trauma—all tied to place.

JONATHAN: You know, the *New York Times* reporter Ron Stodghill wanted to do a shadowbox interview with me about Charleston. And Mother Emanuel was going through a major mourning period. Clementa Pinckney [the senior pastor of Mother Emmanuel church in Charleston and state senator killed alongside eight others at Bible study by white supremacist Dylann Roof in 2015] was my cousin, though we were not very close. After the interview he said, "I'm amazed you're so comfortable with this city, with the harshness and the racism." I said, "For me, Charleston is a living museum of the work my people have done. Every building you look at in Charleston that has any type of historical marker or any of the buildings on this peninsula was built by Black people, maintained by Black people."

GLENIS: We built this.

GABRIELLE: There's biological kin and there's our cultural kin and I do want to ask you both about choosing your cultural kin and the place of collaboration in your work. I'm thinking of the collection of prose and poetry that responds to your work, Jonathan, called *Seeking*, edited by Kwame Dawes and Marjory Wentworth. I'm thinking of your work on a rice symphony. Jonathan, you've worked with composers and dance companies well before Lynnette and Glenis and I approached you about how your work helped inspire my scholarship and Glenis's poetry and our performance collaboration with Lynnette. And there are lots of visual artists who don't do that at all. As a poet, Glenis, we've been working together now for ten years. Can both of you talk about what place collaboration has in your work and its importance?

JONATHAN: I love collaborations. Through those engagements, I can be more explorative with ideas like us talking here, all the things we can talk about. Well, you can't talk about that by yourself. That's why I'm always engaging in collaborations.

GLENIS: But do your collaborations come out of you, or are they sparked by the work that you've created? Or are you going back and forth with others too? Because I always see that you set a precedent and then people want to join what you've created.

GABRIELLE: Your work on Dave was different, right? They asked you to create a series.

JONATHAN: I think it's both. Once I engage in a project, like the book [of poetry that responded to my work,] *Seeking*, and what I've learned from involvement with this project, then I know that my next creative expression is to include other people into the work.

GLENIS: And it's going to live. Doesn't that feel very African that it belongs to the collective now, it's in the collective realm? Like I've done this and it's whole. It's not just for me. What's that proverb? "If you want to go—

UNISON: "Fast."

GLENIS: "go alone. If you want to go—"

UNISON: "Far. Go together."

GLENIS: My first collaborations weren't what you think of particularly as collaboration. I felt like I was collaborating with, you know, writers and poets whom I'd never met when I was fifteen living in Piedmont, South Carolina. That was the only way I was going to stay alive. I read their books and then they would speak to me and I'd write. So it was this kind of imaginary collaboration.

GABRIELLE: Spiritual and genealogical connections.

GLENIS: Exactly. When I read *I Know Why the Caged Bird Sings [whoosh]*.

JONATHAN: And she was smart. When you have a level of intelligence that is appreciated by other people: writing, music, art, whatever, I think it's a whole conglomeration of things. Those are your tickets out.

GLENIS: It was an exit strategy. *[Laughter.]* And I didn't bend to peer pressure in high school. Because I knew I was going somewhere. And then people would say, "Oh uppity" or "aloof" or, you know, "who she think she is?" But there was no reason for me to go into art because I was a first-generation college student and I said I gotta do something with this, "I cannot do art." You know? *[Laughter.]* And I think that was self-imposed, because my parents didn't care. They were just like,

"Get married." I mean literally, at eighteen, "Get married. Find you a man." And I was a feminist at, I think, probably twelve. Because I had seen the relationship between my mother and my father and I said, "Okay, I'm not going to do that." So, poetry became a liberating act of me saying what I needed to say that I didn't say all those years. So, I found people to collaborate with who were liberated. When I saw that spirit of freedom, I was like, "That's who I want to sit down with. That's who I want to talk to. That's who I want to be on stage with. That's who I want to be on the page with. That is me."

GABRIELLE: What does it mean to work with those whose creative output shows your work, speaks to your work, dances with your work in a different medium? To see your poetry in dance. To see your visual art in poetry?

GLENIS: Since I write a lot from the autobiographical standpoint, even historically, it's still from the "I" window. Working with artists in different mediums turns the work into a "we." It turns it into a universal. I think it elevates it to another level that many more people can walk in, where people—some people are not going to read this page. Like you were saying, Jonathan, if you could witness an image, that's going straight to the heart before the poem, before the written word. I mean because art is our first language.

GABRIELLE: But poetry is also connected to the griot, right, to the oral tradition? The griot and the visual artist, to me, speak in primal languages.

GLENIS: I would put imagery before the griots. I mean, I think their job is to carry on history and lineage and engage and connect and call-and-response.

JONATHAN: You know when you said that, I could not help but to think of music.

GLENIS: Oh, well, music is universal. Music was ever present too in our household because of my father. In many ways I was blessed that I really did have an artistic household, we just didn't call it that. I think that's in the Black community a lot, like in the church. I mean, there is art happening all the time in the church.

JONATHAN: So, in the Black community, can we say that we are a manifestation of the arts? Arts and culture.

GLENIS: We are. At a workshop, we were asked: "So when did you first witness arts integration?" And I was the only one in the room who couldn't remember a time when arts weren't integrated in my home. I pretty much got my sense of rhythm in the womb, because my mother was always swaying to father's music. If we learned something, we learned it through song. We learned it through dance. I think if I were to be called anything, I think I'm more a kinesthetic poet.

GABRIELLE: I love the way *kin* is in *kinesthetic* too.

JONATHAN: Well, that certainly is the definition of our Dave performance and collaboration, that was my interpretation of it.

GLENIS: Yes. To bring it to the body.

JONATHAN: Poetry, music, and movement. All personified by visuals.

GLENIS: That's what happens—is that it rises up and becomes a living thing.

JONATHAN: That's why we cannot separate it. I mean, people ask me all the time, "When did you learn to do art? When did you start doing art?" I don't know. *[Laughter.]* All I know is that I've been doing it.

GLENIS: Always doing it.

GABRIELLE: Like you, I grew up in an artistic household with a father, Kent Foreman, who was a poet and with kin-claimed uncles who were photographers and performers, like Oscar Brown Jr.

GLENIS: I went back and listened to that haiku your dad did on *Def Poetry Jam*. And it's like—it's a lovely turn because it's just seventeen syllables.

GABRIELLE:

> "Oh! She wants me to
> love her the way she would love
> her if she was me!"

JONATHAN: Conclusion.

GLENIS: Done. *[Laughter.]*

GABRIELLE: Drop the mic.

GLENIS: "Epiphany."

GABRIELLE: Yup, "Epiphany" is the poem's title.

GLENIS: The thing in that poem is the turn. Can we talk about turns? Turns happen in sonnets. You know, they happen in prose where we have that moment in novels and I think, that is what your work does, Jonathan. It always delivers. There's always a moment, an element of surprise that happens and it works every *[snaps fingers]* single *[snaps fingers]* time *[snaps fingers]*. That's why you're a master artist because you deliver that and you're like, "Well, I don't know when I learned it," but of course you've done it in a way that is resonating for so many people on so many levels. Your turns take me to my own personal turn. And the fact that you made that turn so early, we benefit creatively and artistically.

JONATHAN: And now I'm benefitting.

GLENIS: Because it comes back. Well, because the love you give out comes back to you.

JONATHAN: That's right and that's why I do collaborations. And I think for me, I never think of an end. It's just a continuum. What we're doing with Sir Dave is a continuum resurrecting someone who very, very, few people knew about, and the reason they cared about him, unmistakably, was because of economics. Dave, Sir Dave, had value.

GLENIS: He has value.

JONATHAN: His pots were the most expensive pots in the history of South Carolina.

GABRIELLE: And still are.

JONATHAN: And *[laughter]* look where they are.

GABRIELLE: In museums around the world. As Theaster Gates says, they made the jump from artisan ware to "high" art.

GLENIS: And that's the "I, Master." I master this. I elevate it. That's a lesson to us all.

GABRIELLE: And it's also a lesson to me about historical patience in some ways—and faith. Keep doing the work, right? Keep mastering the trade. And eventually people will come back and discover the work that is built on the work.

JONATHAN: And that's what you're doing with this book.

GLENIS: As you look at my work, Gabrielle, you know, to have someone to look at your work closely, how beautiful is that? It's scary *[laughter]* and it's also beautiful at the same time. Because most people in my neck of the woods, like you know, don't care. I mean until you make them care.

JONATHAN: As a painter, I deal with that a lot. They don't know how to care.

GLENIS: "They don't know how to care." That's very lovely.

GABRIELLE: Well, let's turn to that. What does criticism mean to your work? What does having critics look at your work mean to you? I'm not talking about reviews. I'm talking about people who deeply sit with your work and write. Does criticism play a role in your work, in your career?

GLENIS: It's so after the fact. I'm appreciative, but it's after the fact because the work is written. I wrote my master's thesis on Rita Dove's *Sonata Mulattica*. So, as a person who was critiquing that work, looking at it so closely, that actually taught me what I wanted to do next. So, when someone's looking at my work, I'm grateful because we don't get to be in conversation unless we're around workshopping with people. And that's very different.

You're too close to it as the writer. Some of the stuff I do is intentional. Some of it's very subconscious. And when someone pays that close attention, I'm not used to being heard on that level. Who's used to being listened to on that level?

So, when someone with an expansive mind takes time to take their gaze—actually pay attention—that is a great honor because that also elevates the work too, in a very different way. It extends the work.

It introduces it to another audience.

JONATHAN: Absolutely. That's exactly what happens.

JONATHAN: It elevates the work, sometimes, I may say in a way that I don't quite understand. But I'm willing to follow and allow for that reinterpretation, that reunderstanding of someone else's perspective on what I have done.

GABRIELLE: And of course, that happens with viewers all the time. What they're taking from your work is not necessarily what you saw in your work either.

GLENIS: Isn't it about being in conversation? Because critiquing is another form of having a conversation. I have students do that with my work all the time. I think the work, if it's worth it, it continues to unfold and unfold. It is still living.

The conversation then turned to the experience of artistic resonance and beauty before moving into the multidimensionality that both artists brought to their representations of Dave and the importance of passing knowledge and memory through generations.

GLENIS: I remember being at the Tate gallery and seeing—I can't remember the artist but it's—a painting called *Intimacy* and I think I must have been going through a breakup at the time. It was just a man and his wife. She was knitting by the fireside and he was smoking his pipe. And I thought, "This is a performance art." It might have been Sargent. But I was brought to tears because of how it resonated.

JONATHAN: The part of our performance piece that moved me so much that it brought me to tears was "Shards." I didn't see it coming; I don't know if I could have even envisioned it even though my painting inspired it. The dancers as autumn leaves and shards, I was mesmerized by that.

GLENIS: So, what is the role of beauty in all of this? To take someone like Dave's life, you're not just looking—and looking for [what's been forgotten]—a lot of times when we're looking at what's broken—you know what I mean?—all of it isn't broken. There's a lot of wrong with history, but you find a way to celebrate.

GABRIELLE: We have to find beauty in the shards, in history's broken fragments.

JONATHAN: I appreciate the fragments because the fragments came from a whole. And to appreciate the fragments also speaks to your imagination of the whole, and where it came from, and its purpose.

GLENIS: And I think that's a metaphor for the whole African American experience. Our lineage, which has been fragmented.

GLENIS: I still go back to Edgefield cotton field, because there's beauty in that cotton field.

JONATHAN: The person who bought that painting is an attorney.

GABRIELLE: And a potter.

JONATHAN: He was so mesmerized by that painting. And that painting had to be included in that series. I remember driving through Edgefield before I did the series and I thought, "How beautiful."

GABRIELLE: I love that piece; the empty rows and rows of cotton and that there's no one in the fields, for me that is so suggestive. I write about that piece in my other work. And Glenis's poem that corresponds to that piece takes my breath away.

GLENIS: I think it's one of the first pieces I wrote. And I think it's the first piece that I read to the collective.

GABRIELLE: And it's the strongest ensemble piece in the performance too.

GLENIS: I was living at my mom's. I had left Asheville, thought I was moving to D.C. and she had gotten sick. But we were doing this collaboration; y'all would send me stuff and I was looking at your painting of the cotton and my mother was talking to me about picking cotton, because she had picked it. So she was telling me the stories. I was thinking about beauty and sorrow and hard work. Do people even see it as beautiful when they were bleeding, you know?

GABRIELLE:

> "We stand not on the edge, but in the middle of the field
> in between this white blaze that God made.
>
> Our minds not fixed on the North Star, but grounded
> to the weight in our bones as we pick, prick and bleed."

GLENIS: I was thinking about what a luxury it is for me, for us in this generation and where we are now. I mean, we are privileged.

I remember I was in Washington State giving a keynote and I took my mother to see Gee's Bend quilts. And they had a video of the women who were talking about the quilts and the process, and they were singing gospel music. I was just caught up in it, you know, feeling my hypersensitive self. My mother was over on a bench, staring that thousand-yard stare. I was like, "This is not art." I mean, it's art but it's not entertaining. This is my life.

JONATHAN: That's the importance of what we're doing with Sir Dave, Dave Drake, is we're bringing the real Dave Drake into the lives of his cultural kin, from the historical perspective, from a cultural arts perspective: literature, poetry, music, visual imagery. We're usually not discussed like this. We're usually depicted in one dimension. And that's real close to that word *slave*.

GLENIS: It really is. I get to see you the way I want to see you. I work with a group of teens and I have two stellar twin girls who are white. And when I got finished with Dave poems, one of them just put her fist down and said, "Why haven't I learned about this? Why don't I know about this?" And I said, "It's one of the biggest tricks in education." We want our kids engaged, but we don't want to give them what will make them engaged. Like, we don't want to tell them the stories that will really bring them in. We don't want to do it in a kinesthetic dynamic way; instead they're just teaching to the test.

JONATHAN: We know these teachers are certified, but are they qualified?

GABRIELLE: That's why you do the kind of teaching work that you also do, Glenis, which is about bringing an embodied sensibility to history and that is what this project is about. It is about history, but it's also about communication, passing on, generationally. That's another kind of teaching.

GLENIS: Right. We weren't included in the equation. So, when somebody says we were all brought here as immigrants—wait a minute, no we weren't. If people are trying to be apostles of forgetfulness, then they're not qualified to teach, because they're not looking. You have to look deeply to teach Dave.

GABRIELLE: I love that phrase—and of course, structurally it's a supremacist culture and society that structures and produces apostles of forgetfulness. So, what does it mean for so many people to be teaching with windows instead of mirrors as their model? We won't answer this question if we don't pose it. This is how we get Black history without Black people involved in its narration. We get Black subjects as a spectator sport with us sitting on the sidelines. This is a really interesting moment of erasure, where our work is very much valued as a commodity, but our presence, our history, our spirituality, our cosmology—

JONATHAN: Absent. And that's what I wrestle with every day. Not for me personally, but in terms of the images I paint. I can't tell you how often my white friends say, "Well, don't you ever paint white people?"

GLENIS: I get that with the poems. "Why do you always write about Black things?" Said no one to a white person ever. They can write about an apple. But if I write about an apple, then it's a Black woman writing about the apple. Or, "Why do you have Black art in your house?" "Where are the white people?" Putting yourself in the center of somebody else's narrative, it's a disease in this country.

GABRIELLE: Infectious. Endemic. *[Laughter.]*

GLENIS: And so I think what is revolutionary about Dave is he was able to center himself in the center of his work in a time when it was—

GABRIELLE: —all but impossible.

JONATHAN: You know, I'm just reamazed by what we're doing. To get to now from our earlier discussions . . .

GLENIS: That's what a potter does; they have to center for the pot to be. And Dave's at the center of what we are throwing—to use potters' language—what we are creating.

That is what amazes me, that I just kind of find ways to be in the center of my own world as a Black woman. We're always being pushed to the margins. It's like how dare you? How dare you be Black and intelligent and have something to say?

GABRIELLE: If you do not put yourself in the center of what you spin, what you turn, then the walls collapse. The walls of the pot will collapse on you.

GLENIS: History has been a whole series of taking us out of our centers.

JONATHAN: That was my description of creating work.

Remember I said, "I'm in the center?" And now we're coming back to the center again.

GLENIS: You also centered us. You allowed us to inhabit a space, and in this collaboration, we're centering our art in a very different way than you would individually.

JONATHAN: I just could not have imagined this. I don't always know. I just have an idea.

GLENIS: It's not your job to know, because if you knew all the time, then where's the creative element? You wouldn't be as expansive. I think if you knew all the time, then you would be going back to something. Instead, you're recentering all the time.

GABRIELLE: Dave had to wait centuries for his work to be rediscovered and your work was part of it, Jonathan, then your work on Sir Dave got forgotten too, and—

JONATHAN: Rediscovered by us.

GABRIELLE: And in the rediscovery of Dave, there's this interesting moment where your series gets publicly erased and ends up in private collections, and then twenty years later comes up again in this collaboration.

GLENIS: For the catalog, the curator only wanted one piece to put on the cover, right? I never had heard that story before.

You do a whole series and then—

GABRIELLE: Fourteen pieces are in the series. And four or five pieces travel with the exhibit, but only one piece goes in the book.

GLENIS: And like what happened to Dave, we get marginalized again.

GABRIELLE: And pushed to the outside of the resurrection of the story of your own genealogy—

GLENIS: —your own culture.

GABRIELLE: That is part of a society that always suggests that we don't have the right to be at our center.

JONATHAN: And then I've become esoteric as the Black artist—

GABRIELLE: Rather than central.

JONATHAN: So, tell me this then. Here I am asking questions, right? *[Laughter.]* This is for both of you. So, how do your academic colleagues relate to what you're doing?

GABRIELLE: Almost all the work I do is collaborative. It's almost all about building collectives. Academics outside of the sciences and those who have labs rarely know how to measure that or value it. In literary studies and history, academics are largely invested in individual work. And again, this is part of a European tradition of individual liberalism.

I have literally been told not to put this work on my CV or on my résumé. The first performance and poetry piece we and artistic director Lynnette did together was about [the author, entrepreneur, and religious speaker] Harriet Wilson; it is adopted in classrooms all over, but I was told by my interim department chair that this was not the kind of scholarly work that would be counted. And I had been told that at my previous college about digital collaborative work when I came up for promotion there too. One of the most famous scholars of our era once asked me why I coauthored a volume with an independent researcher when I could have just paid him instead of acknowledging him as a full collaborator.

JONATHAN: So, you're answering my question because that's what I deal with all the time as an artist. Glenis?

GABRIELLE: In what way?

JONATHAN: Remember when I came up to Delaware? And they took me through the museum? And the curator was aghast that my work was not a part of the Paul Jones Collection?

And the explanation was Jones didn't want to pay for it. *[Laughter.]* It really was that simple. I knew Mr. Paul Jones. I had known him for years. And I use him as an example, but I can speak of a number of African American collectors or people that were interested in the arts in my twenties when I garnered the reward for my work. They did not feel that I was legitimized as an artist.

GLENIS: I know that walk because I didn't come through academia. I got my agent because of a Ku Klux Klan rally in Asheville, North Carolina. They saw me there and said, "We want to sign you." At that time, poets weren't being signed. This was not a literary agent; this was a booking agent. So, I go to these showcases where they put you in the room with two thousand people, and bright lights, and you've got ten minutes.

JONATHAN: Your rise, Glenis, was so fast.

GLENIS: It was, but it was unconventional. At these showcases, there was me and white male singers and comedians. So, once my mother and my favorite aunt came with me. I should have known that something special was going to happen because they just said, "We comin' with you." There was a jazz band and a rock band and I'm in the middle. When I get finished, I get a standing ovation and I'm booked for two years solid. That's not the poetry world. So therefore, in academia—they're looking at that like, "Well, what is she doing? She's getting paid."

JONATHAN: Girl, it was so fast. *[Laughter.]* She went way up. *[Laughter.]*

GLENIS: I think that was the ancestors speaking, because literally—somebody said, "Ku Klux Klan's marching. We're going to do a unity rally. We not going to protest. Do you want to come and do some poems?" And I said, "Yeah, I'll come do some poems." I was a nonprofit girl. I was a teaching artist. I was doing social activism in the classroom. And I was writing. I was doing poetry slams at night. I don't know if that makes me illegitimate, but I felt that way. I felt like the archetype of the loner. Like I put myself in this space and I'm glad that I can make a living from this and buy a home and raise my children. But, at the same time, it's made me an Other again. Which I wasn't setting out to do. I had always had in my mind that I wanted to go get my master's.

And people asked, "Well, why do you want your master's?" People who were getting their master's, they don't have a first book. I wasn't ever trying to go to a university. That was never my goal; I wanted to create intentional spaces.

GABRIELLE: It's as if being commercially successful detracts from talent and recognition.

JONATHAN: I'm fascinated with this. My grandmother would always say, "Be ready. Just be ready." So, you were ready by going there to that rally. You were ready by your interest in the work of Dave. I was ready when Jill Koverman asked me to work on Dave. And these things happen to us so often when you're ready. But when you're ready, you also always get in trouble with people.

GLENIS: What catapulted you? I know it's your work and your art. But when did you know you were operating, when you went to the galaxy, what was that shooting star?

JONATHAN: My rise was premeditated. I won the lottery on two accounts. One, the ability to go to the Art Institute of Chicago, and secondly, to have met Richard. The Art Institute school had an arrangement with the museum; they would select paintings from the seniors to go into the Morton Wing. Well, they selected my work, but I was a freshman. [The next year,] when I met Richard, I was a sophomore in college, and I was working two jobs and going to school full-time. The job I most prized was being a security guard at the Art Institute. Because that just allowed me access to the work, to people, and to that whole experience. My second passion at the museum, aside from the works, was the gift shop. Because the gift shop told me, "If you want to be successful and stand the test of time, then your work has to be in the gift shop in a museum." Being on the walls is one thing; no one can buy that and take that home. They can only look at it and admire it. But if they're buying a little handkerchief or a little cup, for me, that was success. So, I made my mind up and I said to Richard in my junior year, "I'm leaving this school as a *professional* artist. I'm not going to wait until I get out of college." And I had my first show right across the street from the Art Institute in the gallery. A one-man show. That's just being ready, diligent.

GLENIS: And being bold.

JONATHAN: And walking with your head up like you own the world.

GLENIS: I think some people who are in these positions act as if they're afraid. Like, "I can't go out there and do that until I have permission." If you're an artist, you do it because you have to. But you're not going to wait till someone else says, "Now you're ready, now you can do this." I mean who gets to say when?

GABRIELLE: This gets to the question that you were discussing earlier, Glenis, about making your own way. Some of us who were embedded in family or enough community have been able to also say, "I'm going to make my own way." I've never needed people's permission.

JONATHAN: We all have that in common.

GABRIELLE: Peers telling me what to do? Please. I feel very much that way in my profession.

GLENIS: Because you're not typical. You're atypical. When you hear her speak, you know that she's atypical, because she is a poet. I hate the word *performance*. But what you do is interactive, and I haven't seen many academicians who can pull that off.

GABRIELLE: Well, I'm a poet's child.

GLENIS: You can pull from here, here, and here and make your work a living thing. It's a gift. To diminish someone because they have made their way in the world is an unfortunate response and it's a lazy response too.

GABRIELLE: It comes out of these interesting maxims. The nail that sticks out will get hammered first. And, the way in which people take your wanting to be your own person as a personal assault, as if it means you don't want to be them . . .

GABRIELLE: Well, Dave certainly didn't seem to ask for permission in an era when Black people, free and enslaved, were beaten and murdered for such things as "impudence." The way he incised his name—bold and deep and attention catching—on the pots he made signaled he wasn't scared to make his own way.

What are your hopes for this volume? How do you want it to impact how people approach the work and legacy of David Drake and your work about him?

GLENIS: I hope this volume uplifts David Drake's work, so that he is a household name. I want David Drake to be taught in K–12 as well as colleges and universities. His story is remarkable and so is his craftsmanship—his pots and his poetry. He is inspirational. One never knows how his legacy will impact others as he impacted us. That is the power of telling our stories. A student might be driven to create, or a future scholar might be inspired to do further research.

David Drake is a South Carolina son. His story speaks for itself. We are just stewards making sure his story continues to travel. As artists, composers, dancers, poets, and scholars, we feel compelled to treat his work in our own mediums because it is worthy of such attention. We're transformed by his work. We want to extend those opportunities for future transformation.

Paintings, Poetry, and Place

GLENIS REDMOND

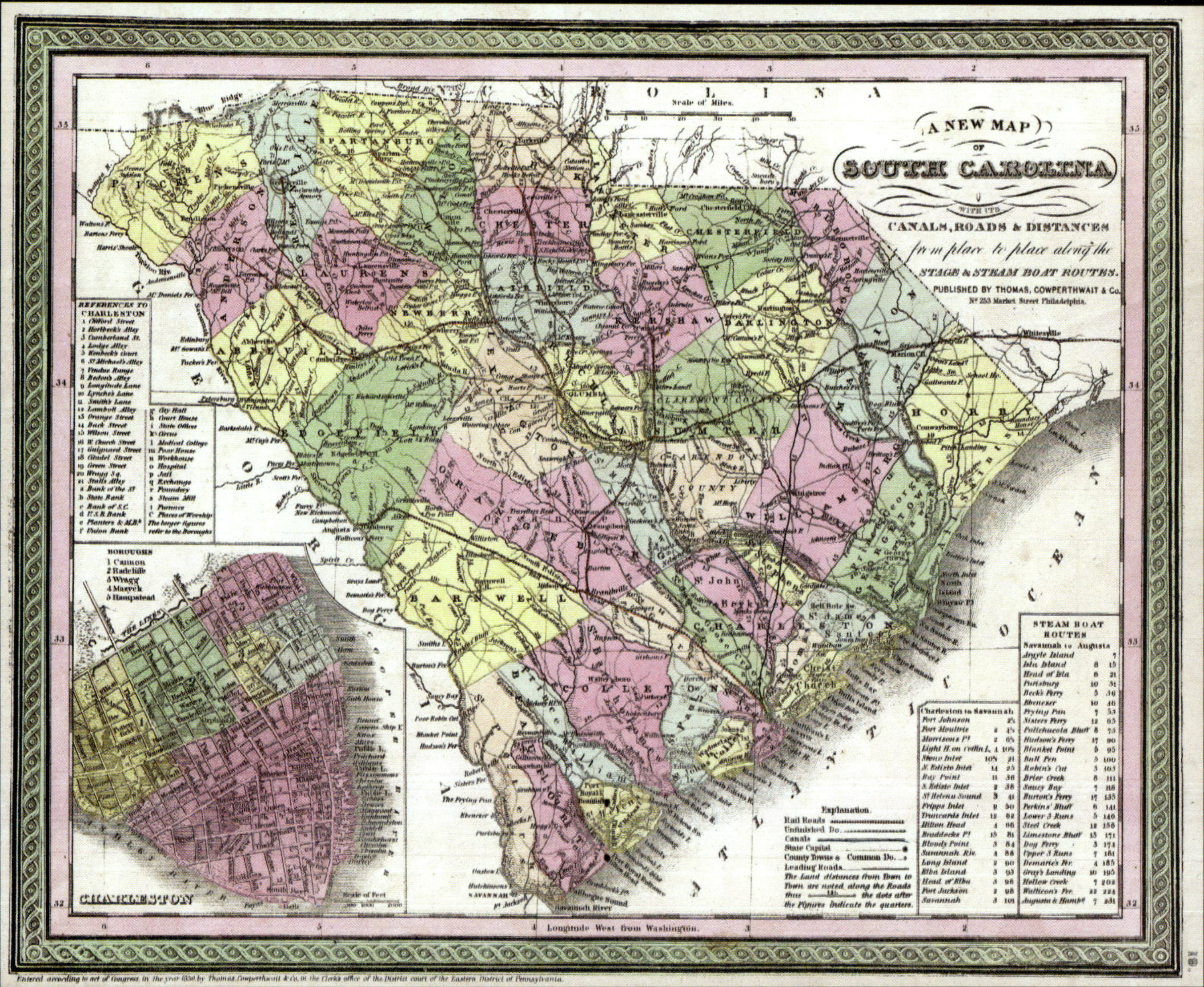

OVERLEAF:

Administrative map of South Carolina, c. 1850.

I HAVE ALWAYS LOVED ART, and in the early 1990s, I hung paintings liberally in and about my home. The art in my home definitely proved that we did not have much money, but I made do. So I hung my own original works. I was also gifted works by a few of my local artist friends. Prints were affordable. Jonathan Green's works entered my world first through prints, postcards, and calendars. I cherished them the most, the loudest, and the deepest, and it has taken me many years to unpack the impression Jonathan Green's artwork made on me.

Our house was a two-story brick starter, but it felt more substantial because it was the nicest house in which I had ever lived. Back then, I was married, and we were raising our twin daughters, Celeste and Amber. We lived in Simpsonville, a small city in Greenville County. To honor this milestone, we hosted a housewarming—gathering our family and our friends. What a joyous occasion, as our house was to be warmed by their good wishes.

I remember being shocked when my dad walked through the front door, because he rarely visited. Our relationship was tense. I always braced myself in his company with an inhalation of breath, because he tended toward the negative when talking to me or about me. So, it should have come as no surprise when he had finished looking round the house and asked, "What does your husband think about all of this Black art that you have hanging on your walls?"

I remember being thrown by his question because I was hoping that my father, for once, would be proud of my accomplishments. I naively hoped he would say, "Congratulations on your lovely home" or "Job well done." Nope—his gaze was elsewhere—not on our home or the beauty of the art displayed. His pointed question was a barbed inquisition.

His verbal jab caught me off guard. At that time, I did not have a sense of agency to unpack his jagged question. I am not sure how I answered, but I am sure of what I thought: *Dad, he married me, your daughter, a Black woman—most women decorate the home and I love art, so I adorned our home with what I love and want to see every day. Not to mention, we are raising two brown girls who need to see themselves reflected so they can walk out into this mainstream white world strengthened by having their beauty reflected.*

His words hurt and stunned me into silence, so I stuffed them, but his question has always rankled me. Underneath his query, I felt his point. What right do you have, even in your own home, to surround yourself with paintings and reflections of the Black experience? He was reminding me that I was Black, and that my husband was white, and that I had no right to uphold my heritage. My father's subtext: My husband would leave me if I asserted myself or my Blackness too much.

My father, Johnny Redmond, has been dead and gone for seventeen years now, and while writing this essay, I realize that our ideologies and stances still clash. I understand now why my father was so obsessed with the white gaze, because he grew up in Jim Crow South Carolina and he had to keep his eye on white people—what they thought and also what their proximity was to him—in order to stay alive. The threat in the 1930s, 1940s, and 1950s was still very real for him.

In the 1990s, my father still radiated with the unspoken injustices doled out to him and his family of origin. He knew that they had been beaten, harassed, and imprisoned for no crime other than being Black in Fountain Inn, South Carolina. Growing up in Greenville County, my father found that there were many places that he simply could not inhabit because of the Jim Crow laws. He lived with Colored Only and Whites Only signs hanging overhead. He and the rest of our family were barred from entry to pools, restaurants, and bathrooms. Everywhere he walked he was threatened. He was acutely hemmed in by the tight margins in which he operated. He had a very real fear of white people—not so much of them but of the power they wielded over him and the whole Black race. He had learned how to navigate around white people. He rarely trusted them or befriended them because of the harsh incidents he had endured. The art in my house spoke of a rebellion he did not possess.

However, my father rarely let his fear of white people override his intolerance to suffer fools. If ever he felt wronged or violated, he would forget his fear and would rise up in defiance, without any thought of consequences. Fortunately—or unfortunately—I inherited this characteristic from him. I saw my father's rage erupt on many occasions. Once a line was crossed, all his fears dissipated. For instance, later in life, I heard through family lore how my older sister, Velinda, (seven years my senior) was not allowed to attend the school on Shaw Air Force Base in 1963 because the elementary school was still racially segregated. My father, enraged by this injustice, wrote a letter to the base commander requesting that Velinda be allowed to attend the school on the base. His request was approved. Though this was a win for civil rights, my sister endured the perils of being the first to integrate the school. She was the Ruby Bridges of Shaw Air Force Base, without the benefit of federal marshals to escort her to class or when walking home—it was just my sister facing her white agitated classmates. She is now in her sixties, and when she recalls that time, I still hear the trauma in her voice. She recounts being called out of her name, being called "nigger" and chased by white boys with sticks when she walked home. She walked home alone every day and every day she was harassed.

I do not know the extent of what my father encountered in his youth, but I have some idea that it was horrific. He never talked much about what he had endured during his childhood, but I felt his internalization of it. He radiated fear and rage. Yet, the self-righteous aspect of his personality both perplexed and empowered me. Though he advocated for the family, when it came to civil rights, he never brought his own dreams to fruition. He played the piano for Bethlehem Baptist Church, and he also played as a fill-in for nearly every Black church within a fifty miles radius, when asked. Still, he never broke out of the tight box of religion in which he was placed by his family.

When we lived away from South Carolina on air force bases across the world, my father always had a jazz and blues band, but when he retired in 1975, and we moved back to his native state, he never played secular music professionally again. He adhered to his mother's belief: "You either play for God or the devil." I witnessed how he wrestled with this chasm. To me, my dad was Langston Hughes's quintessential dream deferred—he never could self-actualize. Hughes's poem "Harlem" asks, "What happens to a dream deferred?" The final line queries, *"Or does it explode?"* I watched my father both implode and explode.

Dad's Dr. Jekyll and Mr. Hyde schism was horrible for all of us, but especially for someone of my constitution: skittish and high-strung. His unpredictable emotional eruptions wrecked and unmoored me. Around him, I was always on high alert. When he entered our home, I was an inheld breath; I never knew when his rage would strike and shred me into many emotional pieces. My father did his best to both suppress and oppress my voice. He did his best to quash my artistic dreams with his unrelenting belittling and bullying. So, when he asked the question about how Blane felt about the Black art in our house, his query felt familiar—reminding me how he always tried to assert his dominance and control over me, trying to put me back in my place as a woman and as his daughter. This haiku tells some of our tumultuous history.

How I Learned to Dance and Read the Weather

On eggshells I danced.
Grooves to fit my father's moods:
Tap dance. Bebop. Dirge.

Unbeknownst to my father, I had already started to climb out from underneath his foot. I had already begun to purge the hate he had poured into me as a child.

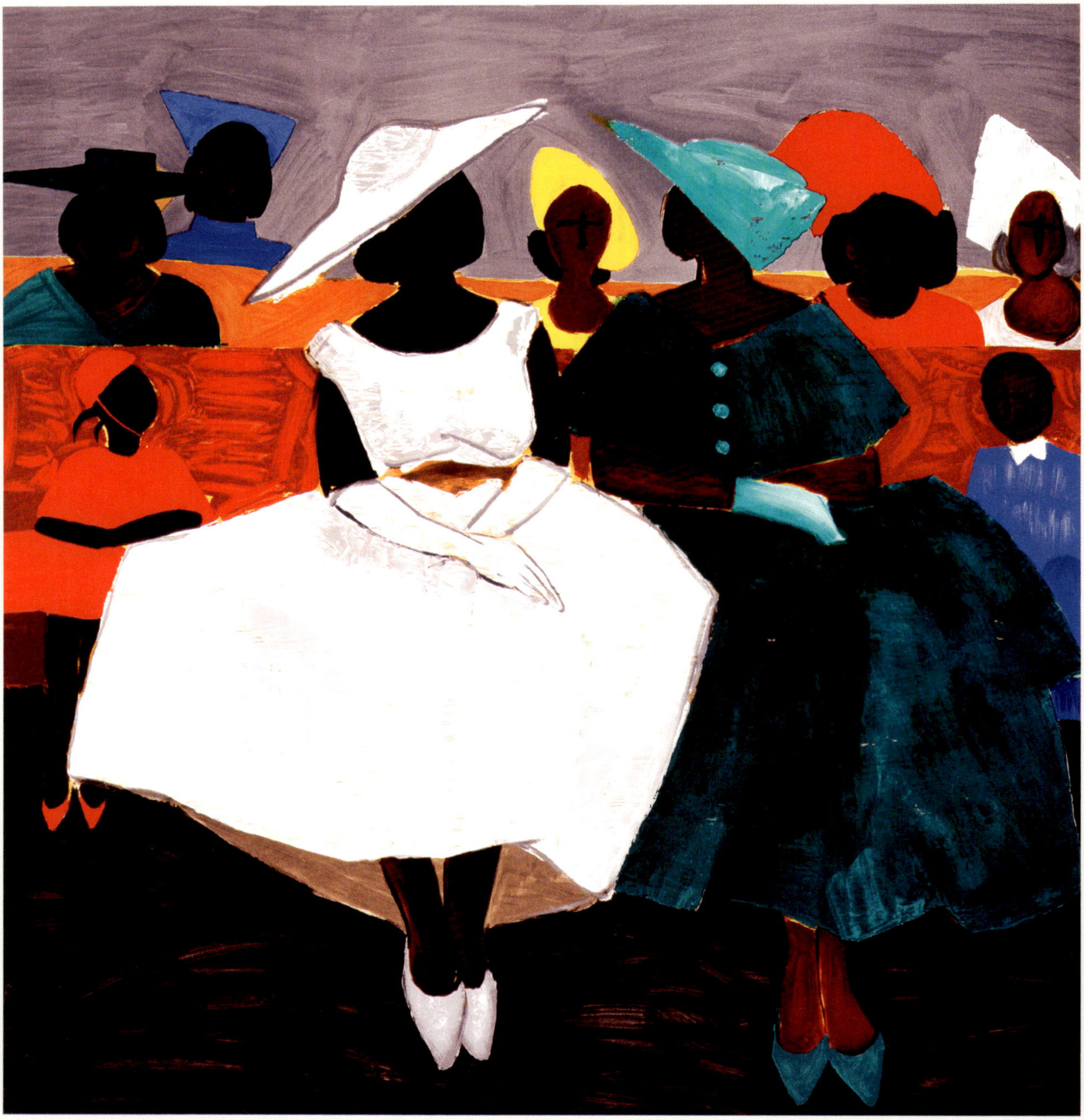

First Sunday, 1994. Jonathan Green. Original hand-drawn lithograph, 18.9 × 19 inches. Courtesy of Jonathan Green Studios. © Jonathan Green.

Strengthening Power of Art

The art in my home spoke to me and for me. The paintings, especially Green's, resonated affirmation-like: *I am unapologetically Black, and I am a powerful, beautiful, bright woman.* I had begun to nourish my Black woman-self with art in ways that replaced what he and the white world had depleted. I took solace in Black art. It was not that I was just high-strung and skittish, it was also that I was born with a poet's soul and a poet's heart, so I sought out and relished beauty whenever possible. The art that I chose acted as an instructive roadmap, leading me to where I wanted to go and what I wanted to ultimately become: a griot, a poet storyteller, and whole. The paintings began weaving a much-needed narrative about myself and the African American story.

Green's paintings showed up in my world and began to combat the negativity that I had absorbed from my home, and especially from the white mainstream world, in a way no other artwork did. His portrayals of South Carolina's landscapes and people transformed me—changed how I saw myself and others in the Black community.

Through his unapologetic brushstrokes and intentional technique of painting black, brown, and golden faces without features, Green made room for me to see myself and my family, as well as the whole of the African American collective. I loved his vibrant use of reds, yellows, blues, and greens. I loved how he portrayed multiple stories—especially how Black people love to dress (peacock) when we go to church or other special occasions. He captured us at church, in the field, or when we gathered outside, under and around an old oak tree, telling stories. His paintings resonated as both a history lesson and an affirmation in one glance, because Jonathan Green's work placed us in the center of our own narrative. When I found his work, it was as if the universe had written a prescription for me to witness his masterpieces for my own well-being—his work made me come alive in ways that I had never been—and his work began to counteract the three decades of being bombarded by racist experiences and stereotypical images every which way I turned.

Internalization of Hate

I graduated from Erskine College with a BA in psychology in 1985. From there, I went to work on a PhD in counseling psychology at Virginia Commonwealth University, in Richmond, Virginia. Though on a full fellowship, I soon learned that I did not want to spend seven years studying in academic towers. I also resented the downtown drive along the Confederate-lined Monument Avenue every morning. I knew that I was on the wrong road, literally and figuratively. We moved back to South Carolina with our toddler twins in tow. I stayed in the counseling field to make ends meet in 1991 and 1992, working as a Clinical Counselor II for the state of South Carolina.

I felt like I had the flu all the time. When I finally went to the doctor, I was diagnosed with a chronic illness, a condition many people had never heard of—fibromyalgia. The doctor described it as a musculoskeletal disorder that resulted in muscle pains and aches, accompanied by a host of other conditions, such as brain fog, temporomandibular joint dysfunction, irritable bowel syndrome, and carpal tunnel syndrome. I had a host of these physical manifestations, but many doctors believed that there was a psychological component to the illness too. I would agree that growing up under my father's tyranny had been traumatic, but I also believed that I was soul sick from not being fully connected to my origin story.

My rheumatologist, Dr. Jeffery Lawson, told me my prognosis. "You are not going to die from this, but you are sure going to wish that you would have." That scared me. Just a year prior, I had presented as a healthy young adult. Dr. Lawson's news of my condition was alarming, but as any good doctor would, he also offered me words of hope. As I was leaving his office, he said, "You need to leave your position as a drug and alcohol abuse counselor, because you are way too sensitive. The work is too taxing and is weighing on you emotionally. I imagine that you take every one of your clients home with you psychically. You are a smart woman, and you will figure it out." I was both depressed and elated by his prognosis and his assessment of me. On the one hand, he'd given me horrible news, while on the other hand, he'd given me my freedom. His affirmation "You are smart" sparked a light within me. I knew instinctively that I would figure out my way forward.

Guidance came in the form of a television program on PBS narrated by Bill Moyers, called *The Language of Life*. The program showcased the renowned Dodge Poetry Festival. My happening upon the show felt quite mystical, in that the language of poetry handed me back my life. As a reference point: at that time, I had no idea that poetry festivals even existed. I believed poets existed only in books. But then, Lucille Clifton stepped up and read a poem and charged me with her Dahomey spirit as she delivered her iconic powerful poem "won't you celebrate with me." Her poem spun life on its axis.

Her words acted as lightning rods to my heart and weary body. Clifton's last lines of the poem became my mantra: "everyday / something has tried to kill me / and has failed." Through my aching muscle pain and brain fog, her poem lit me up from within. After hearing it, I knew I would not be long on my sick bed/couch and I would not spend my days being pinned down by this unseen disability, even though I was told the condition was both degenerative and progressive. Long story short, I had this disease and it was only going to get worse. My body, spirit, and relationships suffered from my fast decline, but poetry became a soft place to land. It became a healthy distraction. I never thought of poetry as a profession; I only thought about it saving my life. Clifton's verse "Every day something has tried to kill me and has failed" was a clarion call. I woke up and rose to her words. The poem acted as an invitation to celebrate my life through poetry, and I did. I began writing poems again.

This was not my first brush with writing poetry. I began writing in Ms. Sergeant's eighth-grade English class at Woodmont Junior High School. She had us freewrite every morning for fifteen minutes, and I never stopped writing in my journal after that. I began writing in a form unbeknownst to me at the time—praise poems and elegiac poems for friends and family. My family's home church, Bethlehem Baptist Church, took my role as a poet seriously. I tried to echo a Black Baptist preacher's cadence. I also was immersed in a blue-collar/sharecropping family, where the men swapped lies, jokes, and stories at family gatherings. It did not matter whether they were on the porch or in the den or the backyard. I absorbed their timing and rhythm in my poetry.

Jonathan Green came to Greenville not long after my spiritual/creative renewal. He was exhibiting work at the Greenville County Museum of Art. I was ecstatic to meet the artist whose prints hung in our home. His work had already shifted my way of being by strengthening my personal identity. A woman named Diane asked me to be part of a group of African Americans in Greenville who would purchase his work titled *The Christening*. It became a part of the museum's permanent collection. It feels like it was yesterday, though it was another lifetime—as I am listed on the nameplate as Glenis Sherer, which speaks to my past life. Now divorced, I have gone back to my maiden name, Redmond. After meeting Jonathan, I stayed in contact with him via letters and phone calls. One day, he asked me, "Why are you still counseling? You are a poet." Jonathan's origin story included being born with the caul over his face. In the Gullah community, this means the child will have the gift of sight and prophecy. With Lucille Clifton's poem and Jonathan Green's prophecy, I did not need to be told a third time. I embarked on my poetry road.

Cultural Background

I did not find many literary mirrors at school—textbooks rarely reflected African American history. If we were lucky, we had a week for Black history. Then, by 1976, we had the whole month. Still, we were likely to get only a paragraph or footnote here or there that mentioned Martin Luther King Jr., Frederick Douglass, or George Washington Carver. Later, I learned about Harriet Tubman and Sojourner Truth. I leaned into the educational silence and footnotes of African American obligatory mentions. Within those tight margins, I absorbed the mainstream's message that our story was not important or significant enough to highlight or teach. My positive cultural mirrors came from books that I read on my own, from church, and from home.

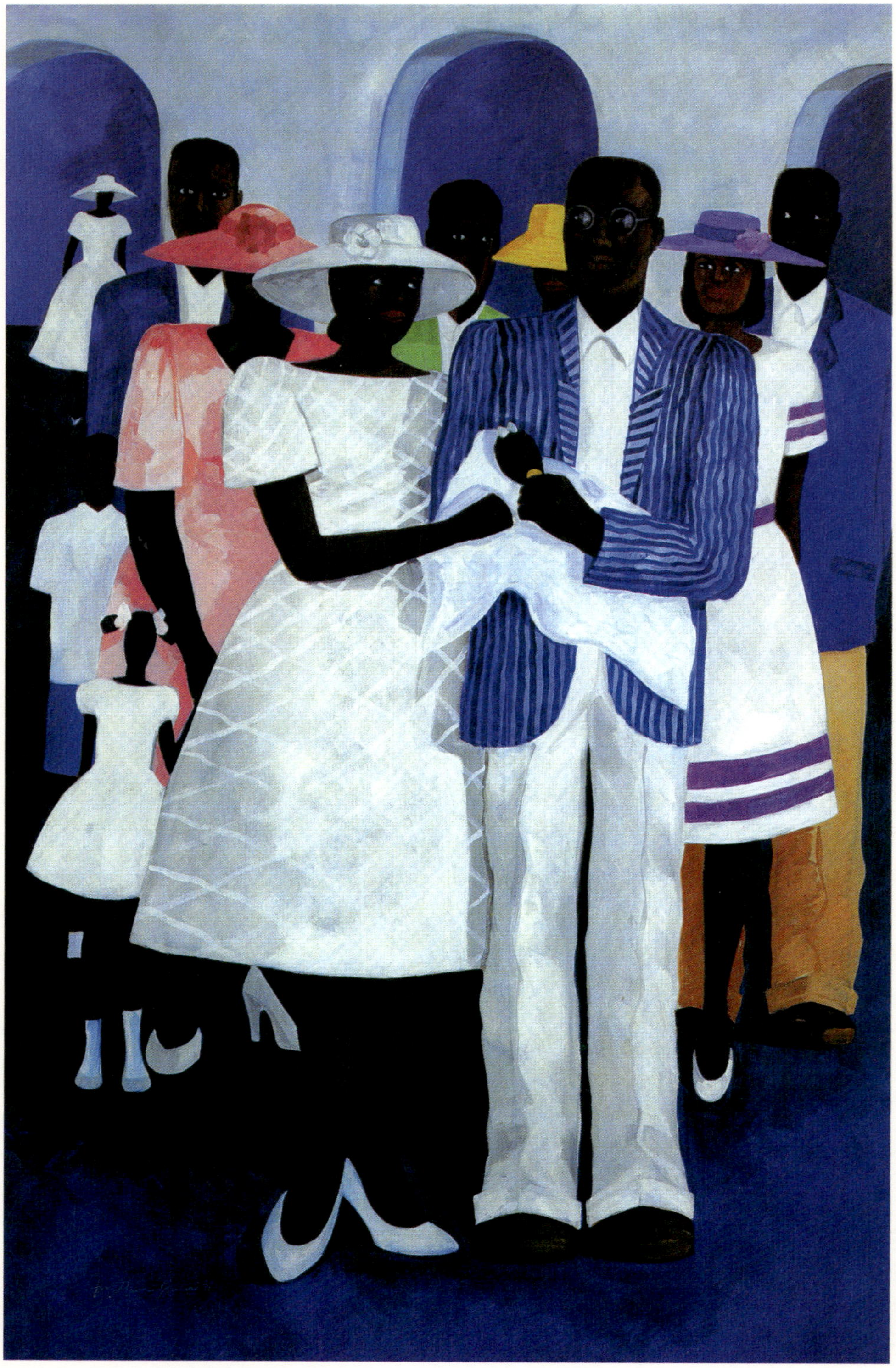

The Christening, 1991. Jonathan Green. Oil on canvas, 52 × 34 inches. Collection of Greenville County Museum of Art, Greenville, S.C.

My mama was great at mothering, with her huge heart—constantly serving us home-cooked southern meals, no matter where we lived in the world. She made most of our clothes—many of mine were sewn to my specifications. She replicated what her mother, born on a farm in 1901 in Waterloo, South Carolina, had taught her: resourcefulness. Though Mom hated farming, the lifestyle had given her many undeniable homemaking skills. In other words, we ate very well, no matter on which air force base we lived. Though all the houses on bases were uniform—they all looked alike on the outside—on the inside, ours had Mama's distinct touch. Though she never wrote a poem, I often say that she was poetry in the kitchen. Her rhythm and timing were impeccable—knowing how to put each item on the stove or into the oven so that all the dishes would be piping hot on the table when it came time to eat.

I watched her with great interest, and I rarely saw her consult cookbooks or recipes, though she did. Yet, like most masters, she put her own spin on her meals. She cooked all things southern for us, which meant a whole lot of fried: pork chops, fried chicken, and crackling. Her family had kept chickens, and so she grew up making every incarnation of yard bird: fried, baked, broiled, hashed, and barbecued. Vegetables—especially collards—were accompanied by fatback. Homemade bread was served at every meal: drop bread, biscuits, or cornbread. Grits and salmon croquettes, with homemade butter biscuits on the side, smothered with grape jelly, is to this day my favorite meal made by my mama's hands. I come from capable and can-do women. They were skillful in the kitchen and outdoors, too—they chopped wood and carried water from the well. And they picked over their weight in cotton—250 to 350 pounds a day. Mama did it all with ease.

My father enriched us with music. We experienced Black history through the lens of our father's musical repertoire. In our household, we sang and danced to the music of the day (R & B proliferated), and we were fans of James Brown, Diana Ross, the Staple Singers, and so on. Daddy, in his heyday, preferred Ray Charles, Muddy Waters, the Clovers, and Howlin' Wolf albums. Gospel was how we understood our culture best. As Daddy practiced his songs for Sunday service, we would sing along to "Just a Closer Walk with Thee" and "Oh Happy Day." Mahalia Jackson, Shirley Caesar, and Marian Anderson reverberated from our home. Our father made sure we knew the words to the Black national anthem, "Lift Every Voice and Sing."

Our household was always inundated in and by music. Our father relished all the arts. Yet, the visual art that I hung on my walls triggered him. We grew up with him telling us stories and jokes, reciting poetry, and performing mime skits that he'd picked up from his air force travels. We held talent shows and dance-offs. I was fifteen years old when I learned that all people were not raised in artistic households. I asked a friend of mine about what music her family sang and danced to in the evenings or on the weekends. She replied, “We don’t do that.” It was an epiphany that we were different. My parents handed down many African American southern traditions.

The difficulty came when we moved from Aviano, Italy, and from McGuire Air Force Base in central New Jersey to Piedmont, South Carolina. It was a complete and utter culture shock. Black lawn jockeys still littered the countryside. Confederate flags flew on the state capitol and in people’s yards. They frequently waved from cars and trucks. They also drove straight into my psyche. Dixie memorabilia was abundant in convenience stores all along the Interstate 85 and 95 corridors. I was not ready for the segregation of the South. It felt like the civil rights movement had never happened at Woodmont Junior/Senior High School. The *Roots* miniseries aired in 1977 and almost caused a riot. This was the first time most of us had had our collective stories told. Alex Haley’s book recounted the horrors of the Middle Passage, slavery, and sharecropping. It was a timely movie, and I felt both a sense of pride and anger. The tensions in the halls of our school were palpable. White teachers and white students were not ready for the Black students’ reaction. They joked and called us Kunta Kinte as a put-down. We found their mockery and insensitivity a cause to stand up for ourselves. This movie was revolutionary and necessary for us. It located us on the American timeline in a way we had never been placed. The poem below speaks to my culture shock of moving back to my parent’s South.

You Know You Are Not from Here

when your dad retires and announces, *we’re going home*
when South Carolina is just a concept not a place
when it would never dawn on your parents
to *preview* or *set the context* for the South
when they just load all five of you
into that 1974 puce green Chevy Nova
and head south on I-95
when you are eyes-wide and full of questions
when you see Sambo depicted on a roadside billboard
when you do not understand the color lines
at basketball games or on Sunday mornings,
but then you wake to charred and smoldering grass
from a cross burned in your neighborhood
when you see a plantation for the first time
and you are not awed by its beauty
but haunted by the history not told on public tours
when you learn to navigate the historical land mines
when your steps become fluid dance moves in the margins
and your tongue follows with fluent code switch and *switch backs,*

criks, hollers, and *down yonders*
when you do not know the word *kin,*
but when you been here long enough
you feel how blood circles back to here
when you understand Dorothy's double-edged decree
There's no place like home. There's no place like home.

I had to make sense of the world racially in my early teens. I watched characters on television, like Stepin Fetchit, who reinforced Black stereotypes. His tagline was: the laziest man in the world. I was fascinated and horrified by his wide-eyed clowning. Though the show stopped airing in 1953, reruns played well into my teenage years in the 1970s. Even later, while I was in graduate school at Texas Tech University in 1986, the student newspaper published a picture of a pickaninny to respond to Black students wanting to celebrate MLK Jr. Day.

I was incensed and offended. However, these are a few of the many racial assaults that I endured daily. Literature followed suit: *Gone with the Wind,* with its stereotypical mammy character. Even children's books contained harmful and hateful imagery. As late as the 2000s, while working at a school in Hendersonville, North Carolina, I went downtown on a break between performances. While I was in a secondhand shop to pass time, the owner of the store followed me, as if I were going to steal. I left abruptly because of that profiling. As I walked out of the store, I turned, and I saw a piece of history staring back at me: a golliwog in the storefront.

What's in the Bank?

I scour downtown Hendersonville.
Find an antique store.
In the window a gleam catches my gaze,
a black ceramic face
Mouth shaped like a crescent moon,
framed with a red golliwog grin.
I am stolen in plain sight,
plantation snatched on Main Street,
pulled further down the southern road
where a price hangs around a Black man's neck.
$995.00 the tag reads, penned
in the most careful delicate hand,
Happy Nigger Bank.
The face holds nothing funny
just history, a sneer holding back a silent scream.

Jonathan Green's Direction

When I began taking writing workshops, instructors often advised, "Write about what you know." They did not give any specific suggestions on how to tap into what I knew. I was operating out of a cultural void, but Green gave me not only inspiration, but also an idea of how to strengthen my voice and how to speak up and out about what I had internalized and suppressed about being Black and living in the American South. Jonathan Green's paintings gave me permission to write about my immediate surroundings, family, people, and culture.

I rarely had access to my parents' past, as they had been traumatized by growing up in a separate but not equal South Carolina. They have suppressed many of their memories of the South for psychological perseverance, and they rarely doled their personal experiences out to me or my siblings. I believe that it is difficult to come into this world both poverty stricken and Black, into apartheidlike conditions, and remain unscathed. Occasionally, we would get glimpses of their histories. As for South Carolina, they adopted the "don't want to go there" mentality. I am sure this was a form of self-preservation to ease their psychic pain. As a sensitive child, I read in between the lines. I understood and felt the emotional load that they carried. As a poet, I had to learn to unpack these heavy silences. This poem tells the story of my family's migration in the midfifties.

Boy

I say, boy, pay attention when I'm talkin' to ya, boy.
—FOGHORN LEGHORN

Boy is a weighted word
aimed and hurled, meant to maim—
Slow kill preferably.
He's pock marked, and bullet ridden
Learns to dance, duck, and dodge,
head either raised or lowered, he knew either way,
they coming for you.
Boy be another way to pin you into place.
Grind metal into precious flesh.
At the Poinsett Hotel,
he's back bent busboy busy
clearing tables or washes dishes
trying everything he knows to grow full height
into becoming a man.
The change is so short in his pocket,
he figures, he can't get there from here.

One day, he's triggered.
One more time, if I'm called boy, I'll kill 'em.
The next day, instead of punching the clock,
he finds Uncle Sam's office.
Signs his legal name: Johnny Clifton Redmond.
Exchanges apron for fatigues.
Swaps battlefield.

Jonathan Green's work changed my perspective of African American history from a generalized understanding to a more pointed look at my own lineage in South Carolina. He helped me to absorb and unpack the southern African American experience in a positive way, while Lucille Clifton's poem helped me solidify my identity as a Black woman. With their artistic direction, I began to write about place, specifically South Carolina. Jonathan Green's paintings specifically connected the dots from South Carolina to Africa. "Mama's Magic" was written out of Jonathan's prompting. It took time for to me to finally connect the dots. A black-and-white photo reminded me of my humble beginnings. I was trying to hunt and dream up inspiration on how to write about low-income housing—all I had to do was go back on the timeline to my humble beginnings. This was my first true poem of origin. After a failed attempt, I believe my subconscious continued to search and work on the poem. One morning, I woke up in tears and I wrote this poem as a tribute to my mama and as an anthem of how we spiritually overcame poverty. As Alex Haley wrote: "Find the good and praise it." I learned, too, from Green's work that it is a radical act to celebrate amid the struggle.

Mama's Magic

My mama is magic.
Always was and always will be.
There is one phrase that constantly bubbled
from the lips of her five children, "My mama can do it."
We thought my mama knew everything.
Believed she did, as if she were born full grown
from the *Encyclopedia Britannica*.

I could tell you stories of how she transformed
a run-down paint-peeled shack into a home.
How she heated us with tin tub baths from a kettle on the stove.
Poured it over in there like an elixir.
My mama is protection, like those quilts her mother used to make.
She tucked us in with cut out history all around us.
We found we could walk anywhere in this world and not feel alone.

My mama never whispered the shame of poverty in our ears.
She taught us to dance to our own shadows.
"Pay no attention to those grand parties on the other side of the tracks.
Make your own music," she'd say as she walked,
as she cleaned the sagging floorboards of that place.

"You'll get there. You'll get there."
Her broom seemed to say, with every wisp.
We were my mama's favorite recipe.
She whipped us up in a big brown bowl,
supported by her big brown arms.
We were homemade children.
Stitched together with homemade love.
We didn't get everything we ever wanted,
but we lacked for nothing.

We looked at the stars in my mama's eyes.
They told us we owned the world.
We walked like kings and queens,
even on midnight trips to the outhouse.
We were under her spell.
My mama didn't study at no Harvard or Yale.
The things she knew you couldn't learn in no book!
Like . . .
How to make your life sing like sweet potato pie sweetness
out of an open window.
How to make anybody feel at home.
How, at just the right moment, to be silent and, with her eyes, say,
"Everything's gonna be alright, chile. Everything is gonna be alright."

How she tended to all our sickness. How she raised our spirits.
How she kept flowers living on our sagging porch in the midst of family chaos.
My mama raised children like it was her business in life.
Put us on her hip and kept moving,
keeping that house Pine-Sol clean. Yeah, my mama is magic.

Always was and always will be. Her magic?
How to stay steady and sure in this fast-paced world.
Now, when people look at me with my head held high,
my back erect, and look at me with that . . .
"Who does she think she is?"
I just keep on walking, with the assurance inside.
I am Black Magic!
I am Jeanette Redmond's child.

My work has progressed since then in many ways. Yet, I continue to mine my culture creatively. I have delved into learning about how my family and my ancestors arrived in the upstate during the "second middle passage." The second migration was known as the domestic, or internal, slave trade. Once my people were brought to the port, they were then displaced to other regions in the South. When my ancestors left Charleston, I do not know. I also do not know who the first person was in my father's line or in my mother's line that took that forced march to Greenville, Simpsonville, Fountain Inn, and Laurens.

However, when I witnessed my first Jonathan Green painting, my soul shouted a resounding "Yes!" I felt a déjà vu from his painting. *Burning Sheets* especially made me remember other past lives, when midwives or spiritual elders burned sheets after birth or death. He began to connect the dots of my lineage. It was Green's use of ritual that instructed me. In the poem below, I attempt to convey my appreciation for Jonathan Green and his work.

Vision Is a Complicated Thing

For Jonathan Green after Lucille Clifton
Jonathan Green
Burning Sheets

A picture is worth all the words.
—GLENIS REDMOND

Capture the image. Relish green
and how it deepens the landscape.
Verdant may not be in your vocabulary,
but let it touch you. Expand your palette.
Feel the story growing underneath the story.
With a careful eye, drink in green.
See how it colors everything,
even in the cobalt dash from the Atlantic
and the crimson drops.
Remember: the first layer is always dressing.
Celebration is the pressure applied to stop the bleeding.
In the background, there's always more
—alabaster streaks that cover the land.

Cruelty is at the root. That's why cotton
will never just be soft harmless tufts;
that's why the soul sings of the trouble
nobody knows.
If you let it, the eye will go back to the past:

the hands dark, rich, and burnt,
forming rays from pearl to midnight
—hands that picked and plowed,
but still made time to clap, pray, and praise.

Vision is a complicated thing,
but those who have the sight
understand how history blurs the edges.
Sit still long enough.
Peer through the veils
until it becomes clear
—how green turns the head
to the struggle and beauty at hand.

Writing to Right History

Though I said that I would never live in Greenville, South Carolina, I learned that I should never say never. When my mother got sick, I went home and lived with her for a year. The first poem I wrote while living with her was about South Carolina. It was for Clayton Bates, known as Peg Leg Bates, a one-legged tap dancer who in the 1950s taught my mother and father at Fountain Inn Colored High School.

I'm Fly for Clayton "Peg Leg" Bates

Some people got two good feet
and still don't know what to do.
My smoothness makes the argument
for just one. My other leg be long gone,
sacrificed to the cotton gin god.

They pinned my mangled mess down
to the kitchen table. Made me suffer more
under the hand of an unsterilized knife,
with only a cotton bit to bear the pain.

I got up and spit out that terrible taste of Jim Crow
and pity. Spun my mama's guilt and worry into a dance
that twists past the neighbors' prayer, gossip, and stares
of how he gonna make do with just one leg?

I strap on my dreams with tux, tails, and flair.
Turn can't into can, without losing time, not even in my mind.
This Fountain Inn son done good. I knock beats on wood.

I'm a worldwide showstopper, all right.
Shout rings around all those two-footers.
I'm the master of my own fate.

'Though the world cut me below the thigh,
I don't shuffle off in misery.
I get up on my one good leg and fly.

She also told me about Willie Earle, the last Black man lynched in Greenville, South Carolina. She was eleven years old when a white mob of twenty-six men shot him in the head on Bramlett Road—two hours from where she lived then and an hour from where she lives now—and not one man was convicted.

Nature Lesson

1947.
At age eleven,
my mama learned
how a rope turns into more than a rope,
looped around a branch where a tree
becomes more than a tree,
where memory twists around
more than the mind,
like Willie Earle's life
and my mama's young heart.
In Greenville, South Carolina,
mama sees how memory hangs
on each and every tree.

Dr. Gabrielle Foreman urged me to investigate a poet-potter, David Drake, because of his extraordinary story and because he was from South Carolina. At the time, I was not ready to write about him because I was working on another project, but then poetry began its mystical swirl—everywhere I traveled, people would ask me if I knew about David Drake and his beautifully crafted pots. After the third person asked me, I relented. I began to research and study and muse about David Drake. Of course, I discovered that my artistic guide, Jonathan Green, had already painted David Drake in the 1990s.

This was a full circle moment. I began writing ekphrastically to David Drake via Jonathan Green's work. Discovering a South Carolina poetic forefather grounded me. On one of his pots, he wrote this couplet: "I wonder where is all my relation / friendship to all and every nation." Viscerally impacted by the horrors of slavery, Dave found a way to record his story. Dave's wondering in the 1800s furthers my wondering about our ancestral links. His pots and poems serve as partial missives to us. His "I wonder" couplet speaks specifically to me about the African American torn lineage that we strive collectively to piece together. The place-based poems that I write about David Drake set in motion a call-and-response creative cycle. David calls out as he looks for his people; I look back to him to discover and recover our ancestral links. As a South Carolina poet, too, I reply to Dave's query. My poems are a direct address to Dave: We are your relations. I feel compelled and driven to preserve and uphold his legacy. I say to Dave: I am here. I say: Those who neglect their past have no future. Working on these David Drake poems, I have been inspired by two visual artists: David Drake and Jonathan Green.

I took the liberty to respond to David Drake via persona, which means I put on a mask of Dave and wrote through his lens. The questions that I asked were: What would David say? What would he feel? It is an imaginative experiment to take on an enslaved man's perspective. However, it is one that I find informative and gratifying. When I ask these questions, I am also posing the questions: How did my ancestors feel? How would I feel? As a poet, I dream and create to fill a void in our history. I am attempting to create an emotional resonance that speaks to this artist and outlier. David Drake's remaining pots and Jonathan Green's *Sir Dave* series provided art in which to converse poetically. With both paintings and pots, I continue to explore and discover our Afro-Carolinian history. In the first poem in this collection by me, "Forefather," I express how David Drake inspires me as a poet and as a Black daughter of South Carolina and how knowing of him and his works empowers me.

Artist Statement

My poems are necessary and urgent missives that percolate from the core—words born from joy, anger, rage, celebration, and sorrow. I pour what burns onto journal pages. These hot-inked scribblings are handwritten epiphanies that morph into soul-driven manifestos. This drive comes from a deep-seated oceanic need to explore my dismembered (Middle Passage) lineage. My poem making is a creative way for me to make peace with the many pieces of my disrupted family tree. With this red clay–weighted history, I strive to weave beautiful bold lines speaking unapologetic colloquial anthems. In my poems, I say the unsayable. I am inspired by the unknown multitudes of my ancestry. They stand ten thousand strong at my back. I am a griot, a storyteller, a poet, and a holder of history. These works stitch and sing my heritage back into being. I write to right history the best I can, giving permission for my poems to dance and sing on both page and stage.

Dave the Potter

A Theatrical Production Sharing His Legacy

LYNNETTE YOUNG OVERBY

Pretty Girl

from *Dave the Potter*

Ralph Anthony Russell

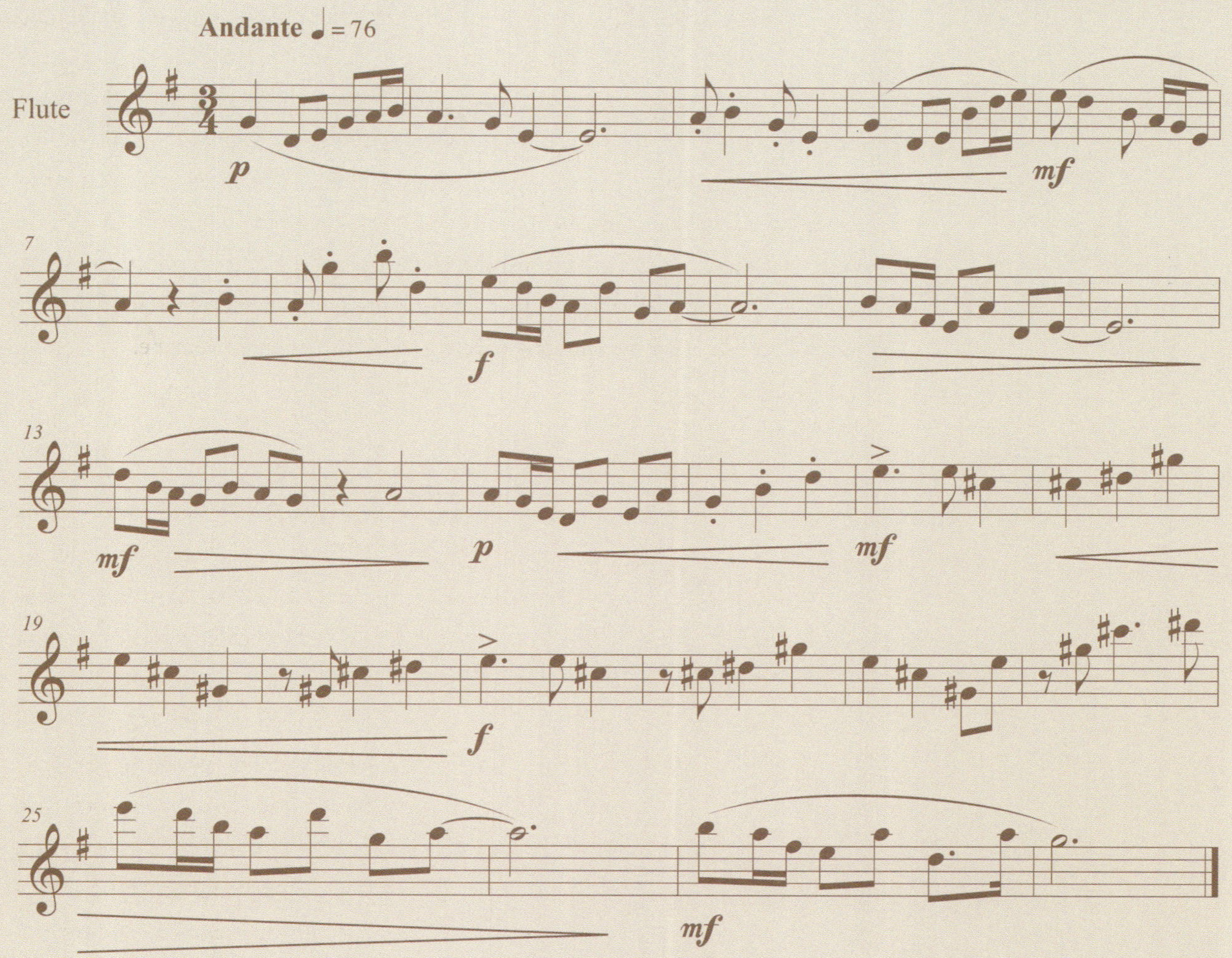

OVERLEAF: Score from "Pretty Little Girl." Courtesy of composer, Ralph Anthony Russell.

PREMIERING AT THE UNIVERSITY OF DELAWARE on March 14, 2014, the theatrical production of *Dave the Potter* was a collaboration of multiple artists and scholars. It featured paintings by Jonathan Green, poetry by Glenis Redmond and Gabrielle Foreman, choreography by me (Lynnette Young Overby), Teresa Emmons, Vincent Thomas, and Gabrielle Hilliard, and music composed by Ralph Russell and Jennifer Higdon. The orchestra was directed by Duo Shen. A forty-five-minute production, it required several months to prepare at the time and has continued to evolve in the years since.

Watching you water and grow this project, this cross-age, cross-interest, cross-time community and collaboration, has been an honor and pleasure. Dave lives on, in, and through us!

—GABRIELLE FOREMAN, 2014

As artistic director, my goal for this project was to create a venue for people to experience a historical time that could easily be lost and to engage with the event in a multisensory, multidisciplinary manner. I wanted them to have a synthetic, meaningful experience. To create this engagement, it was clear that collaboration among artists, historians, and community members would be required. For many years, I have been involved in social justice through arts programming, and *Dave the Potter*, like all social justice projects, called for a similarly collaborative approach. Yet collaborations are not easy. They mean you must be open to the thoughts, ideas, and contributions of others—contributions that may or may not merge with your existing thoughts and ideas. Such was the case with the development of *Dave the Potter* as a multidisciplinary project.

How did it begin? With the history? The poetry? The music? Perhaps it was the paintings, or the movement? In reflecting back on the process, I believe the project was initially guided by the history and by the paintings. The history provided the substantive knowledge that guided the process, and the paintings provided a visual image and structure for the music, poetry, and choreography that came next. Yet, in some ways, the potential for *Dave the Potter*—the genesis for this collaborative, multidisciplinary production—began even earlier. *Dave the Potter* was, in fact, the second collaboration between me, professor and literary historian Gabrielle Foreman, and poet Glenis Redmond. Two years earlier, we had worked together to develop a production based on the life and times of Harriet E. Wilson.

The result of our first collaboration was *Sketches: The Life of Harriet E. Wilson in Dance, Poetry, and Music.*[1] A walk on the University of Delaware campus with Foreman in the fall of 2011 started our journey into the project. At the time, I was looking for assistance in identifying an appropriate slave narrative to depict in a choreographic work. During our walk, Foreman mentioned her discoveries and subsequent publications about Harriet E. Wilson. Wilson, abandoned by her mother at a young age to serve as an indentured servant until age eighteen, lived through constant abuse. Yet she turned her life around and became a successful businesswoman and one of the first African American novelists. After our walk, Foreman left me with a copy of Wilson's autobiographical novel, *Our Nig* (1859),[2] and that began our multidisciplinary collaboration. To help tell Wilson's story, I invited Redmond to create poetry for the project. Lauren Wells, a graduate student in music composition, created original music. This collaborative work resulted in a fourteen-minute performance that is now on YouTube and used in English classes around the country as a means of understanding *Our Nig*.

Arts-based research (ABR) defines this form of scholarship. ABR promotes a deeper understanding of a topic, as well as greater access to it, by transforming the material into an artistic work or creative experience.[3] In this case, the art forms of poetry, dance, and music transformed the topic—the life and times of Harriet E. Wilson—to deepen readers' engagement with Wilson's original text. Productions of this sort require a rigorous form of scholarship that allows one to truly feel the meanings of the work, promoting a deep cognitive and emotional understanding.[4] Multidisciplinary collaborations steeped in research and the acknowledgment of difficult social issues provide audiences, contributors, and performers with the opportunity to experience places, times, and situations through their different senses—visual, auditory, and kinesthetic. And this is what we did by bringing several branches of learning together to tell the stories first of Harriet E. Wilson and subsequently of David Drake.

The goals of the *Dave the Potter* production were several: to create, perform, and disseminate David Drake's story through original music, choreography, and poetry inspired by the paintings of Jonathan Green and Dave's historical setting itself; to inform audiences and students of all ages through the performance; and to create a permanent exhibit of materials through web technology. Working together as collaborators, we produced a piece intended to be entertaining, informative, intellectually rich, and emotionally evocative.[5] The choreography included movement sequences that emerged as imagined and improvised scenes based on the times and experiences of Dave's life, with the choreographers as facilitators who structured many of the improvised sequences into a finished work.

Three critical components shaped the production: team visits to Edgefield, South Carolina, where Dave was born and lived, writings by scholar Gabrielle Foreman and Leonard Todd, and paintings by Jonathan Green.[6] Some of the readings provided us with details of Drake's life in Edgefield. Other readings provided us with details about the lives of enslaved African Americans in the South. We also had access to the couplets written on his pots. Finally, the visual history provided by Jonathan Green's paintings gave us a roadmap to use as we told Dave's story in dance, music, and poetry.

Background—the History

Dave the Potter is known for turning large stoneware pots, some large enough to hold up to forty pounds. Stoneware pots were a common commodity in the mid-1800s that were often used as containers for meat and meal on plantations. Mastering the ability to create these pots required many years of training and great skill. Dave's pots were covered with a unique alkaline glaze that helps researchers identify his pots today. However, more important for both the identification of Dave's pots and the history behind them is the fact that he inscribed his name and self-authored poetic couplets on his pots.

Little is known about Dave's early years, only that he was born in approximately 1801 in the United States. In 1818, he was known to live in Pottersville, a homestead in Edgefield County, South Carolina. It is here that Dave learned how to create pots and to read and write. Because of his skill as a potter, Dave escaped the common fate of toiling on a cotton plantation. He inscribed many of his pots with poetry—a remarkable feat considering he was enslaved and thus denied the right to read or write. The poetry he inscribed on the pots was simple but direct, and often told stories of his times, his family, and his friends.

The couplet "I wonder where is all my relation / friendship to all and every nation" (August 16, 1857) helped drive the collective work on the *Dave the Potter* production. Within our multidisciplinary interpretation of his life in the mid-1800s, when David Drake was enslaved in South Carolina, we focused on his time as a potter and his experience as a man who felt the satisfaction of mastering a trade alongside the inevitable horror of slavery.

Artists and Scholars

The collaborators in this production included Gabrielle Foreman, our literary historian, who introduced Dave to the other collaborators, as well as Jonathan Green, a world-renowned painter who created a series of paintings on Dave's life in 1998.

Our poet, Glenis Redmond, was inspired by Dave's story, Green's paintings, and her own South Carolina roots, which enabled her to visualize and create poems bringing Dave's story to life. Vincent Thomas, a choreographer, university professor, and Edgefield native, grew up in the same town as Dave. He walked the same paths and experienced the same South Carolina culture, although over one hundred years later. He played Sir Dave in the original production.

Ralph Russell, the composer, gave the production sound, rhythm, and harmony as he carefully composed and edited music to work with both the theme and the needs of the choreographers. Teresa Emmons, a Dover High School dance teacher, jumped at the chance to create a piece about the marketplace. Gabrielle Hilliard choreographed her piece in response to the evocative poetry recited by Glenis Redmond and Audrey Wright, our undergraduate researcher.

The final collaborators were the dancers themselves. While the choreographers came with ideas for choreography, in many cases they invited the dancers to contribute to the dances by improvising on specific ideas and themes. In this sense, the choreographers were facilitators, shaping and structuring the final dances. As artistic director and choreographer, I supervised the undergraduate research assistant, organized auditions, group meetings, and rehearsals, and served as lead choreographer for the majority of the individual works in the creation of the performance.

The Process

Our journey with *Dave the Potter* began with visits to South Carolina. Vincent Thomas, Gabrielle Foreman, Glenis Redmond, and I visited Jonathan Green in August 2013, where we described the proposed production. Green was very supportive, giving us access to all of his paintings in the *Sir Dave* series. Next, we visited museums where the pots were on display and discussed the project with Leonard Todd. Not only is Todd the descendent of one of Dave's owners but he is also the author of *Carolina Clay: The Life and Legend of the Slave Potter Dave* (2008).

We then began reviewing written sources. First, we conducted research with the assistance of Audrey Wright, a University of Delaware undergraduate researcher. When she initially joined the team, she worked in the capacity of research and choreographic assistant to me. Then, with an undergraduate research scholarship, she spent the summer of 2013 researching the daily aspects of life for enslaved workers on cotton plantations in South Carolina from 1810 to 1860. Through an extensive literature review, she was able to glean information about what one may have experienced living and working during that time.[7]

Our next steps included selecting specific artwork to use for the production and auditioning dancers. For the paintings, we selected representative work from Green's *Sir Dave* series. With the artwork chosen and the historical content in mind, the composer, poet, and choreographers began working on their artistic interpretations in the summer and fall of 2013. Meanwhile, we cast the performers. Because of the racial diversity I desired for the work, I contacted the Christina Cultural Arts Center, a community arts center in Wilmington, Delaware, that focuses on African American arts and culture. I auditioned several of the dancers and incorporated them into a cast that included University of Delaware performers.

Rehearsals commenced as soon as the musical compositions and poetry were set. They included improvisations on specific themes, written and verbal reflections by the dancers and choreographers, the development of movement motifs, and the organization of movements into a cohesive choreographic work. The process was similar to the steps of kinesthetic empathy, embodied exploration, embodied reflection, and "work-in-process showcase" described by scholar Susan Leigh Foster in *Choreographing Empathy*.[8] During the rehearsals, the choreographers and dancers were prompted to create data (movement content) inspired by embodied exploration and reflection on the history, paintings, and poetry. The choreography was completed and taught by February 2014, and grants we had applied for in the early stages of the process enabled us to pay contributors and reserve the performance space.

The Complete Production, Performed March 14, 2014

Dave the Potter's production components integrated original choreography, music, and poetry with the selected paintings of Jonathan Green as backdrop. Several large pots designed and rendered by students in the University of Delaware Art Department were also an important part of the stage set. The following section presents the production in full, highlighting the key narrative, artistic, and conceptual elements of all ten movements. The first full sequence following the prelude, "Field Cotton," receives particular attention to emphasize the multidisciplinary dimensions of the performance as a whole.

PRELUDE

POETRY: "Praise Dave" by Glenis Redmond
PAINTINGS: *Sir Dave* series by Jonathan Green
MUSIC: "Dave the Potter Prelude" by Ralph Russell

In this opening piece, Glenis Redmond performed her poem while the selected paintings scrolled in the background. The sequence introduces Dave, providing a glimpse into his life as a potter, an enslaved man, and a person who overcame significant odds to become a successful African American. In the poem's conclusion, Redmond captures Dave's significance as an enslaved artist and historical figure with her powerful words, "I sign my name Dave. / I don't write slave. / See if my pots and me spin history. / See if we hold hold hold."

FIELD COTTON

POETRY: "Field Cotton" by Glenis Redmond
PAINTING: *Edgefield* by Jonathan Green
MUSIC: "Field Cotton" by Ralph Russell
CHOREOGRAPHY: "Cotton" by Lynnette Young Overby

Jonathan Green's *Edgefield*, the backdrop for this piece, captures the beauty of cotton fields in bloom. But Green's painting does not reflect what went into making these gorgeous fields. Dave lived near cotton plantations all his life, but once he became an accomplished potter, he likely wouldn't have faced a future of field labor. He was certainly affected by cotton slavery, though. Any family and friends he had would have been at risk of working on a cotton plantation. Taking us through the life of an enslaved worker, Redmond's poetry sets the stage for this central facet of life in Edgefield, South Carolina. Her poem brings the fields to the fore, pondering, "How can something so comely turn so ugly?"

"Field Cotton" by Ralph Russell is a lyrical piece that similarly captures the harsh conditions of plantation life. The piece is in F minor and is characterized by a simple vocal-like theme and recurring bass ostinato. The opening bass pattern depicts the slow and exhausting movements of the workers as they pick cotton in the unrelenting heat. In contrast, the songlike theme, which was inspired by African American spirituals and work songs, reflects the workers' humanity. Jonathan Green's bright and distinctive painting of the cotton field generated the piece's musical language and tone, while the piece complements the texts, tone, and timbre of Redmond's dramatic narrative. Her varied melodic phrasing, rhythmic accents, and subtle dynamics reflect in the music's form, thematic presentation, and recurring bass accompaniment.

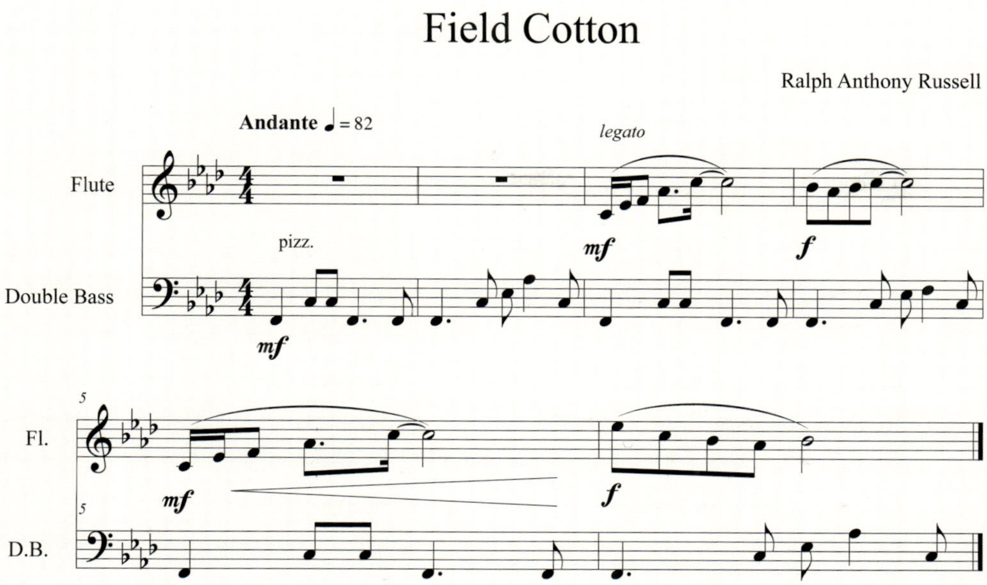

Score from "Field Cotton." Courtesy of composer, Ralph Anthony Russell.

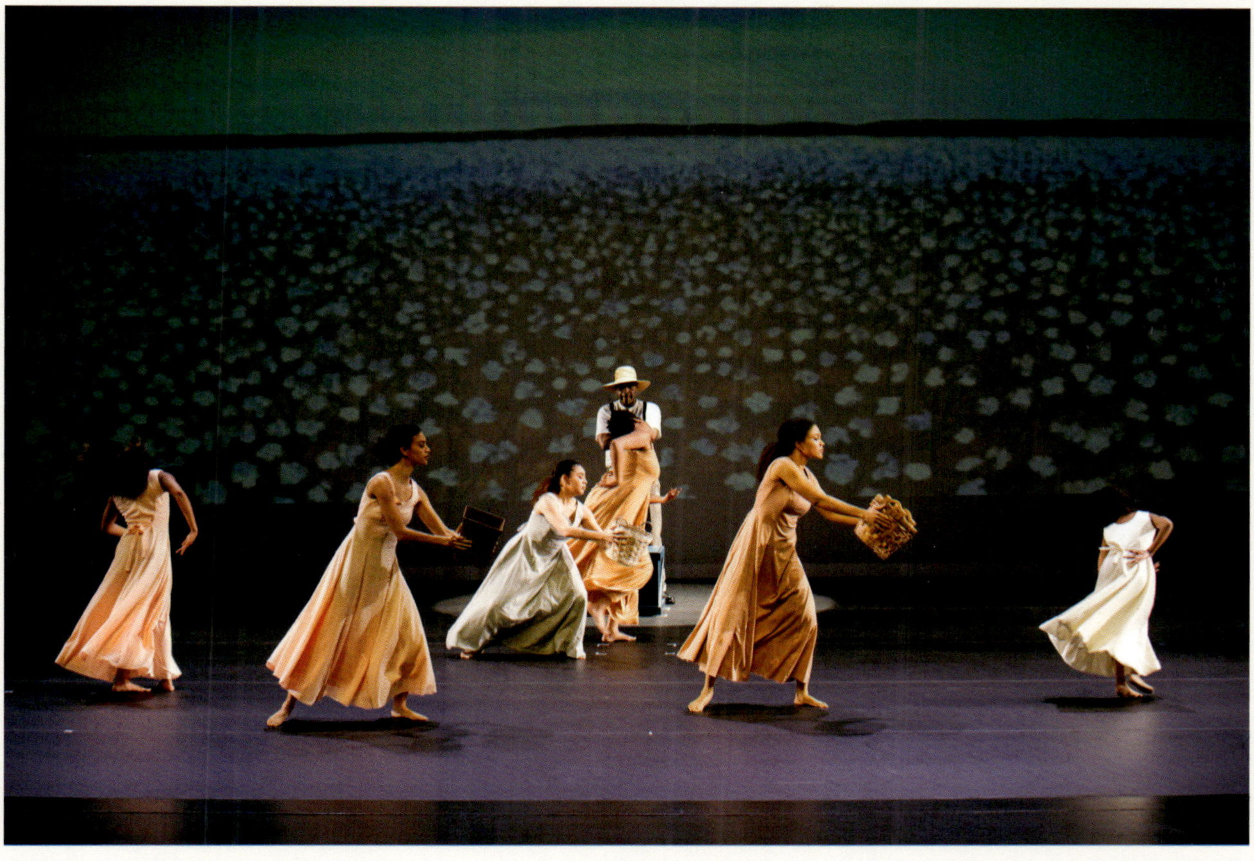

"Field Cotton." Choreographed by Lynnette Young Overby. Performed by Rachel DeLauder, Dianna Ruberto, April Singleton, Amber Rance, Gabrielle Shubert, and Ralph Russell. Music by Ralph Russell. Poetry by Glenis Redmond. Photographed by Amy Randall. Featuring *Edgefield*, by Jonathan Green. February 6, 2019. Courtesy of Amy Randall Photography. All photographs from February 6, 2019, were taken at performances at the Peace Center in Greenville, South Carolina.

Character development was one of the most important parts of the choreographic process. The dancers were encouraged to take part in the choreography and contribute their own ideas and movements. For example, in one of the first improvisational sessions, the dancers improvised interpretations to the words "pick, prick, and bleed" from Redmond's poem. The dancers also created their own personas as cotton pickers to perform on stage. To further empathize with the people who lived in the time period, they were given excerpts from particularly striking personal slave narratives.[9]

On stage, the piece begins with performers sleeping in small groups depicting different families. When they are awakened by the overseer ringing a cow bell, they begin their day. Before heading to the fields, the dancers first portray the preparation of the day's meals. Next, they are workers in the fields, picking row by row under the overseer's watchful eye. This section of the "Cotton" dance portrays the heat and exhaustion that came from picking cotton all day in the hot sun. One of the workers almost passes out from exhaustion; others help her up. Then it is the end of the day, and the cotton picked by each of the workers must be weighed, with the knowledge that there will be punishment if not enough cotton is picked. Three workers weigh their cotton in front of the overseer. Two are fine, but the final worker does not have enough. She is chased by the overseer to an area (off stage) where she is punished. The other workers dance the anxiety and concern for their friend or family member, a scream causing them to freeze in a shape of concern. The punished dancer returns in the final section of the dance as the workers return to their homes to clean, cook, and prepare for bed before the next day in the field. The overseer hits the cow bell to let the workers know that all lights should be out. The enslaved worker who was punished for not picking enough cotton blows out the last candle as a final act, accompanied by the last lines of poetry: "Cotton running in straight rows. / The only train we was ever meant to ride."

PRETTY LITTLE GIRL

PAINTING: *Dave the Potter* by Jonathan Green
MUSIC: "Pretty Little Girl" by Ralph Russell
CHOREOGRAPHY: Vincent Thomas

In "Pretty Little Girl," the dance begins with Dave seated and working on his pots. A young woman—his love interest—enters to meet him, moving lightly as though through a meadow. The two dance together with many connected and balancing movements, then "jump the broom," signifying their marriage. The dance ends with the young woman leaving Dave at his pots, recalling the phrase from Redmond's "Praise Dave" poem: "but everything I love, I lose / so I want what I mold to hold."

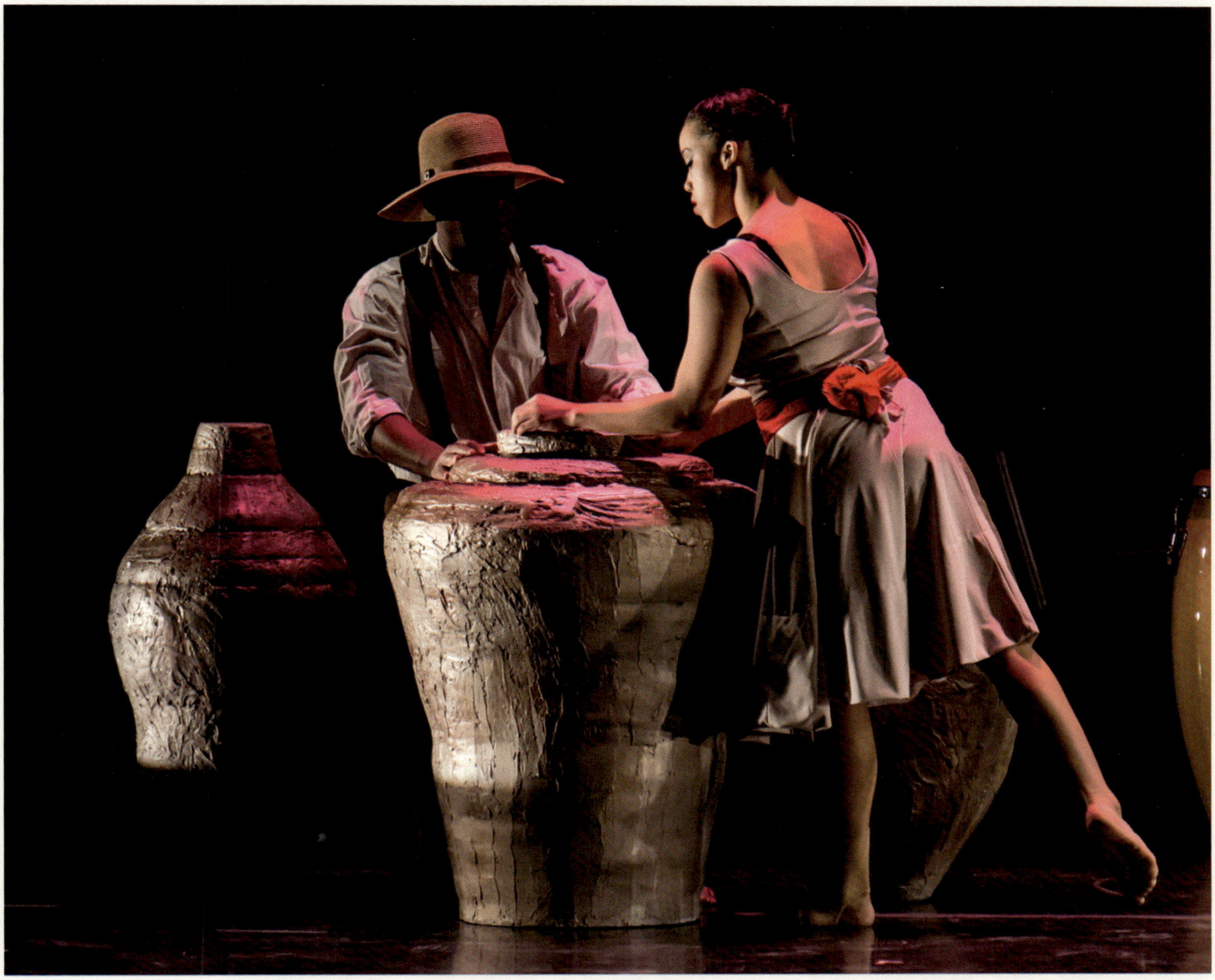

"Pretty Little Girl." Choreographed by Vincent Thomas. Performed by Vincent Thomas and Blair Galiber. Music by Ralph Russell. Photographed by Dan Dunlap. Featuring *Dave the Potter* by Jonathan Green. March 14, 2014. Courtesy of Dan Dunlap Photography.

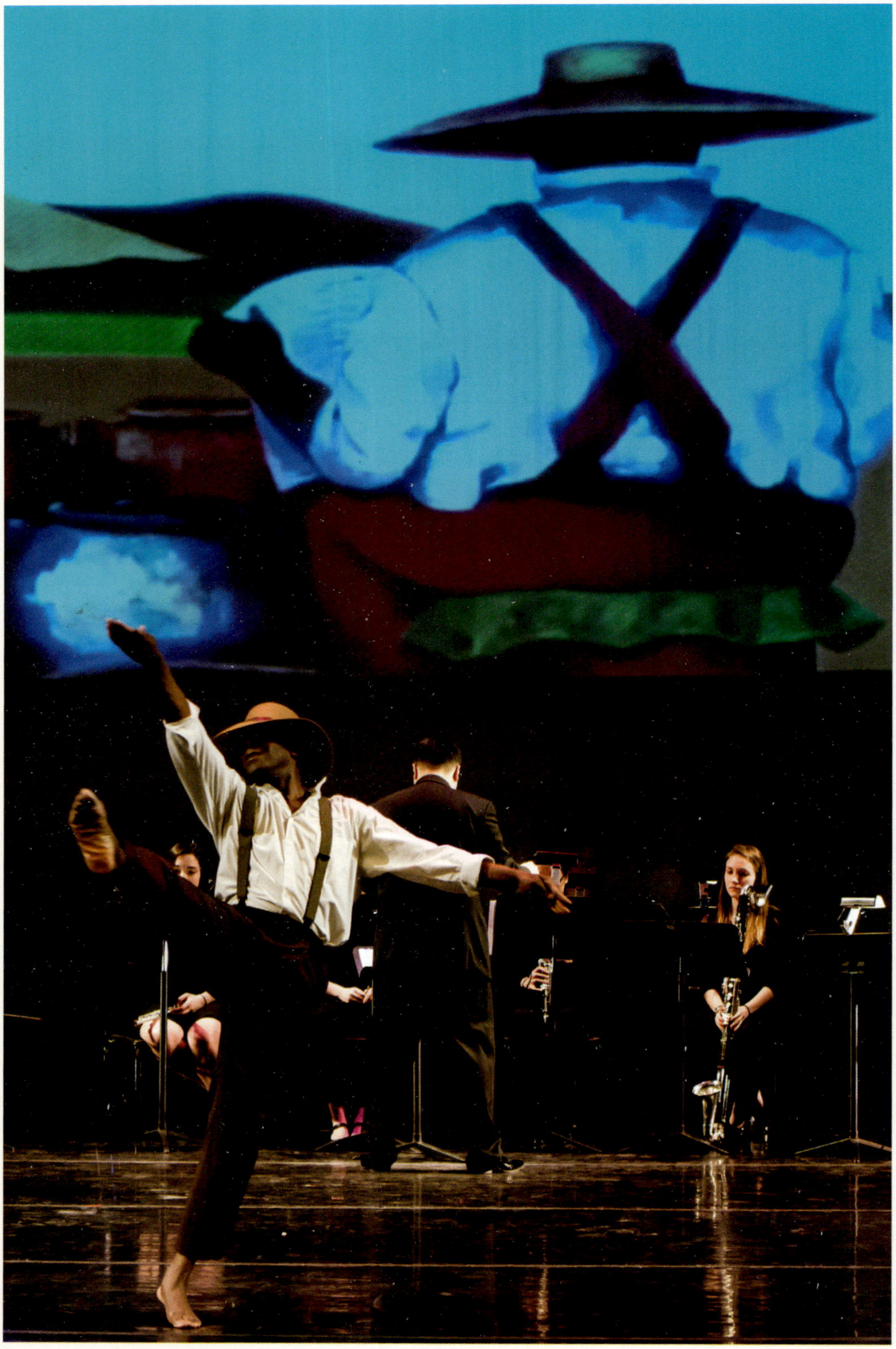

“Sir Dave.” Choreographed and performed by Vincent Thomas. Music by Ralph Russell. Photographed by Dan Dunlap. Featuring *Sir Dave* by Jonathan Green. March 14, 2014. Courtesy of Dan Dunlap Photography.

SIR DAVE

PAINTING: *Sir Dave* by Jonathan Green
MUSIC: "Dave's Song" by Ralph Russell
CHOREOGRAPHY: Vincent Thomas

Vincent Thomas describes choreographing "Dave's Song" as an opportunity to explore his roots as an Edgefield native. Dancing the role of Dave on stage gave him the chance to return to his roots through dance. The piece begins with Dave writing poetry on his pots. He then leaves the pots in order to dance, his movements depicting his strength in the creation of his work. The dance concludes with Dave's return to his pots—he writes on them, then lays his head down to rest.

DAVE'S MARKET

PAINTING: *Dave's Market* by Jonathan Green
MUSIC: "Dave's Market" by Ralph Russell
CHOREOGRAPHY: Teresa Emmons

During our visit to Edgefield in 2013, we discovered that the location of the weekday market was also the place where people who were enslaved in the county were sold on weekends. The dance to "Dave's Market" begins with a colorful market scene

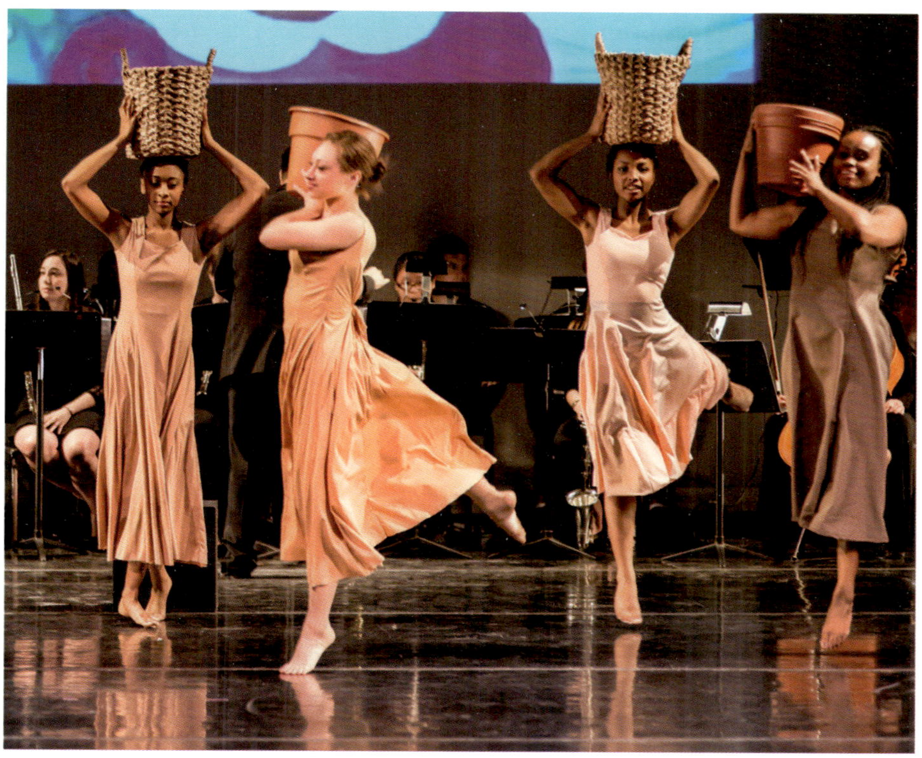

"Dave's Market." Choreographed by Teresa Emmons. Performed by Aliyah Clay, Caitlin Green, Taylor Walker, and Danielle Smithson. Photographed by Dan Dunlap. Featuring *Dave's Market* by Jonathan Green. March 14, 2014. Courtesy of Dan Dunlap Photography.

filled with movement and lightness, the dancers portraying the buying and selling of goods. During the dance, we see enslaved residents of Edgefield accompanying their owners, making purchases and, in some cases, selling goods such as food and clothing. Suddenly, the dance and music transition from the light mood of market day to a somber mood—the market is now selling human beings. An enslaved woman is dressed by her white enslavers in a blue dress, and she then performs a duet with the slave owner. The dance includes lifts and falls; at one point, she defiantly throws her hat down only to have it retrieved and placed back on her head as she is pointed toward the auction block. Other dancers perform movements—reaching and retreating—and finally leave. The enslaved woman walks slowly to the auction block, and the piece transitions into the following sequence.

DREAM OF FREEDOM

PAINTING: *From Earth We Came* by Jonathan Green
MUSIC: "Amazing Grace" by Jennifer Higdon
CHOREOGRAPHY: Lynnette Young Overby

As the choreographer of "Dream of Freedom," I stared at Green's painting *From Earth We Came* a long time. What did it mean—a woman in blue, surrounded by light? I imagined an enslaved woman waiting to be sold at auction. Set to the music "Amazing Grace," the dance tells the story of this young woman, who dreams of freedom. In the first section of the dance, she stands on an auction block, showing her teeth and hands to potential buyers. Then the dream begins: the young woman dances with two friends/children; they romp and play together with joy and abandon as the music builds. But alas, it is only a dream. In the concluding section, the woman in blue returns to the block and raises her arms, heart, and head to the heavens along with the final chords of the music. Dave's couplet "I wonder where is all my relation" echoes through the piece.

GRAVE

POETRY: "Grave" by Glenis Redmond
PAINTING: *Earth to Earth* by Jonathan Green
MUSIC: "From Earth" by Ralph Russell
CHOREOGRAPHY: Gabrielle Hilliard

In the dance drama depicted in "Grave," a woman faces the harsh reality of death and the burial of a loved one. The dance begins with a woman donning a scarf, finishing her housework, and setting off for the grave. Merging the poetic interpretation of painting,

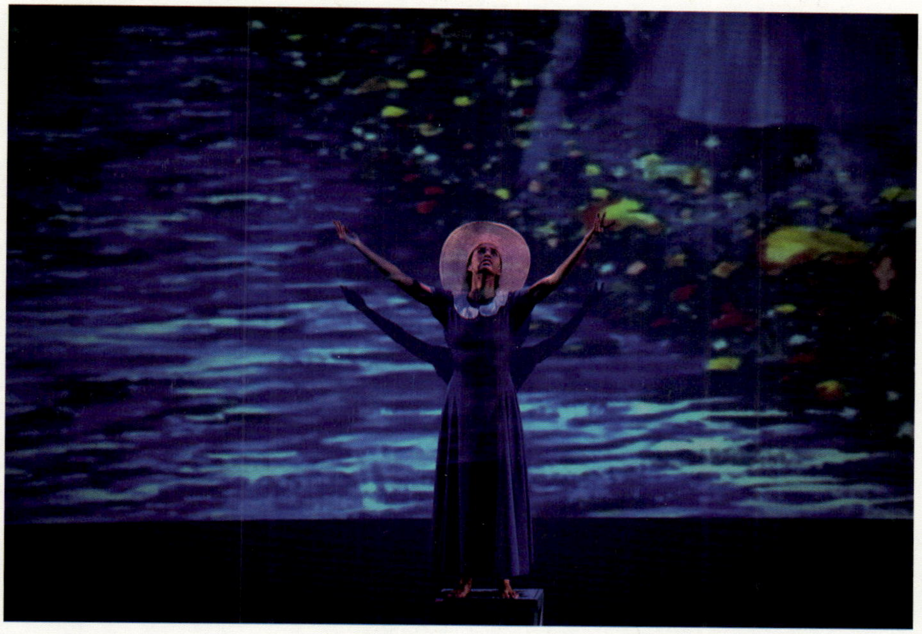

"Dream of Freedom." Choreographed by Lynnette Young Overby. Performed by Melissa Jones (*left*), and by Melissa Jones, April Singleton, and Amber Rance (*below*). Photographed by Amy Randall. Music by Jennifer Higdon. Featuring *From Earth We Came* by Jonathan Green. February 6, 2019. Courtesy of Amy Randall Photography.

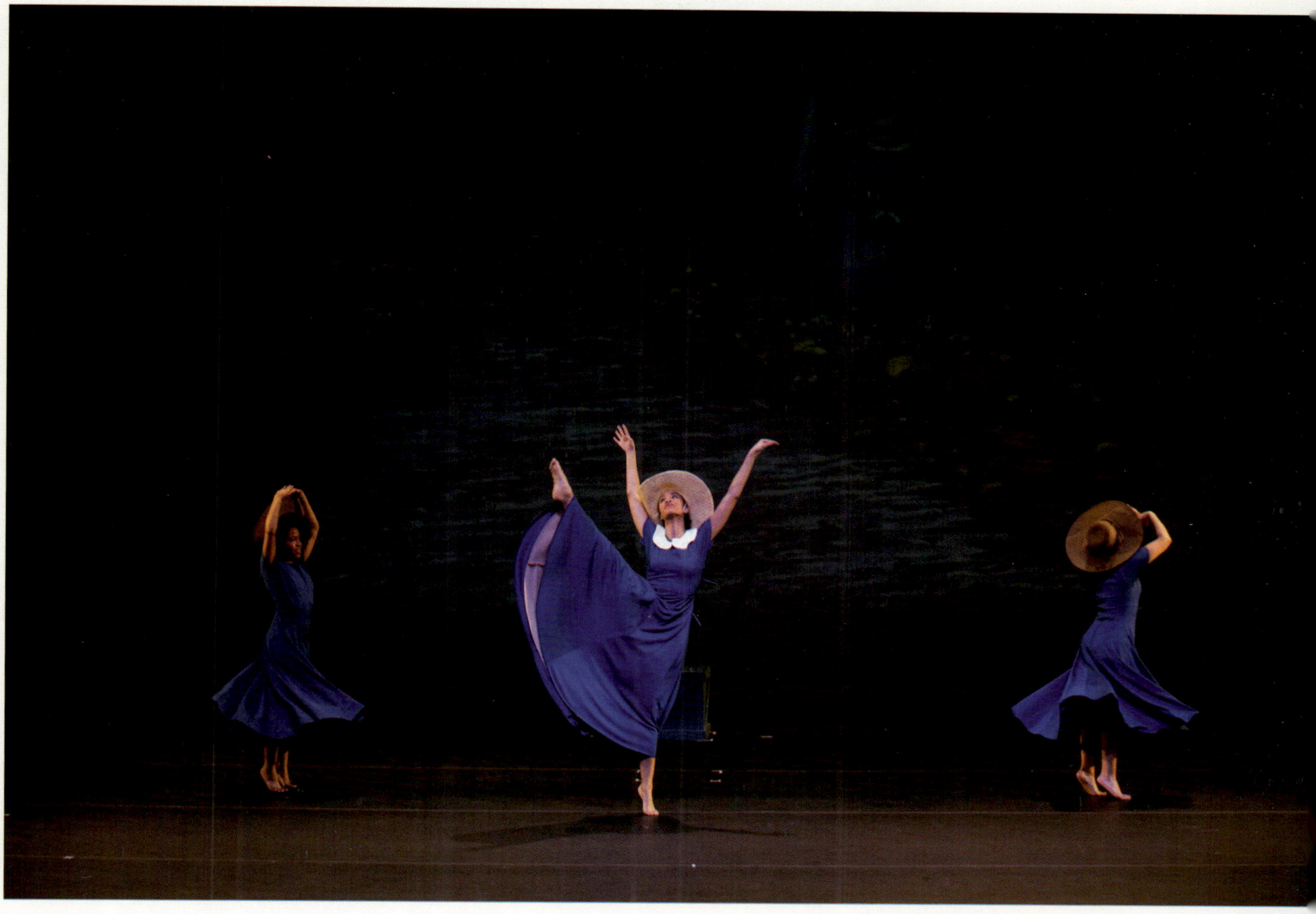

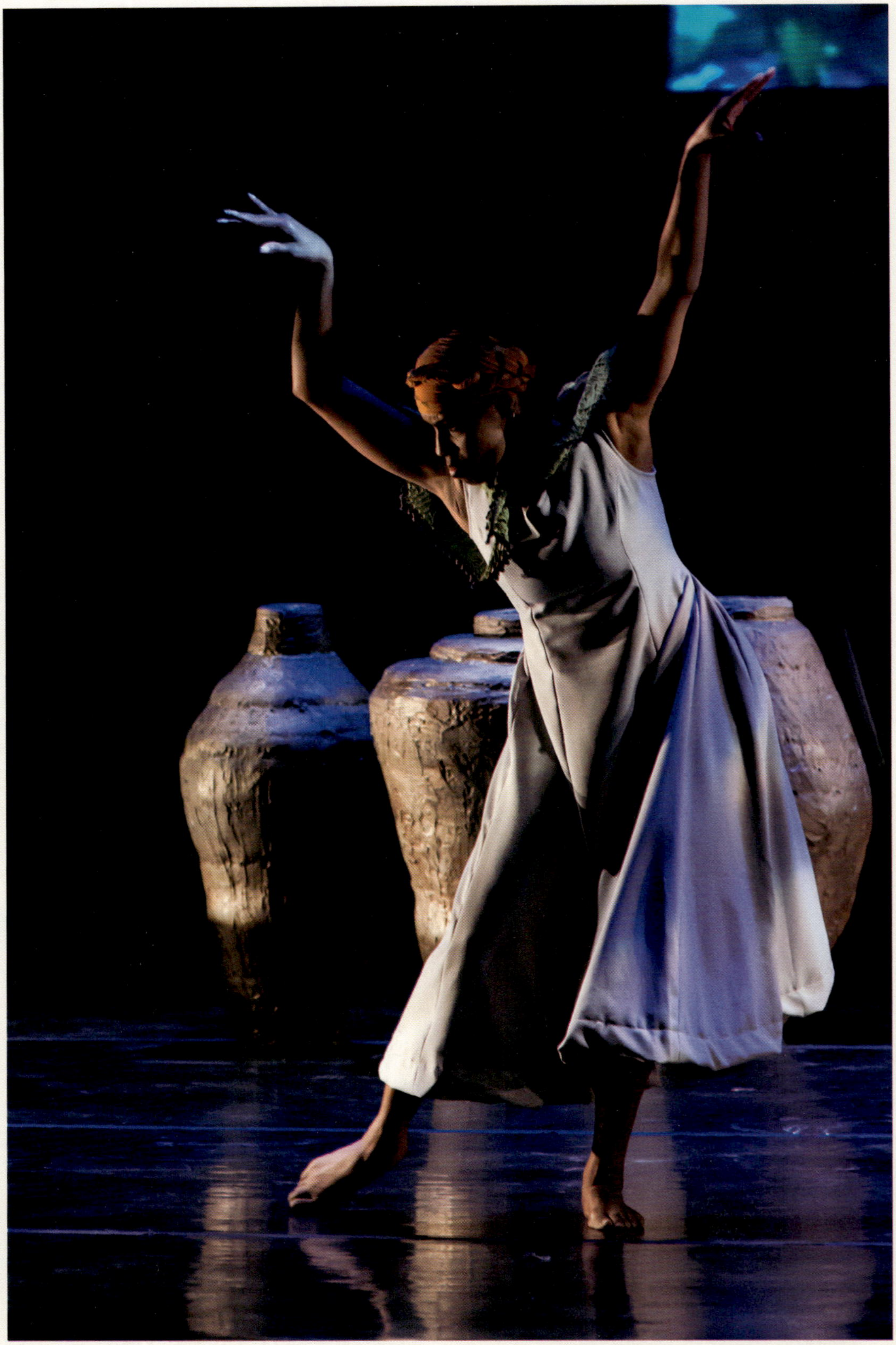

"Grave." Choreographed and performed by Gabrielle Hilliard. Music by Ralph Russell. Poetry by Glenis Redmond. Photographed by Dan Dunlap. Featuring *Earth to Earth* by Jonathan Green. March 14, 2014. Courtesy of Dan Dunlap Photography.

choreography, and music, the dancer and the audience together remember and experience loss, the dancer's movements representative of both grief and resignation. She dances these words: "Dis be de heaviest work I ever done / carrying on / carrying you / living / inside my chest." In the last scene, the dancer returns to her home, only to look longingly back while reaching toward her loved one's final resting place.

SHARDS

PAINTING: *Potter's Fragments* by Jonathan Green
POETRY: "Slavery's Slippery Touch" by Gabrielle Foreman
MUSIC: "Shards" by Ralph Russell
CHOREOGRAPHY: Lynnette Young Overby with contributions from the dancers

In "Shards," literary historian and poet Gabrielle Foreman, accompanied by Ralph Russell's composition and the dancers' kinesthetic expression, created an image of shattered pieces—pots, lives, and relations. An abstract interpretation of pottery shards—a metaphor for the broken shards of enslaved peoples' lives—the dance begins with the poem "Shards," recited by the poet. The dancers enter in groups and form a group shape on three levels. As shards, they dance with specific improvisational prompts for each section of the dance. They dance balanced, ugly, and broken shapes. The costumes are red, yellow, and white—blended colors—with each dancer manipulating a two-foot strip of fabric. The backdrop painting is animated to include images of pottery pieces falling from the sky. The final connecting pose is illuminated with black lights as the poet's final words ring out: "Slavery's slippery touch, its slippery, slippery, touch."

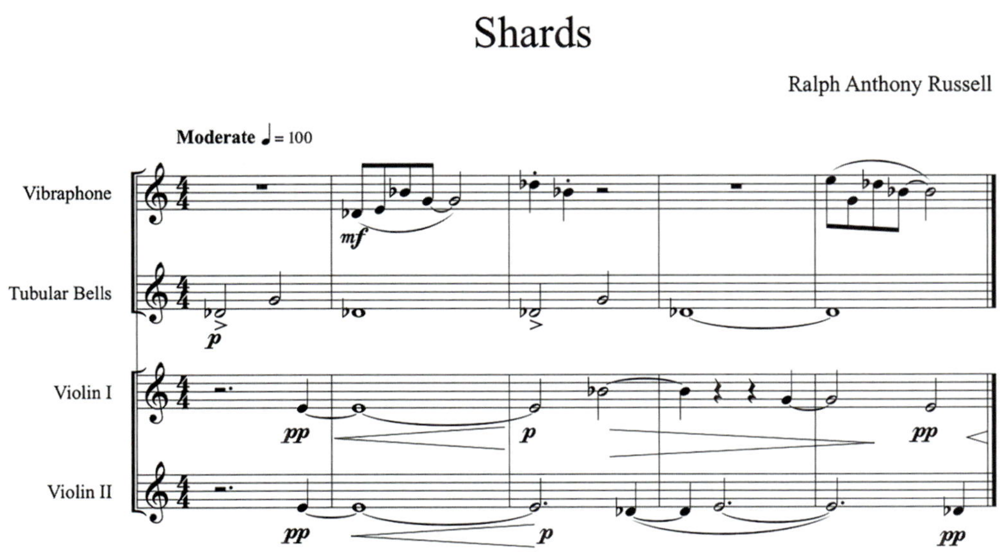

Score from "Shards." Courtesy of composer, Ralph Anthony Russell.

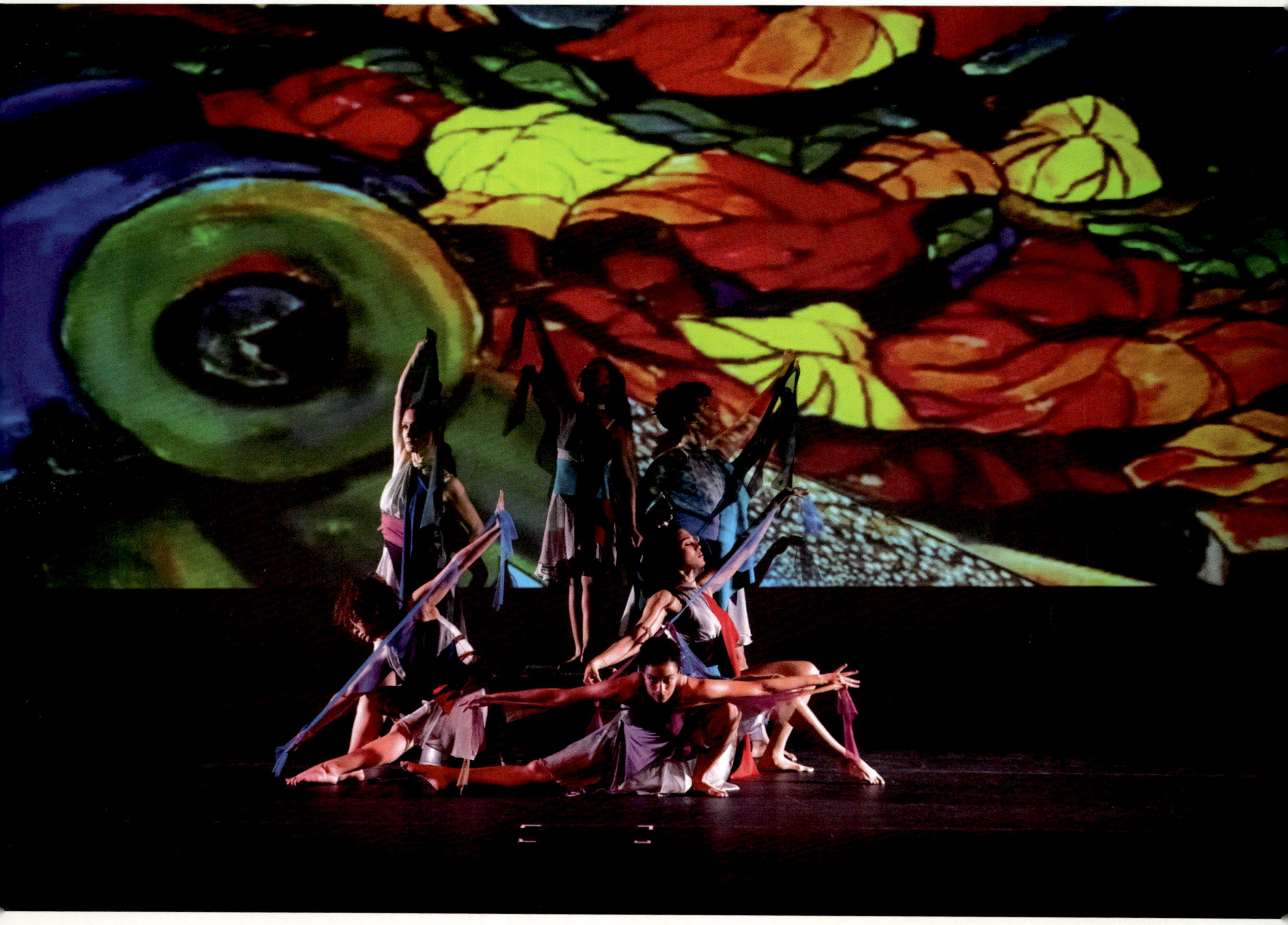

"Shards." Choreographed by Lynnette Young Overby with contributions from the performers, A. T. Moffett, Amber Rance, April Singleton, Dianna Ruberto, Melissa Jones, Gabrielle Shubert, and Rachel DeLauder. Music by Ralph Russell. Poetry by P. Gabrielle Foreman. Featuring *Potter's Fragments* by Jonathan Green. February 6, 2019. Courtesy of Amy Randall Photography.

VESSELS

PAINTINGS: *Three Vessels* and *Vessels for Taking Us Home* by Jonathan Green
MUSIC: Ralph Russell
CHOREOGRAPHY: Vincent Thomas

Vessels provide us with hope, as we see in the legacy of Dave represented in a cast of multigenerational, multiracial dancers. The dancers include three males (a child, an African American man, and a white man) and three females (two white and one African American). Pots are manipulated during this work through reaching and retreating movements that invite the audience to imagine the journey these pots will take across continents, through decades, and with people of all ages and races. The music provides a hopeful serenade and lifts the mood of the production. In this way, "Vessels" becomes a processional that recognizes Dave's humanity and honors his creativity.

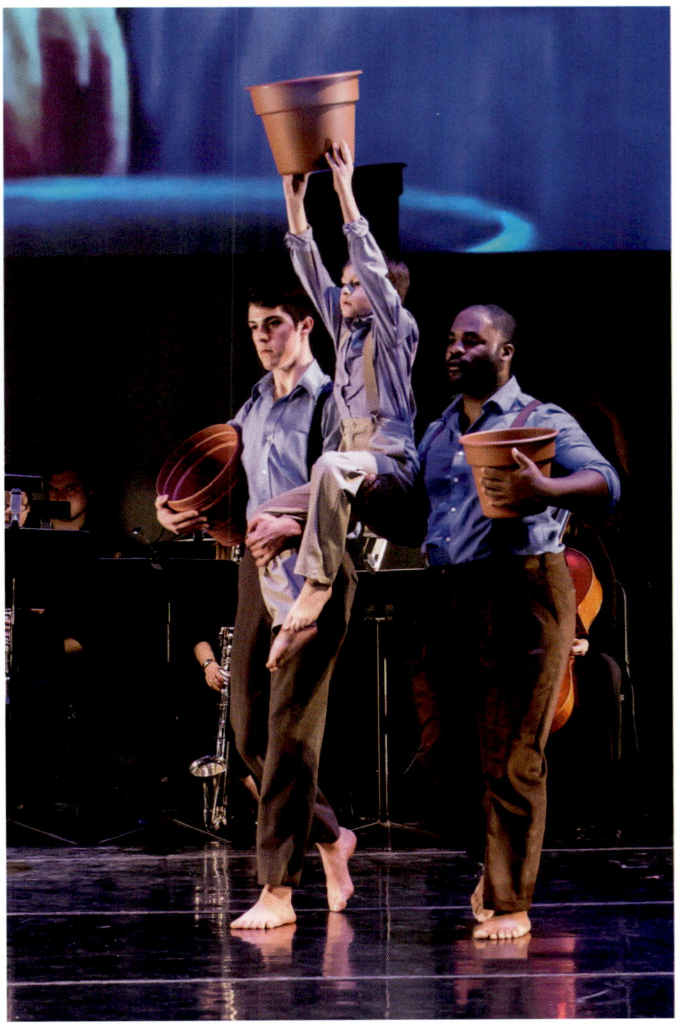

"Vessels." Choreographed by Vincent Thomas. Music by Ralph Russell. Performed by Elliot Ledford, Eli Latshaw, and Alfred Lance Jr. Photographed by Dan Dunlap. March 14, 2014. Courtesy of Dan Dunlap Photography.

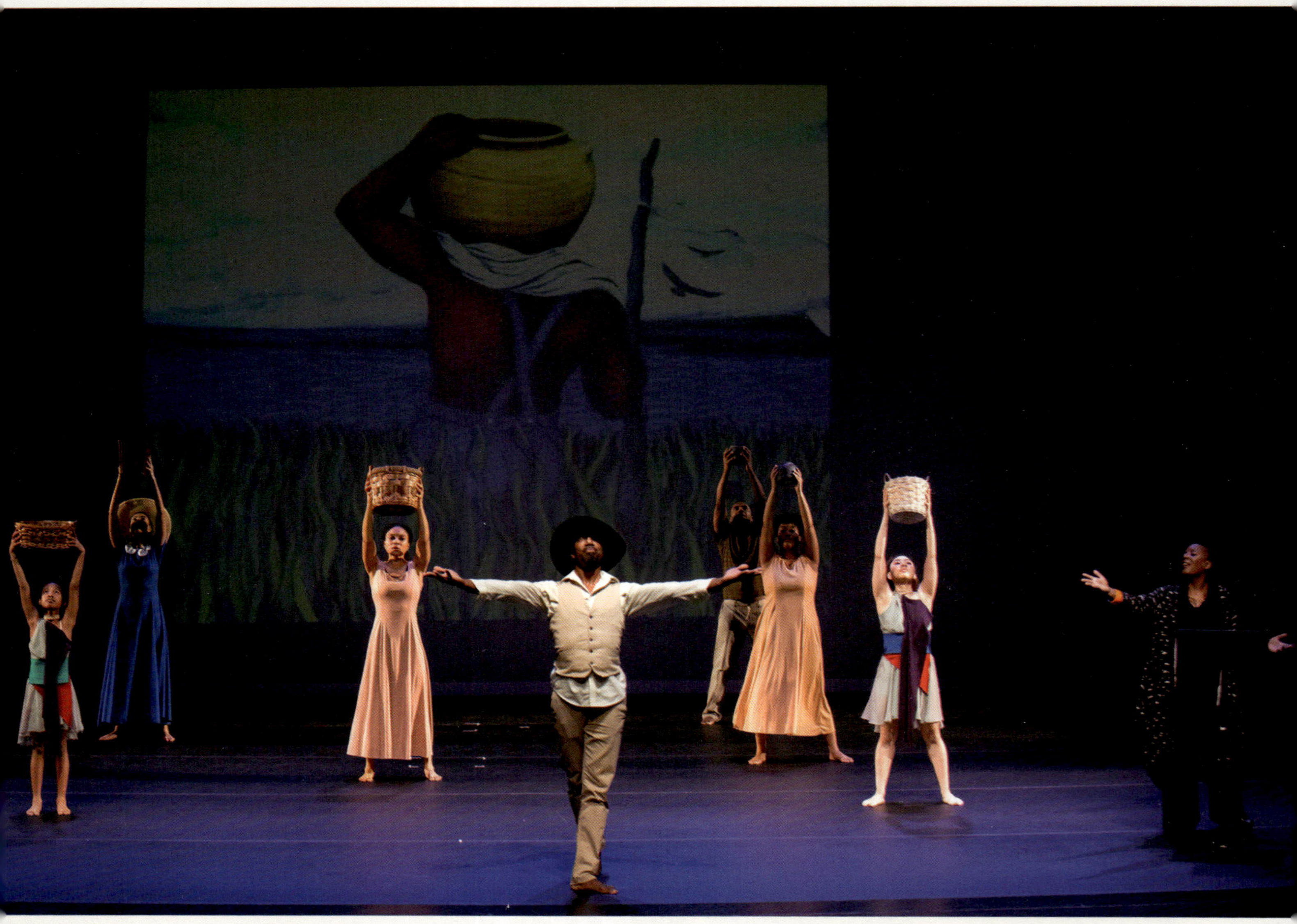

"Postlude." Choreographed by Lynnette Young Overby. Performed by Vincent Vaughan, Rachel DeLauder, Dianna Ruberto, April Singleton, Amber Rance, Gabrielle Shubert, Ralph Russell, Melissa Jones, and Glenis Redmond. Poetry by Glenis Redmond. Music by Ralph Russell. Photographed by Amy Randall. Featuring *Marshland Passage* by Jonathan Green. February 6, 2019. Courtesy of Amy Randall Photography.

POSTLUDE

PAINTING: Images from the *Sir Dave* series by Jonathan Green
POETRY: "Carry Us" by Glenis Redmond
MUSIC: "Postlude" by Ralph Russell

In the final sequence of *Dave the Potter,* Glenis Redmond returns with the poem "Carry Us" to carry us into a more benevolent future. As the *Sir Dave* series scrolls across the backdrop, the dancers move majestically from one side of the stage to the other, ending in a formal bow. They are accompanied by Ralph Russell's "Postlude," whose recurring themes and pulsating rhythms were inspired by African American and American Indian folksongs, African rhythms, and Gregorian chants. The sequence carries the dancers, the audience, and Dave's legacy into the future. Dave himself dances the final words of the poem: "Keep turning this struggle, keep turning this struggle, keep turning this struggle into beauty."

Conclusion

We had three primary goals for our production on the life of David Drake: to create, perform, and disseminate his story through original music, choreography, and poetry inspired by the paintings of Jonathan Green and the historical setting of Dave's life; to inform audiences and students of all ages through the performance; and to create a permanent exhibit of materials through web technology. These goals were realized in the theatrical production itself and through the creation of additional web-based products, including the development and presentation of lesson plans. Developed by history teacher and former ArtsBridge scholar Jennifer Ferris, and based on the integration of arts and history, these lesson plans can be provided to school age students. There is also an exhibit that provides lessons and videos, accessible at https://www.sharingourlegacy.org.

Collaborations require time, patience, flexibility, and perseverance. And it was through our multidisciplinary collaborative effort that the production of *Dave the Potter* became a kinesthetic example of arts-based research. The production promoted a deeper understanding of David Drake's life and times, and it became more than one person or a single discipline could produce or imagine on their own. In keeping with the tenets of arts-based research and ethnotheatre, the collaborators synthesized history, music, paintings, choreography, and poetry into a unified orchestration that was entertaining, informative, intellectually rich, and emotionally evocative.

Dave lives on, in, and through us!

NOTES

1 Overby, *Sketches in the Life of Harriet E. Wilson.*

2 Wilson, *Our Nig*, Penguin edition.

3 Barone and Eisner, *Arts Based Research.*

4 Barone and Eisner, *Arts Based Research*; Moffett, "Arts-Based Research in Dance," 54–62; Overby, *Public Scholarship in Dance.*

5 Saldanya, *Ethonodrama*; Saldanya, *Ethnotheatre Research.*

6 See Foreman, "1857," and the chapter on David Drake and his verse in her book, tentatively titled *The Art of DisMemory: Historicizing Slavery in Poetry, Print and Material Culture*, forthcoming. Also see Todd, *Carolina Clay.*

7 Wright, *Dave the Potter.*

8 Foster, *Choreographing Empathy.*

9 Hurmence, *Before Freedom, When I Just Can Remember*; Jackson, *The Experience of a Slave*; Jacobs, *Incidents in the Life of a Slave Girl*; Wright, *Dave the Potter.*

Black Artists as Cultural Historians

Jonathan Green, Carrie Mae Weems, and David Drake

P. GABRIELLE FOREMAN

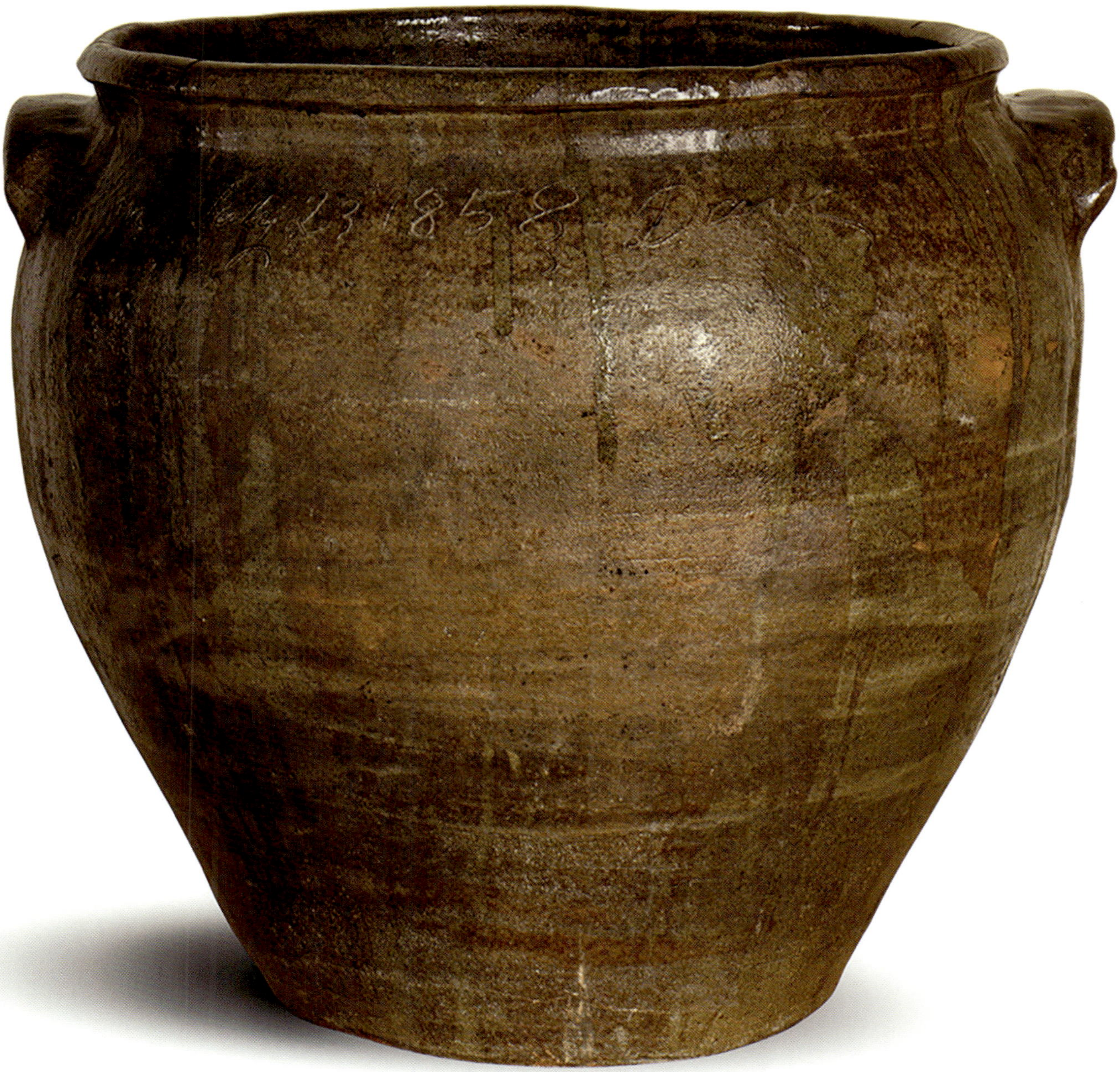

OVERLEAF: Poetic Vessel, "the Sun moon and — Stars =," July 23, 1858. David Drake. Greenville County Museum of Art.

WE KNOW MORE ABOUT what "Dave the Potter" made than we know about who David Drake was. Bringing Drake to life in vivid color, Jonathan Green's *Sir Dave* series raises critical questions as it also seeks to fill a historical canvas full of blank spaces. Green's visual memorial to Sir Dave, like other artistic meditations about Black history, prompts us to query not only *what* we know but *how* we apprehend and approach the archival voids that characterize the long history of U.S. slavery. Raised in a community of elders steeped in living culture, Green affirms that he remains grounded in the depth and "power of memory," particularly the "power of visual memory, hear/say memory."[1] Claiming the importance of visual genealogies alongside Black oral traditions, Green envisions Black artists as storytellers and preservers of history; in his paintings and in his collaborative projects, artists take their place beside griots as caretakers of the past.

As one of the most well-known southern painters of his generation, Green is celebrated for his vibrant palettes; the signature sweetgrass hats that are so ubiquitous in his work often take the place of faces themselves, announcing his subjects' South Carolina roots more readily than their shaded features ever could. Green's love of clothing and textiles appears in billowing fabrics: signature skirts and canvas-filling clothesline quilts and sheets that reclaim the expressivity—rather than the oppressive labor—so often associated with Black women, clothing, and laundry work.[2]

Green has produced multiple historical series and projects. In addition to his *Sir Dave* series, Green also has translated Robert Smalls's fascinating life onto canvas. As an enslaved man during the Civil War, Smalls sailed himself, a crew, and their families to freedom, delivering the gunship he commandeered into Union hands before serving in the South Carolina senate and then as a U.S. Congressman. Green is also the founder and head of the Lowcountry Rice Culture Project, which brings together historians, foodways scholars, artists, educators, and cooks from South Carolina to the upper Guinea coast. The Lowcountry Rice Culture Project examines the source of rice production technologies—Black (enslaved) expertise and labor that seeded the crop cultivation from which South Carolina business has been enriched for

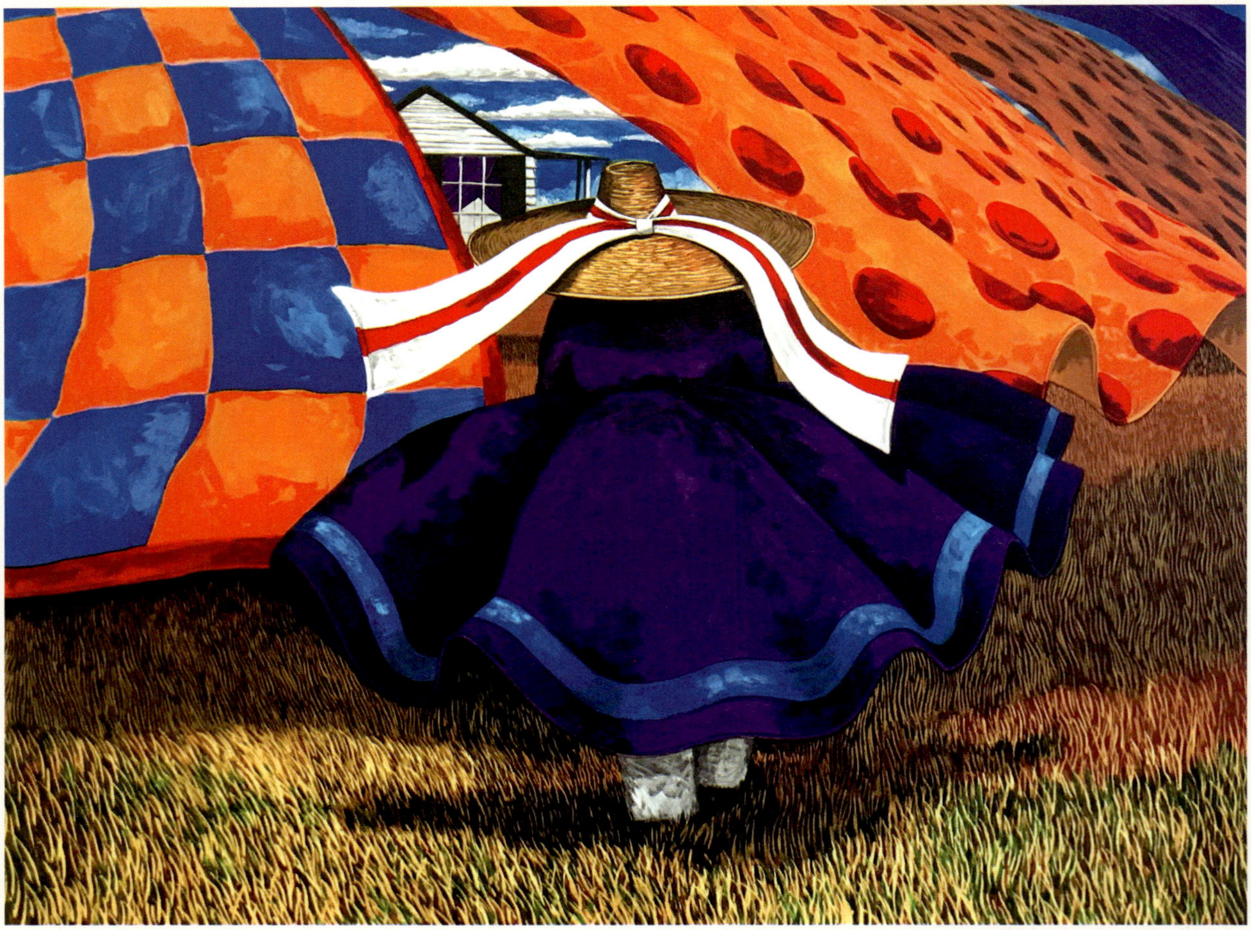

Farm Woman, 2009. Jonathan Green (American, b. 1955). Lithograph, 22.5 × 30 inches. Courtesy of Jonathan Green Studios. Collection of JK Fine Art Editions Co. / Mojo Portfolio, Union City, New Jersey. © Jonathan Green.

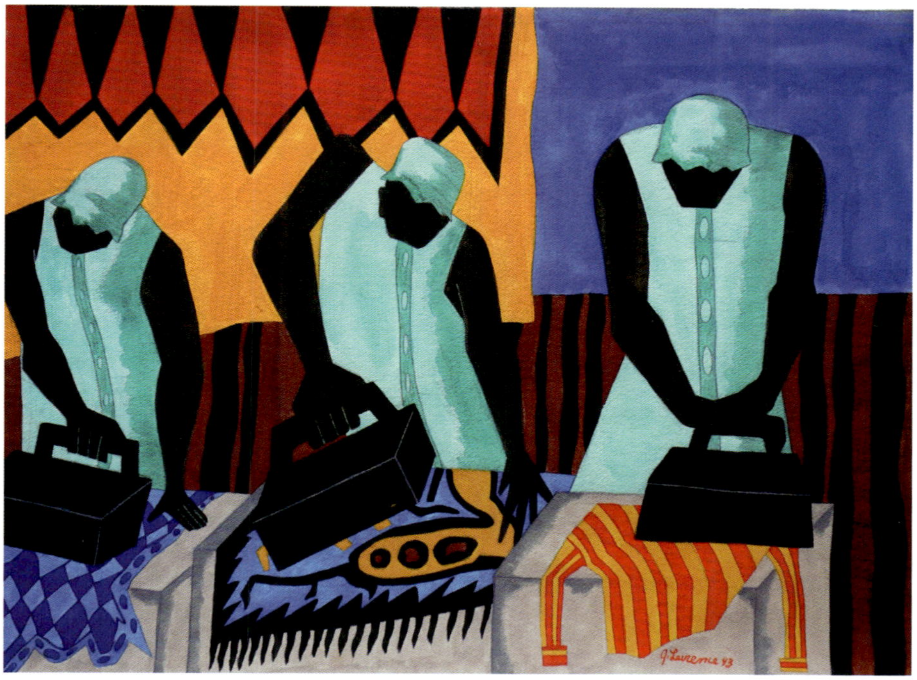

The Ironers, 1943. Jacob Lawrence (American b. 1917). Gouache on paper, 21.5 × 29.5 inches. © 2021 The Jacob and Gwendolyn Knight Lawrence Foundation, Seattle / Artists Rights Society (ARS), New York. Private collection. Photo courtesy of Terry Dintenfass, Inc.

hundreds of years. These collaborations resulted in a *Requiem for Rice*, which was a "a tribute to the suffering, sacrifices, and contributions of Blacks enslaved on Lowcountry rice plantations who remain unburied, unmourned, and unmarked."[3] In a symposium that included partners from a wide array of sectors (from the arts, cultural institutions, higher education, and business), the Lowcountry Rice Culture Project delivered on its mission "to discover and revive the significance of rice cultivation and its legacies."[4]

This volume about David Drake reflects on Jonathan Green's deep and collaborative commitment to working with performers, poets, and scholars to engage Black history, what is often called slavery's contemporary "afterlives," and living culture. Green values the ways in which art and culture move through society and has worked with a long line of dancers and choreographers to extend the expressive reach of his painting onto the stage. One example is a 2005 collaboration that resulted in the Columbia City Ballet's production of *Off the Wall and Onto the Stage: Dancing the Art of Jonathan Green*, which continues in their repertoire.[5] His site-specific painting called *Seeking* was inspired by a visit to South Carolina's unmarked cemetery at Mepkin Abbey where, more than a century before, enslaved families who worked the rice plantation had been interred with no markers. Five years later the collaboration between the father who presided there and Green culminated with the painting being acquired by Charleston's Gibbes Museum of Art. A scholarly symposium on the painting with wide educational outreach included a world premiere performance by composer Trevor Weston and three evenings of poetry and jazz in the city's public libraries.[6] Five years later, in a book named for that painting, poets responded in a volume that is no doubt this book's older sibling. It was edited by Kwame Dawes, who wrote the foreword for this volume as well, and by South Carolina poet laureate Marjory Wentworth.

As the first formally trained painter from South Carolina's Gullah communities, communities with deep root systems from African cultures transplanted in Low Country soil, Jonathan Green is transfixed by how visual and oral traditions are transmitted and "incubated" from one generation to the next. The term *generation*, of course, is another way of identifying cultural kin; it is a term that extends forward to the future as it also arches backward, looking to the past in order to carry what's necessary and useful into the present moment. Still, Green hadn't heard about his South Carolina predecessor while growing up in that state. Green wasn't introduced to Drake's innovative pottery and poetry at the School of the Art Institute of Chicago, where Green had been a star student. He didn't learn about this ancestor-artist, separated by more than 150 years and the horizontal span of their home state, until he was good and grown, as it's said, when Drake was introduced to him by art historian Carroll Greene Jr., who was "a leading proponent of African-American art long before it was a fashionable thing to do."[7] Passing knowledge to artists alongside others, as an elder statesman, Greene kindled Green's interest by sharing the enslaved potter's story.

This essay explores how representations of Black cultural expression and loss, grief and dis/continuity, and mute (artisan) labor under slavery reveal themselves in living color in *Sir Dave*, when they often are rendered invisible in visual traditions celebrating plantation histories.[8] It places Green's rendering of an enslaved South Carolina worker and artisan in the context of the many images of exploited field workers pictured in southern plantation and African American art traditions. It also situates Green's *Sir Dave* in conversation with Carrie Mae Weems's *Sea Island* series (1992). Green's art, like Weems's, displays how "artists as historians" are as concerned with historical subjects as they are "with addressing the history of their mediums and forms," to borrow from Mark Godfrey.[9] How, I ask here, are elements of their work situated in political, historical, economic, and philosophical contexts?

Individual pieces in the *Sir Dave* series gesture toward the (broken) possibilities and (sharded) promises of recovering history buried under slavery's shrouds, while they also invoke Black creative heroism under repressive circumstances. In its "historical sequence that presents a dramatic biography," to borrow from Ellen Harkins Wheat's description of Jacob Lawrence's epic narrative series (1938–1940), *Sir Dave* echoes Lawrence's visual enshrining of Black agency and heroism in Lawrence's well-known *Toussaint L'Overture*, *Harriet Tubman*, and *Frederick Douglass* series.[10] Green adopts the series style of the famous painter who mentored him. Yet by refraining from numbering the pieces in his series as Lawrence does, Green creates more space for the viewer between the stories each individual piece tells. Though Green's *Sir Dave* paintings have not yet been exhibited as a series, when they are, a curator will have to engage the multiple and open possibilities to display them, thinking through the various meanings different sequences might communicate.

As this book's introduction notes, though the paintings are not numbered, defaulting to a sense of chronology would place *Young Dave* at the beginning of the series. From there it gets more complicated, as multiple paintings (*Earth to Earth, From Earth We Came, Vessels for Taking Us Home*) signal that they could serve as the final painting, simultaneously complicating the idea of a singular ending altogether. Together, the work's arc develops through paintings illustrating events thought to have occurred during David Drake's life alongside images of his work as an acclaimed potter in his own time. They are accompanied by abstract pieces that follow the pots themselves as they travel well beyond the orbit of Dave's own life and geography. Green's medium and dimensions serve as close cousins to Lawrence's, especially when compared to the diachronic videos, mixed image and text paintings, sculptural objects, and object and sound pieces assembled by other artists who also answered slavery's reverberating call to those concerned with historical and visual imagery over space and time.[11]

David Drake's life spans the first seventy years of the nineteenth century and overlaps with both the end of the transatlantic slave trade and the U.S. acquisition of the Louisiana Territory; each fueled the spread of slavery into the Deep South through a domestic trade that initiated a second great forced migration for enslaved people. South Carolina's ports and ideology fed the insatiable appetite for the brutal system of enslaved Black labor that enriched the country's elite. Yet Green's colorful palettes and outdoor scenes display an absence of whites, whips, or the signs of compulsion that enforced enslavement's relentlessly oppressive systems. Instead, viewers encounter scenes of Black creativity, contemplation, and joy that show how such communities protected their humanity while enduring slavery's brutal realities.

Some might see work that doesn't depict either slavery's everyday barbarity or Black people's resistance to it through the eyes of such critics as James Baldwin, echoing his derision for the dangers of flirtation with revisionist sentimentality. Yet this critique refuses these paintings' more complex imaginative, narrative, and historical recovery work. To build on John L. Jackson's *Real Black: Adventures in Racial Sincerity*, Green's creative projection of Black community vitality and wholeness can be read as a commentary on the partial and ephemeral records of Drake's history available to Green and others in their research. *Sir Dave* can also be read as a visual projection of colorful Black joy–cum–utopic performance that so often has been necessary for Black survival under the oppressive systems of slavery, Jim Crow, and gross economic, legal, and educational disparities, as well as state surveillance that water the outgrowths and conditions of the current moment.[12] Banishing enslavers from this series affirms an artistic power to elevate alternative Black realities as well as relations between Black subjects. Centering Blackness is to conceive of "representation in art as a proxy for their desired representation" in historical and political memory—to imagine speculative Black futures as well as Black pasts.[13] In this vein, to borrow from Homi Bhaba, "the 'past-present' becomes part of the necessity, not [only] the nostalgia of living."[14] Green's works depict the human interaction, Black creativity, and agency that slipped through, above, or below the domination and will of enslavers and found expression through and in the Black hands that made the potter's wheel turn, in the fingers that made the fiddle or the quill sing—if only for the moments the artist chooses to capture and represent.

Green transforms "the no-place of the archive into the no-place of a utopia";[15] his emphasis is on healing dimensions of art, history, and visual imagination. He engages what's absent in traditional records, archives, and repositories, the "inordinate difficulty of gleaning the histories of the enslaved through the objects and material traces left within the archives of governing classes," as art historian Huey Copeland might put it.[16] Green borrows from the oral and living histories of the South Carolina communities out of which he's sprung. Seen in this way, viewers can detect a deeper current, which moves beneath *Sir Dave*'s seemingly pleasant and placid surfaces. This series speaks to the ancient, dusky, rivers of silence that flow from slavery; his work comments on the ways that such historical "no-places" nonetheless surround, frame, and infuse Black history with "visual and hear/say" memories that "crisscross and accumulate over time."[17]

Green's painting *Edgefield*, named for the South Carolina district where David Drake lived his life and plied his craft, highlights the ongoing field work performed by so many of David Drake's fellow bondsmen and women as he turned pots at his enslavers' behest. Including the painting in the *Sir Dave* series underscores the ubiquity of enslaved labor and the countless visual representations of it; Green riffs on the popular southern painting tradition of the plantation panorama where the landscape draws the viewer's gaze to the grand mansion. In that tradition, the painter acts as surveyor of the benign and patriarchal institution's impressive and masterful accumulations. As art historian John Michael Vlach points out, antebellum painters facing the challenge of portraying "the beauty of nature and the brutality of forced captive labor" often left enslaved workers "out of the picture."[18] In such painting, the architecture of captivity rarely claims space on the canvas: slave cabins, or the buildings in which captives readied raw materials for the market, do not make an appearance. "Instead, the planter's house stands alone in a pleasant, park-like setting."[19]

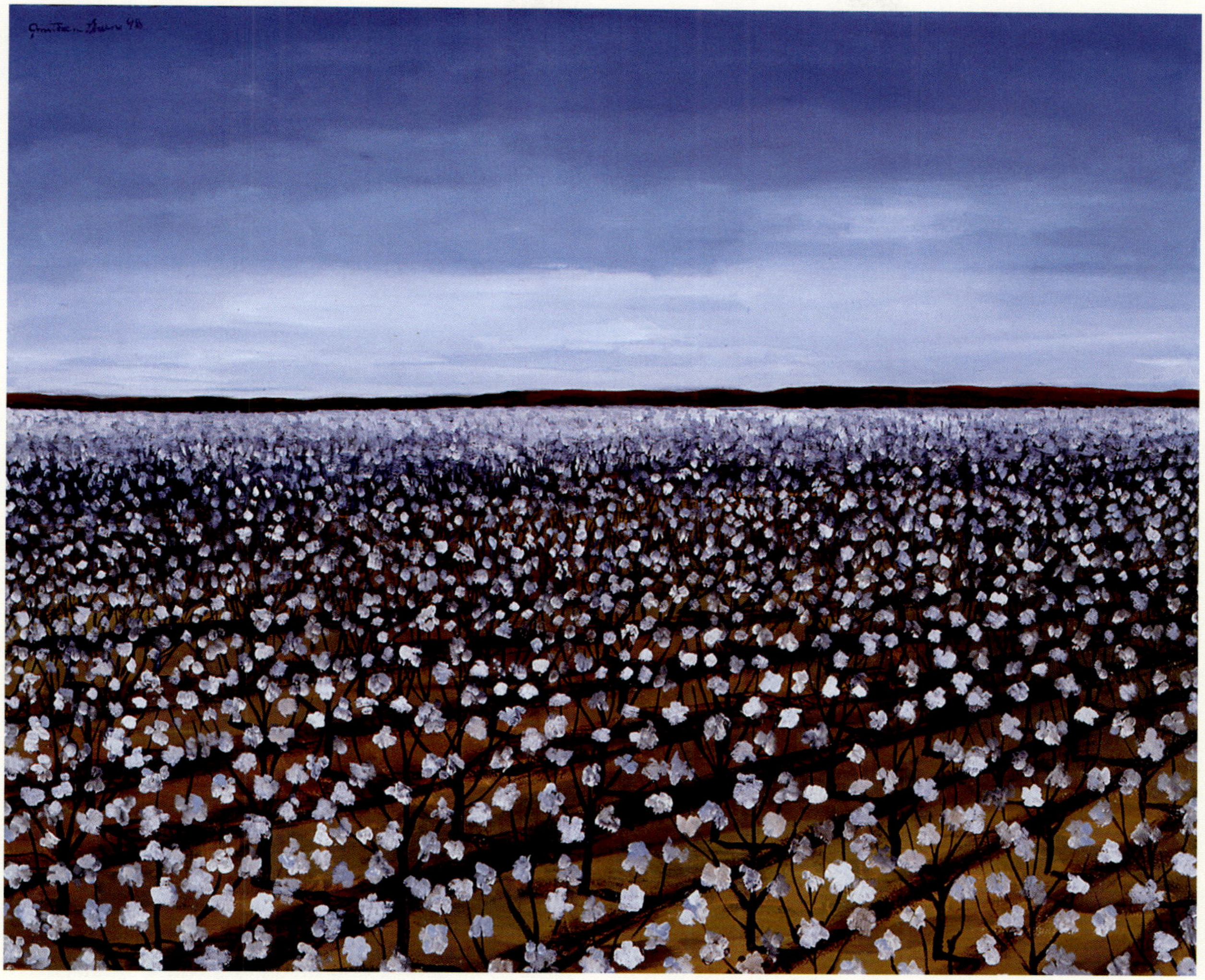

Edgefield from the *Sir Dave* series, 1998. Jonathan Green (American, b. 1955). Oil on canvas, 16 × 20 inches. Courtesy of Jonathan Green Studios. © Jonathan Green.

Though in Green's work figures and buildings are likewise absent, his painting counters southern representations created by the racial elite. As I write in the introduction, unlike traditional plantation imagery, in Green's *Edgefield* viewers encounter cotton directly and immediately. Rows of open bolls reach as far as the eye can see running into the low hills in the distant horizon. The further the viewers' eyes travel the more intense the cotton becomes; it crowds out the brown earth it springs from in the foreground, stems disappearing, converging into a field of beautiful white bolls mirroring a swath of blue-white clouds in a turquoise sky. However bucolic it may seem, however, in Green's *Edgefield*, what there is is endless cotton, cotton now and cotton forever, cotton uninterrupted by buildings or workers, cotton that, in the context of this series, ask viewers to imagine and engage its histories of labor, representation, and erasure.

While Dave was throwing pots in Edgefield District, South Carolina painter William Aiken Walker (1838–1921), a native of Charleston, began to take cotton plantations throughout the South as his subject. His post-Reconstruction *A Cotton Plantation on the Mississippi* is paradigmatic of the nostalgic scenes the landed elite commissioned: master and mistress in the foreground, a Black man reclining on cotton bales lifted high on the wagon that carried the crop to the riverboat in the background. Representations of modernity steam out of the ship and the gin, technological promise paired with the picture of productive Black "workers" in the happy scene. This image became "one of the most popular symbols of the region" and one of the most popular images of revisionist relationships between Blacks and the cotton fields they worked in the first decades of the new century.[20] As John Vlach points out, this image gets recycled again and again in the racial imaginary; indeed, in Washington, D.C., it adorns the Capitol's first-floor hallways—introduced in 1993–1994 as a mural called *Sharecroppers*, which uncannily reproduces the sentiments and structures of paintings such as Walker's. In the visual imagery of the U.S. South, as in African American art, "cotton has a place as landscape and metaphor, real and imaginary, romantic and racialized."[21] Green's *Edgefield*, produced by a Black painter and child of the South, a student of the School of the Art Institute of Chicago, and an artist involved with larger projects of archival art and public history, enters into this contested representational ground to subtly challenge a dominant historical and symbolic plantation order that has enjoyed lasting force.

In Green's cotton painting, the absence of enslaved laborers works as an invitation, asking viewers to imagine the missing actors in the (visual) field who made southern economies not only work, but rich. In this way, one might pair the more intimate *Edgefield* (16 × 20 inches) with Leonardo Drew's sculptural, monument/al *Untitled #25* (1992), which is made up of seven rows of raw cotton stacked eight and half feet high and more than thirteen feet wide.[22] Each piece poses questions about the exploitation and exertion necessary to move cotton through its various stages of production. As Nicole Fleetwood suggests in a broader context, "blackness fills in the space between matter, between object and subject," between, in this case, rows and bales of cotton; it "fills in the void and is the void."[23] The very absence of Black figures disrupts a predictable association between Black labor and white cotton (wealth), asking viewers to feel and think about the image—and associations—anew. Put another way, this disembodied scene is visually vacated of the physical labor or romantic associations that must be produced instead by viewers and their (historically determined) imaginative power. Like the stark space behind the cut-out canvas in Banksy's commentary on Millet's 1857 *The Gleaners* (when one of the three wheat worker figures steps out of the historical and visual frame to take a cigarette break), the weight of Black artistic visualizations of cotton that adheres to Green's *Edgefield* "interrupts the pastoral mood" (as Viv Golding says) of Banksy's reframing of one of the most famously "sympathetic" renditions of the mid-nineteenth-century laboring classes.[24] By not representing individual figures, Green's painting highlights the aggregate, omnipresent, continuous, and fungible nature of plantation work performed by vast numbers of enslaved Africans.

When interpreted as a piece that invites Black viewers to project absent Black figures back into the frame, Green's *Edgefield* is in conversation with Jay Lynn Gomez's *Domestic Scenes* series (acrylic on magazine, 2013). Gomez's paintings of Latinx workers on advertisements—or on iconic images of Southern California domestic environments—disrupt sunny portrayal of wealth's promise "devoid of the people tasked with maintaining those environments."[25] Green's invitation for the viewer to project the worker into his painting is testimony to the association between cotton fields and the Black people who so often labored in them. Gomez brings to the day-bright scenes of late-stage capitalism the faceless workers who are largely erased in images of luxury that leave no traces of labor. The hauntings in Green's image—absent but imagined workers—and Gomez's gossamer projections function similarly. As Gomez puts it, her "paint on the magazine interruptions [advertisements she uses as canvas] is applied lightly, and can be scratched off easily"; "the artistic decision to focus on their transience comes from the realization that these workers will eventually disappear without a trace in the history books."[26] Green's cotton-filled cotton field similarly announces the permanent traces of Black labor that ghost cotton's visual representation as a "residue that hovers, lingers, emanates, and circulates long after the moment of the marking."[27]

While Gomez's series of *Domestic Scenes* complement Green's *Edgefield* as haunted reflections of how Black and immigrant labor go unrecognized in wealthy environments they build and maintain, John Biggers's *Cotton Pickers* (1947) functions as their opposite, like a photographic negative. In it, the bodies of four fatigued Black field

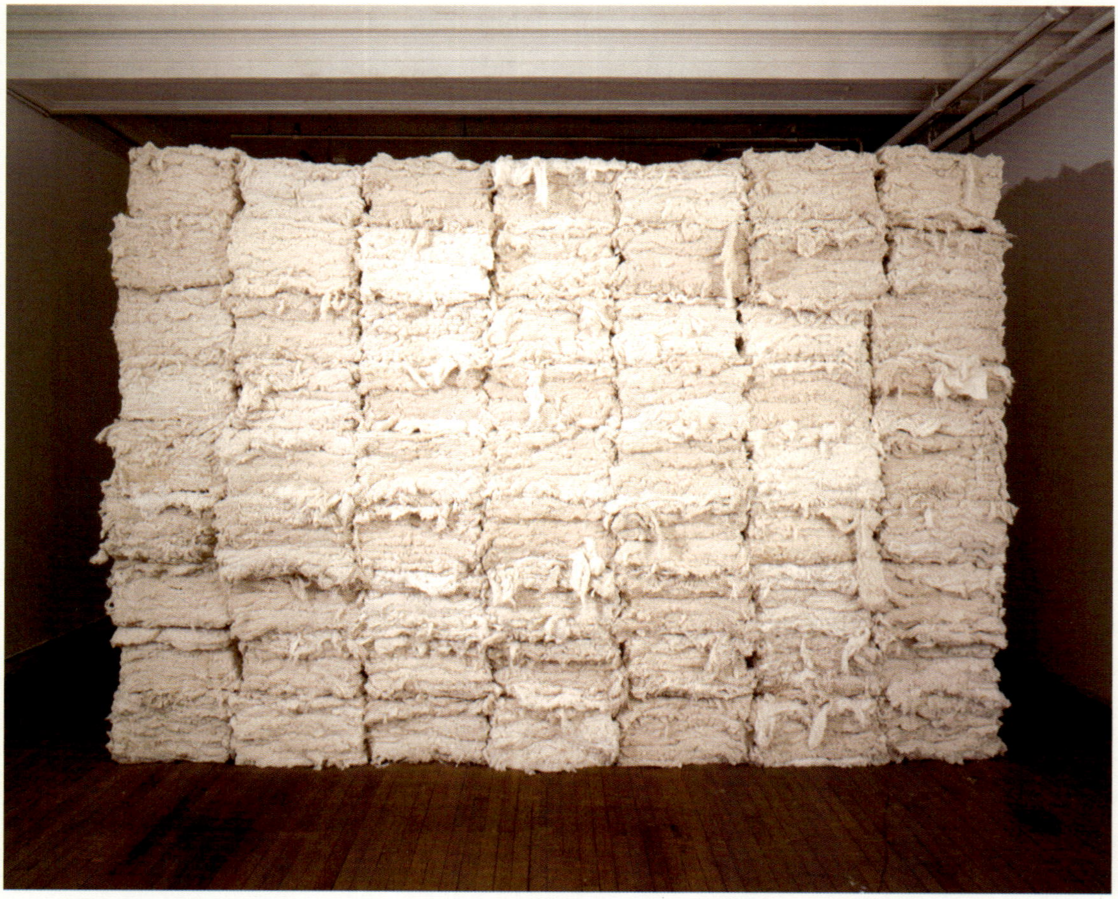

Untitled #25, 1992. Leonardo Drew (American, b. 1961). Cotton, 108 × 120 × 56 inches.
© Leonardo Drew. Courtesy Galerie Lelong and Co., New York.

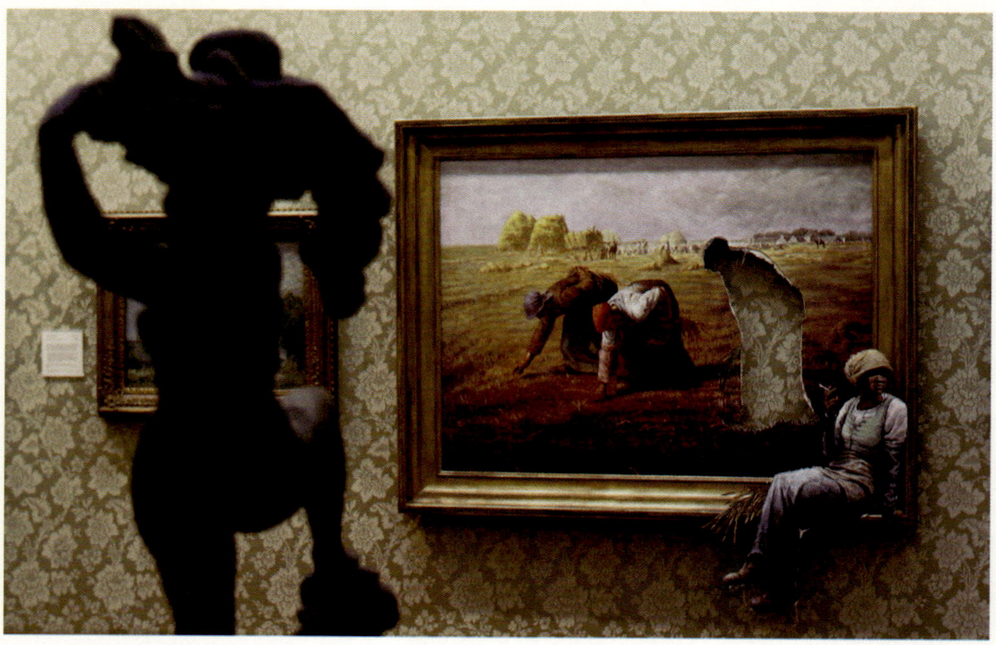

Jon Mills's photograph of Banksy's *Agency Job (Gleaners)*, mixed media. Courtesy of Jon Mills. © Jon Mills.

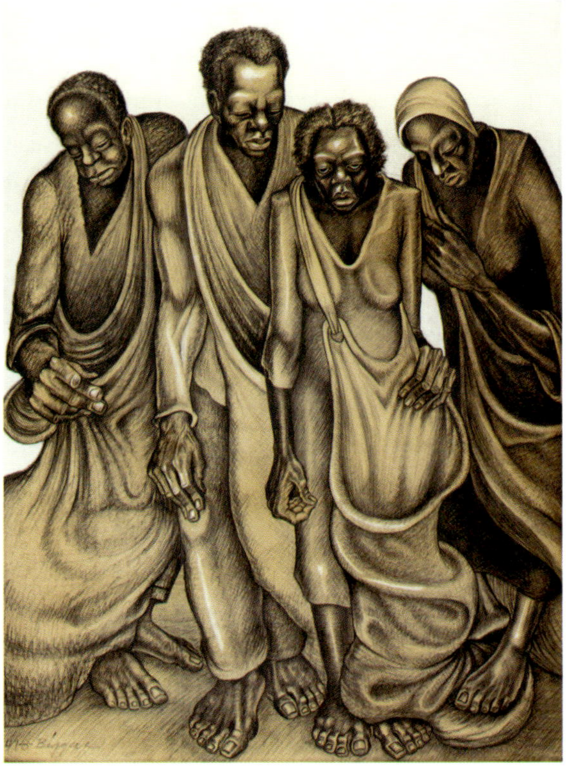

Cotton Pickers, 1947. John Biggers (American, 1924–2001). Conté crayon and gouache on paperboard, 39 ⅝ × 29¾ inches. © 2021 John T. Biggers Estate / Licensed by VAGA at Artists Rights Society (ARS), New York. Estate represented by Michael Rosenfeld Gallery.

hands fill up the frame, standing without any landscape in the foreground or background. With only space as blank as their expressions serving as backdrop, the figures emerge at once like stooping bronze sculptures and restless demi-ghouls. Biggers's cotton paintings bring attention to the toll of Black toil. He emphasizes the physicality of their knuckled fingers and large bare feet. Likewise, the contoured cotton sacks that the four both muscular and defeated men and women tote are as empty as their downcast postures and gazes tell us they are. Biggers's choice of materials, like his sober and constrained use of color—gouache on brown paper with only charcoal and white pencil (and a tinge of red on the figures' mouths)—accentuate the limited landscape of his subjects' life choices. Indeed, the materials themselves provide a commentary on the process (and rapid rate) of human disintegration that his work depicts. As a fetishized art object that degrades easily and so is rarely on view, the painting *Cotton Pickers* enjoys a level of protection that was never extended to Black field hands themselves.[28] If Green's painting invites viewers to insert subjects into the visual field, Biggers asks those who encounter *Cotton Pickers* to imagine the fields of labor these figures encounter and to confront labor's enervating power.[29]

As I've suggested, throughout Green's *Sir Dave* series, the paintings both affirm and unsettle a return to the "no-place of the archive," transforming it into "the no-place of a utopia" through his own commitment to amplifying Black vibrancy and wholeness.[30] In the unpeopled cemetery depicted in *Earth to Earth* (page 78), neither visitors nor mourners dot the scene, just as there are no enslaved workers in *Edgefield*'s cotton rows. Yet the graveyard exudes the connection between the seen and unseen, the living and the dead, what is depicted and the indelible traces that (don't quite) appear on its surface. The foreground is busy with objects: a large earthenware pot and jug occupy its center, a teacup and saucer to one side, a face jug to the other. A framed portrait of a young woman is perched aloft the large jug turned on its side, aligned perfectly with the huge white tombstone cross careening slightly to the right as if toppling off the canvas itself. Green's use of dimension makes the objects in the small painting bigger than life;[31] death cannot contain nor keep them at a safe and comfortable distance. Nor, as the perspective pans out widely in a spatial geometry that itself seems otherworldly, does the painting's outer border contain the burial site's scope and extension. Tombstones dot the intermediate fore- and middle ground for what seems like forever. The burial ground is ongoing and continuous—death spills out and over the image's borders, over death's supposed limits.

Earth to Earth bristles with kinetic energy and movement, while its face jug serves as a visual ar/resting spot, a punctum, to borrow from theorist Roland Barthes, that simultaneously educates, confronts, and holds viewers' attention. Traditionally placed on a burial mound to ward off evil spirits, the face jug gazes out directly at spectators. Vertically aligned with the bush (far) behind it, it draws viewers into the visual frame, functioning both spatially and anthropomorphically as the midpoint between the painting's outer limits and viewers themselves. The painting is bifurcated by the gray and white tombstone-as-cross that dominates the other half of the image and shortens its depth of vision. There, everything is on uneven footing, chaotic, upended. Objects surrounding the cross-stone tilt in different directions, as if on their own planes: the teacup tipping just slightly to the right; the cross leaning with more force, to a greater degree, in the same direction; a jar just under and behind it, inclining away. Seen in person, the piece's horizontal correspondences (the face jug and the portrait) and vertical alignments (the face jug, the bush, and the viewer) coexist with the eruptive energy at its center to unsettle any sense of conventional dimension. The result is not only otherworldly but surreal(istic); death, memory, and history persist both outside and inside knowable material, temporal, and dimensional realms.

The featured face jug provides quite specific historical depth to the collective story of Black cultural production that informs Jonathan Green's series and David Drake's history. Edgefield District, where Drake lived and worked, was a prominent center of face jug production. Though reportedly found throughout the Diaspora, those made in Edgefield were wheel-thrown and kiln-glazed vessels attributed to the early 1860s; indeed some are attributed to the stolen Africans illegally transported to the region in 1858 on the *Wanderer*, one of the last known U.S. vessels to traffic stolen Africans.[32] The type of jug featured in *Earth to Earth* is what art critic John Vlach would call one of the "most refined of those pots," featuring a three-color format with "white matte finished eyes and teeth, shiny green or brown vessel body and eye rims and lips of either a buff or reddish brown color that were left unglazed."[33] In Green's work, such a master pot placed alongside other pots and shards suggests an homage to David Drake and to a community of Black master potters who are too often unrecognized and uncelebrated. *Earth to Earth* provides a commentary on such (art) historical absences. If Drake lies in an unmarked grave, if no one knows exactly what happened to him after the Civil War, Jonathan Green, as his cultural and artistic kin, offers him a final resting place, one full of cultural resonance and continuity in place of the gaping absence that is one of slavery's enduring legacies.

Green's 1998 *Sir Dave* series is in conversation with Carrie Mae Weems's 1991–1992 *Sea Island* series; each take South Carolina, cultural retention, and the natural world as their subject.[34] Green's *Earth to Earth* speaks directly to Weems's *Boneyard*, a quadriptych (three gelatin silver prints and screen print text panel) made up of a vertical triptych of graveyard photographs with a conjoined text panel. Weems functions as both documentarian and conceptual artist, inviting and augmenting meditations on the evidentiary nature of her black-and-white photographs with text panels and ceramic plates. *Earth to Earth* and *Boneyard* formally reverberate: a bush in the background corner, tombstones jutting out at different angles, the familiar gray-white cross headstone.

Certain visual components of Green's and Weems's work resonate strongly because they draw from a shared cultural history. In *Earth to Earth*, tombstones are surrounded by shards of pots, cups, and jugs—as is customary in African burial customs that traveled across the Atlantic. Nowhere was the continuity of such continental cultures stronger than it was in South Carolina, where Africans who had endured—and had survived—the Middle Passage mingled with those "of country born" in greater numbers than in any other state and where the influx of captive Africans was particularly strong in the years before the end of the transatlantic slave trade in 1808, the years of Drake's youth.[35] "The use of fragments," in such Black burial grounds, affirms art historian Robert Farris Thompson, is "deliberate."[36] As one formerly enslaved woman told a WPA interviewer: "them dishes and bottles what put on the grave is for the spirit to feel at home"; "you put . . . all the pretty pieces what they like on the grave," breaking the objects to break the chain between death's hold on the ancestor and their living descendants.[37] Once functional objects, they appear in the *Sir Dave* and *Sea Island* series as sacred vessels, broken pieces connecting across space and time to traditions and practices with far-reaching power and dominion.

Formal and thematic echoes underscore how Weems and Green each function as "a witness and a guide" leading their viewers into Black culture and history.[38] In *Boneyard*,

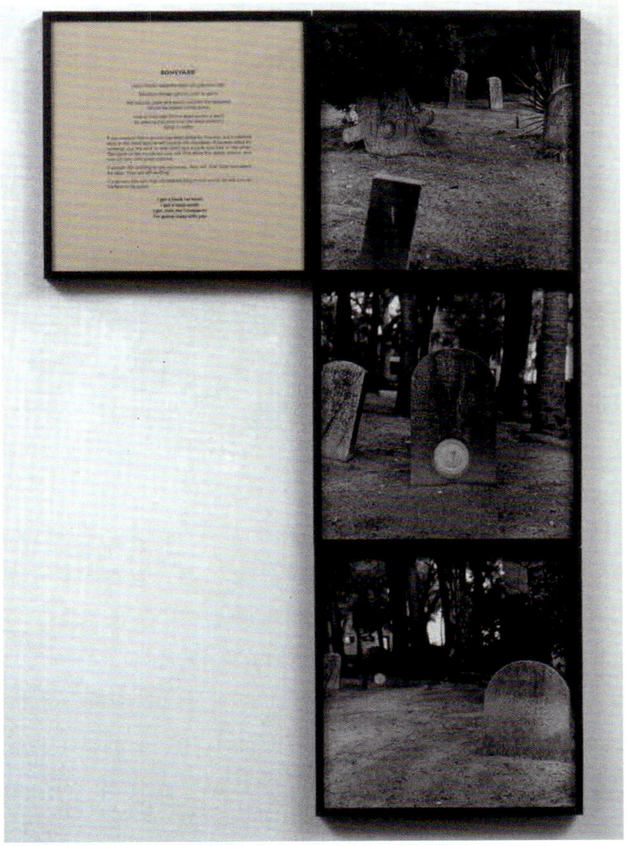

Untitled (*Boneyard*) from the *Sea Island* series, 1991–1992. Carrie Mae Weems (American, b. 1953). Photographs and text panels. © Carrie Mae Weems. Courtesy of the artist and Jack Shainman Gallery, New York.

the cups and scraps of ceramic wares also present in *Earth to Earth* (page 78) appear in the conjoined text panel. With its centered couplets and stanzas on the top half and its left-justified dream book/folklore catalog of seemingly disparate sayings and translations on the bottom, the text panel includes the line: "the last cup, plate and spoon used by the departed / should be placed on the grave." Green's *Sir Dave* and Weems's *Sea Island* installations continue a dialog about shared cultural landscapes; another piece from Weems's series, *Ebo Landing*, resonates loudly with one of Green's three homegoing images, images that could be grouped together as his own closing triptych. Presented as a narrative shape poem in the form of a pot, Weems's *Ebo Landing* is the middle (text) panel in a vertical triptych that includes black-and-white photographs of coastal Low Country / Sea Island moss and palmettos on either side. With neither human nor human-made markers of time—no buildings, material objects, or technologies to help date them—these black-and-white photographs invoke a seemingly timeless past. It is the text panel that intervenes to populate the tableau.

Weems's text panel expresses both a "poetics of exile" that disrupts the natural environment and also a "pot-etics of exile," as if such a tragic forced migration calls for a vessel with sacred powers to hold it.[39] The pot poem relates the historical events

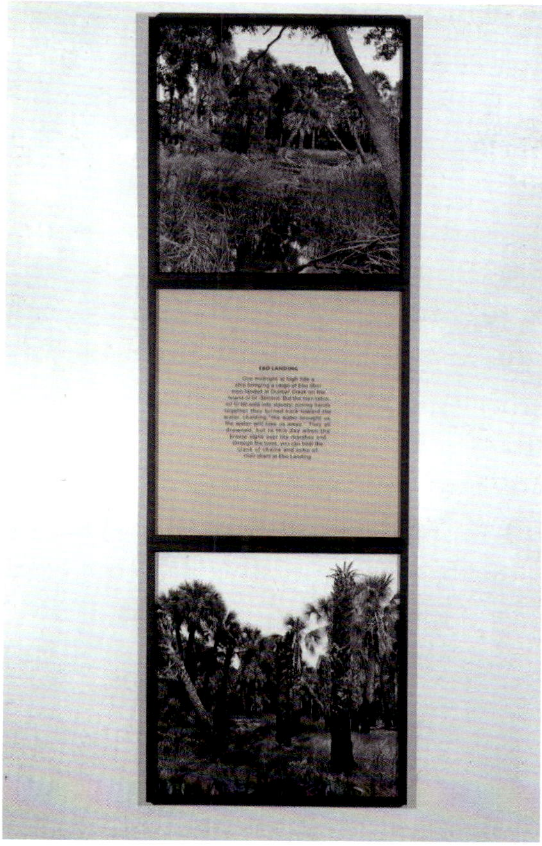

Untitled (*Ebo Landing*) from the *Sea Island* series, 1991–1992. Carrie Mae Weems (American, b. 1953). Photographs and text panels. © Carrie Mae Weems. Courtesy of the artist and Jack Shainman Gallery, New York.

(and familiar story) of a group of captive Ibos/Ebos who mutiny near the end of a transatlantic slave voyage in 1803 to St. Simons Island in coastal Georgia. Bending history's arc away from the trajectory of their expected route from free Ibo people to ever-owned New World cargo, the mutineers turned their backs on the (additional) capture, punishment, and enslavement that would follow the loss of white life that their revisionary acts of resistance engendered. Instead, as Weems's poem shares:

> . . . joining hands
> together they turned back toward the
> water, chanting "the water brought us,
> the water will take us away." They all
> drowned, but to this day when the
> breeze sighs over the marshes and
> through the trees, you can hear the
> clank of chains and echo of
> their chant at Ebo Landing.

It is worth noting that it's not the (historical and) natural tableau of proud Ibos re/turning to the water that appears in the photographic panels that vertically bookend the text panel; instead it's the "this day" of memory—marsh sighs and echoing chants—that Weems's work brings into view. Throughout this exhibit, Weems's work does not, to borrow from Homi Bhaba, "merely recall the past as social cause or aesthetic precedent; it renews the past, refiguring it as an 'in between' space that innovates and interrupts the performance of the present."[40] The cultural connections between Carrie Mae Weems's *Sea Island* installation and Jonathan Green's *Sir Dave* series underscore Green's vision of "in between" space where the "between" is the slip between individual and collective oral histories and the representational vessels that contain and express them. Though the works share visual touchstones and temporal sensibilities, Green's painting doesn't stress the collective suicide at St. Simon that is contained in Weems's shape poem but rather depicts a celebrated version that has lived on in Black oral, literary, and visual culture, one in which the Africans defy social death and fly away, to recall the well-known Black spiritual. Like Weems's text panel, Green's large *Vessels for Taking Us Home* (page 90) is dominated by pots. Visible in person, though not in reproductions, Green has signed "Dave" on the large green pot in the right foreground corner where artists often sign their names. In doing so, Green brings the two artists, himself and David Drake, together across time and medium to claim collective and creative ownership over an artistic legacy that includes both pots and paintings. The vessels in the back-row distance tilt toward the ocean in the painting's horizon as if the ancestors themselves offer the pots as a holding place where stolen souls can take refuge, as mentioned in this book's introduction. Just above those tilt-away pots, set against otherworldly orange clouds, people-sized black birds are in flight away from the coastline, flying back to Africa, as oral tradition testifies, "taking us home."[41] The painting's visual cues point toward the sacred power of Ibo Landing. The title, "*Taking* Us *Home*" (emphasis mine), not only points to the collective us, but also (in the gerund form, tak*ing*) to ongoing action. In doing so, Green embeds his work in the continuity of slavery and its afterlives.

Flying Africans are a recurring motif and topic in African American arts and culture. They appear in twentieth-century WPA interviews, in children's books by the most celebrated Black authors, and as the basis of classic Black novels and films from Toni Morrison's *Song of Solomon* and beyond. Yet, for centuries, no memorial marker has been dedicated to Ibo Landing. Instead, Black cultural memory has taken root and wing against the state's erasure of Black sacred history. In using visual art to elevate the cosmological contexts of captive Africans in the Americas, Jonathan Green, like Carrie Mae Weems, "serves as the historic agent of memory."[42]

In his work honoring David Drake, Jonathan Green joins a generation of Black artists who mine African American histories seeking to gather the shards of the past that are "often lost or displaced" and make them "physically present."[43] His *Sir Dave* series not only elaborates on surviving objects, Drake's tremendous poetic pots, but also meditates on legacies and genealogies that have been lost and found. In his turn to a history that invites viewers to think about the past and make connections between events, characters, and objects, Green joins contemporary artists who engage the archive of slavery to revisit, revive, and revise their ancestors and antecedents, and alongside loss and along with grief, to revel in the archive's possibilities as they also extend its reach.

NOTES

I would like to thank Curtis Small, Julie McGee, Kimberly Blockett, and Denise Burgher for their critical feedback and Emily Luiken Gessmann for her research assistance.

1 Green, unpublished interview. Also see "Seeking Jonathan Green."

2 Green notes he was "always fascinated by textiles" and that when he enrolled as a student at the Art Institute of Chicago, he had imagined he would become a fashion designer. He quickly figured out that it was the paints that were calling to him, as he put it ("Seeking Jonathan Green"). For more on Black women's labor, see Hunter's *To 'Joy My Freedom*. The Jacob Lawrence image here graces the cover of her prize-winning book.

3 The symposia resulted in several collaborations and performances, one which Jonathan Green organized and which debuted in 2017 at Mother Emmanuel in Charleston, and the other centered in Pittsburgh with scholar Edda Fields-Black and composer John C. Wineglass. Quoted from "Casop: A Requiem for Rice."

4 "Purpose and Mission," The Lowcountry Rice Culture Project website.

5 *Off the Wall and onto the Stage*, Columbia City Ballet website.

6 Wentworth and Dawes, *Seeking*, xi.

7 Greene had curated the 1967 exhibit *The Evolution of Afro-American Artists: 1800–1959* with Romare Bearden and is said to be responsible for saving Mt. Moriah Church, which became the Banneker-Douglass Museum of Afro-American Life and History. Maryland Commission on Afro-American History and Culture, "A Tribute to Carroll Greene Jr."

8 For more on this tradition and terminology, see the critical anthology Mack and Offius, *Landscape of Slavery*.

9 Godfrey, "The Artist as Historian," 168.

10 Wheat, *Jacob Lawrence*, 15. The reference refers to Lawrence's 1938–1940 Frederick Douglass and Harriet Tubman series.

11 These include artists Glen Ligon, Lorna Simpson, Fred Wilson, and Renée Green, as Copeland so deftly displays in *Bound to Appear*. They also include Carrie Mae Weems and Kara Walker and, of course, Theaster Gates, whose exhibit is *To Speculate Darky: Theaster Gates and Dave the Potter*, Milwaukee Museum of Art, 2010, also takes David Drake as its inspiration. Green uses oil on linen and on canvas on 16″ × 20″, 18″ × 24″, and 60″ × 48″ canvases; Lawrence uses tempera on gessoed hardboard, all 12″ × 17⅞″ for his series.

12 Jackson, *Real Black*, 18. He writes that "racial sincerity" allows for "ephemerality, partiality, and social vulnerability" and "the possibility of performative ad-libbing."

13 See Wilson, *Specters of Democracy*, 7. It reads, "The project interrogates the ways in which antebellum African Americans conceived of representation in art as a proxy for their desired representation in politics."

14 Bhaba, *The Location of Culture*, 10.

15 Foster, "The Archival Impulse," 22.

16 Copeland and Thompson, "Perpetual Returns," 2.

17 Trouillot, *Silencing the Past*, 27. Some readers will also hear resonances of Langston Hughes's "The Negro Speaks of Rivers," which is widely anthologized and reproduced online.

18 Vlach, "Perpetuating the Past," 16.

19 Vlach, "Perpetuating the Past," 16.

20 Vlach, "Perpetuating the Past," 21–22.

21 McGee, "Field, Boll, and Monument," 37.

22 For an extended reading of Drew's *Untitled #25*, see McGee, "Field, Boll, and Monument," 47.

23 Fleetwood, *Troubling Vision*, 6.

24 Golding, "Creolizing the Museum," 207. See the Banksy image on page 192.

25 See Charlie James Gallery for images https://www.cjamesgallery.com/artists/jay-lynn-gomez.

26 Jay Lynn Gomez, interview by Kinsey Lane.

27 Though Fleetwood does not write about Green or Gomez, her language applies to each of them. Fleetwood, *Troubling Vision*, 24.

28 Since this work is easily degradable, it is on view an average of four months every five years to protect the work, shared Devi Noor, curatorial assistant, American art. Visit to LACMA, February 24, 2014. Materials confirmed in a follow up email by Noor to the author, February 28, 2014.

29 On the ways in which Green and Biggers comment on Winslow Homer's popular *The Cotton Pickers* (1876), see the chapter on Green's and Theaster Gates's work in Foreman, *The Art of DisMemory*, out of which this essay is excerpted.

30 Foster, "The Archival Impulse," 22.

31 Like *Edgefield*, this is one of the smaller canvases in the series, 16″ x 20″.

32 One vessel found in Philadelphia, for example, and now on exhibit at the Philadelphia Museum of Art (and featured on PBS's History Detectives) was traced back to Edgefield. See "Face Jug Investigation Update."

33 Quoted in Baldwin, *Great and Noble Jar*, 80.

34 The exhibit signage announces: "By presenting particular African American cultural details, especially those with direct links to Africa, these photographs portray a complex and persistent heritage." Weems, *Three Decades of Photography and Video*; Guggenheim Museum, visited May 6, 2014.

35 See Stuckey, *Slave Culture*, and Michael Angelo Gomez, *Exchanging Our Country Marks*.

36 Green extends the ways in which "pieces are aligned to show the length of the grave in a simple axial statement." Thompson, "African Influence on the Art of the United States," 150.

37 Quoted in Stuckey, *Slave Culture*, 41.

38 Weems explains this as her (symbolic and autophotographic) role within the 2006 series *Roaming*. Museum text, Weems, *Three Decades of Photography and Video*, Guggenheim Museum, January 24–May 14, 2014.

39 Bhaba, *The Location of Culture*, 7.

40 Bhaba, *The Location of Culture*, 10.

41 Buzzards appear in African American folktales—including those about the flying Africans of Ibo Landing.

42 Enwezor, *Archive Fever*, 16 and 46.

43 Foster is not talking about Black art here—but his sentiments obtain. Foster, "The Archival Impulse," 4.

Afterword

A Praise Song for *Praise Songs*

EVIE SHOCKLEY

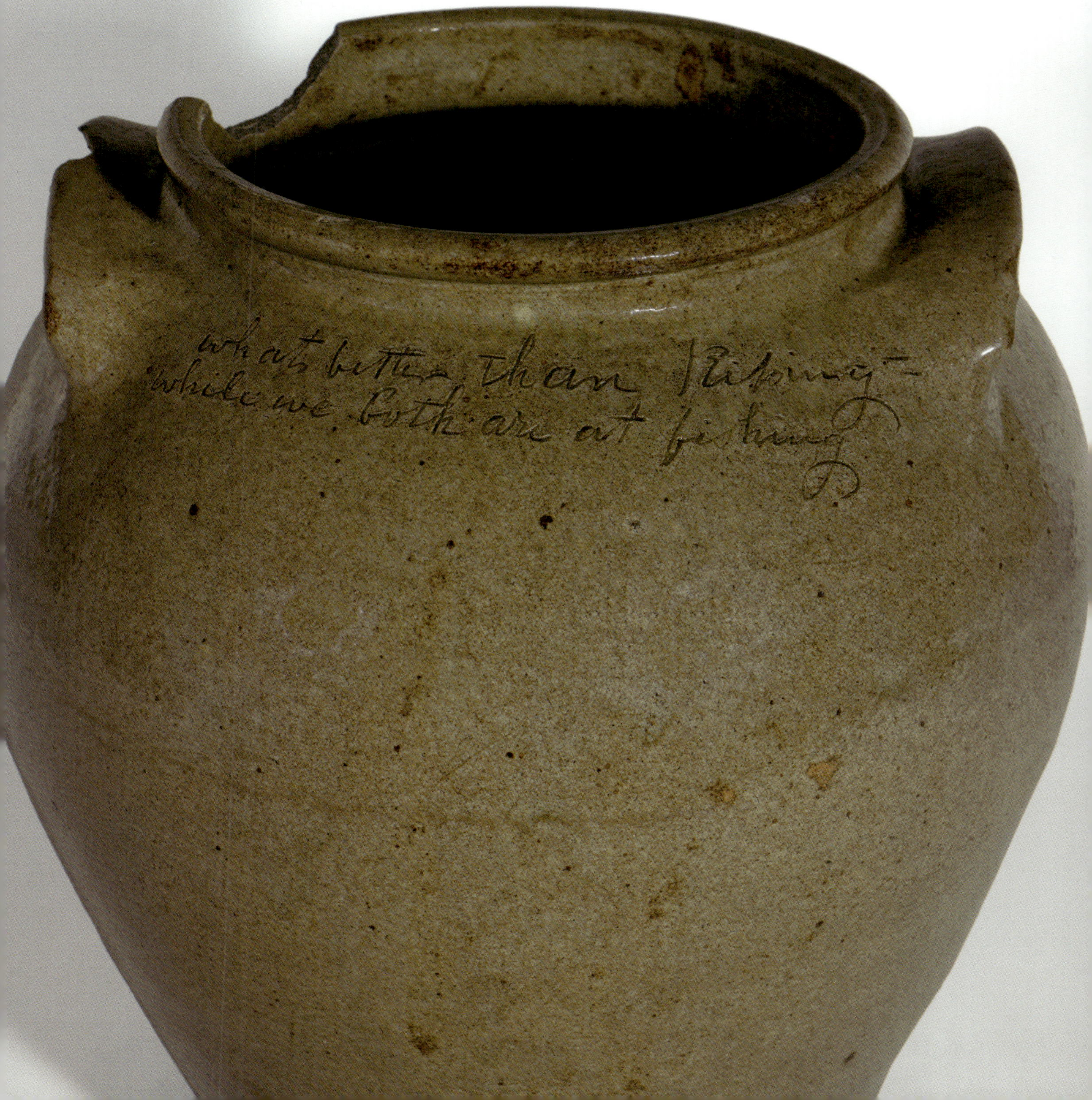

OVERLEAF: Poetic Vessel, “whats better than kissing =,” July 10, 1840. David Drake. Greenville County Museum of Art.

DAVE THE POTTER. DAVE THE POET. Dave the Son. Dave the Observer. Dave the Bold. Dave the Reader. Dave the Uprooted. Dave the Jokester. Dave the Lover. Dave the Theologian. Dave the Bereft. Dave the Marketer. Dave the Husband. Dave the Disabled. Dave the Confident. Dave the Wonderer. Dave the Mourner. Dave the Freeman. Dave the Artist. Dave the Ancestor.

We find ourselves at the end of an amazing experience, dear reader, sister viewer, fellow dreamer. Are you still spinning, too? I feel as if, many pages ago, I stepped up onto a potter's wheel, thinking I'd enjoy the ride, not expecting my living clay to be transformed. But in the expert hands of our primary guides—David Drake, Jonathan Green, Glenis Redmond, and Gabrielle Foreman—I have been reshaped, made larger, stronger, more open. I am more capacious *and* more full.

I came to *Praise Songs for Dave the Potter* already familiar with all four of these figures. But I nonetheless learned a great deal about how and why they make their work, and with what results. I was reminded as well of a truth I'd forgotten: collaboration is not simply additive. The whole of this collaborative project is greater than the sum of its parts.

The volume, like the artistic and intellectual activity it documents, is a process and is *about* process. If we, as its audience, have been spun on its wheel, it is also true that we have stood at the shoulder of its editor and watched her turn the life and art of Dave the Potter round and round before us. Beginning with Foreman's introduction, David Drake and his South Carolina habitat appear in 360 degrees. We see Edgefield County as birthplace, site of families, growing, dividing, and being ripped apart; as seat of instruction, in reading, perhaps typesetting, certainly in throwing pottery; as economic hive, where stolen labor, forced labor, transformed clouds of cotton—and unparalleled artisanship—into "silver or; either Gold." And we witness a Black man coming into view: the strength and skill of his arms and hands; the power of his legs—and then the rumored loss of one of them; the keenness of his eyes; and the aliveness of his mind. Foreman coaxes what she can out of slavery's wretched archive, of course; as a historian, she knows how to wring drops of narrative from the most arid of sources. But that's not her destination. She keeps turning the wheel. Because as a reader, viewer, and maker of art herself, her editorial vision is to situate David Drake's pottery and poetry within a creative context his work helped to engender. This volume reveals not simply the faint traces the archive provides but a visual artist among visual artists, a poet among poets, a Black South Carolinian artist among Black South Carolinian artists: we are gifted with the David Drake of Jonathan Green's paintings and Glenis Redmond's poems.

I loved learning about Green's discovery of "Dave the Potter," the artist-forerunner whose name and story seem to find his descendants as if fated to do so. The importance of the enslaved potter's existence to Green is evidenced by his decision to invest *years* in generating a whole series of works imagining this man, who had grown from the same soil, but under much different conditions. For me, seeing David Drake in Green's bright, deeply saturated jewel tones was not unlike the moment when I first saw the drab, gray Dorothy of Kansas wake up and walk out into Technicolor Oz. Green is indeed a wizard, casting a spell over cotton fields and pottery shards, and waking us all up to the simple, yet awe-inspiring beauties of the South Carolina landscape and rural life that must have informed Dave's potting and enlivened his musings. Dubbing the potter "Sir Dave," Green turns the seat at the pottery wheel into a kind of throne. Though he draws no connection (in these pages) to Stevie Wonder's unforgettable song "Sir Duke," I hear the musician's tribute to his admired predecessor, Duke Ellington, echoed in Green's title for his series and the figure it honors.

Foreman's thickly textured essay situating the *Sir Dave* series within Green's illustrious career and African American art more broadly makes a wonderful counterpoint to the piece she writes on Glenis Redmond's moving poetic sequence. Redmond takes the (Black) poet's prerogative to write lines that are double-voiced, singing David Drake's life and work and Green's artistic vision of it at the same time. As it turns out, the trio of South Carolinians are a real *concatination*, to echo Dave's first known inscription; it was Green, whose images had long adorned the walls of Redmond's home, who called her into the serious pursuit of her art form, we've learned. Moreover, similar to Green, Redmond tells us that Dave's story found *her*—chased her down, one might be tempted to say—and she, too, was compelled by the knowledge of this forerunner to create in his honor. If the paintings deepened my ability to *see* David Drake moving through his life, Redmond's powerfully oral poems invite me to *hear* him, but in the most intimate way: through her imaginative rendering of his interiority, his unspoken thoughts. "What my mouth don't say my hands do," Redmond's Dave tells us, but what his pots don't convey is conjured in her economical, yet musical stanzas. Like her subject, Redmond knows her way around a couplet and how to tighten consonants and vowels till they hum: "I pulls people like I pulls pots / from miles around dey come // to see what I got on spin." This is, as she suggests in her own essay contribution to the volume, fundamentally a poetry grounded in the "echo [of] a Black Baptist preacher's cadence" and the "timing and rhythm" of the voices she heard in her South Carolina adolescence. A God-fearing man like David Drake, who testifies in his own poetry to feeling "the need of Grace," is lucky to have a poet so attuned to his wavelength re-presenting him in words.

Perhaps the most exciting section of the volume for me—and that's saying a lot, because the whole book is engrossing, and each of you will have your own favorite elements—is the transcript of Foreman's interview (call it a rap session) with Redmond and Green. The three of them speak quite openly about their experiences of living with, without, and for Black art: the fortuitous (or spirit-given) way they have encountered the works and people they need to grow and become; the obstacles of other people's low expectations that they've gone around or overcome; and the art they surround themselves with and rely on to nurture their spirit. Poems are recited and punchlines are anticipated. Advice is given, too, for those who know how to hear it. Their conversation is a masterclass on how to be conscious—and consciously appreciative—of the good and plenty of Black culture, whether the treasure is hanging in a museum or spilling from your grandmother's mouth. The text of their exchange is like a lyric poem: eloquence overheard.

I haven't even mentioned the theatrical production staged at the University of Delaware in 2014, richly recalled in choreographer Lynnette Young Overby's essay for the volume and the gorgeous accompanying photographs. Here we have yet another aspect of the collaboration comprised by this multiyear project, and another whole group of kindred spirits: choreographers, composers, arts education teachers, and dancers, including the choreographer and Edgefield, South Carolina, native Vincent Thomas, who danced the role of Dave. Foreman wrote a poem for this production, an exquisite concrete poem composed of rhyming couplets in the shape of a pot, which I was delighted to discover included in this volume's abundance. The final essay, Foreman's consideration of "Black Artists as Cultural Historians," brings Carrie Mae Weems's *Sea Island* series alongside the artistry of South Carolina's native sons David Drake and Jonathan Green—the icing on the cake (or should I say the glaze on the pot?). It is hard to express how satisfying this book is to me, as a poet-heir of Sir Dave, an admirer of Green's and Redmond's creative tributes to their forerunner and "relation," and an educator who can envision these lush pages in the hands of generations of current and future artists.

Dave the Potter. Dave the Poet. Dave the Miracle. Dave the Maestro. My head is *still* spinning—but I'm already ready for another ride on this potter's wheel. Dear reader, fellow viewer, sister dreamer, are you with me?

Bibliography

Andrews, William L. “Slave Narratives, 1865–1900.” In *The Oxford Handbook of the African American Slave Narrative*, edited by John Ernest. New York: Oxford University Press, 2014.

Andrews, William L. *Slavery and Class in the American South: A Generation of Slave Narrative Testimony, 1840–1865*. London: Oxford University Press, 2019.

Baldwin, Cinda K. *Great and Noble Jar: Traditional Stoneware of South Carolina*. Athens: University of Georgia Press, 2014.

“Banksy’s *Gleaners*.” Art a Fact. November 20, 2012. Accessed June 4, 2014. https://artforus.wordpress.com/2012/11/20/banksys-gleaners/.

Barone, Tom, and Elliot W. Eisner. *Arts Based Research*. Thousand Oaks, Calif.: Sage Press, 2012.

Bhaba, Homi. *The Location of Culture*. New York: Routledge, 1994.

“Casop: A Requiem for Rice.” Requiem for Rice. Accessed June 18, 2020. http://www.requiemforrice.com/index.html.

Chaney, Michael A., ed. *Where Is All My Relation? The Poetics of Dave the Potter*. New York: Oxford University Press, 2018.

Clifton, Lucille. *The Book of Light*. Port Townsend, Wash.: Copper Canyon Press, 1993.

Conroy, Patrick. Foreword to *Gullah Images: The Art of Jonathan Green*. Columbia: University of South Carolina Press, 1996.

“Contemporary Dance: Sketches (The Life of Harriet E. Wilson in Dance, Poetry, and Music).” YouTube. https://www.youtube.com/watch?v=RJgWgL9Zb4A.

Copeland, Huey. *Bound to Appear: Art, Slavery, and the Site of Blackness in Multicultural America*. Chicago: University of Chicago Press, 2013.

Copeland, Huey, and Krista Thompson. “Perpetual Returns: New World Slavery and the Matter of the Visual.” *Representations* 113 (Winter 2011): 1–15.

Douglass, Frederick. *Narrative of the Life of Frederick Douglass, an American Slave*. Documenting the American South. Accessed July 8, 2018. https://docsouth.unc.edu/neh/douglass/douglass.html.

Dungy, Camille. “In Others’ Voices: The Millennial Poets and Personae.” *Black Issues Book Review* 8, no. 2 (March/April 2006).

Enwezor, Okuwi. *Archive Fever: Uses of the Document in Contemporary Art*. New York: International Center of Photography, 2008.

"Face Jug Investigation Update." History Detectives: Special Investigations. PBS. Accessed June 24, 2014. http://www.pbs.org/opb/historydetectives/video/2030307324/.

Fleetwood, Nicole. *Troubling Vision: Performance, Visuality, and Blackness*. Chicago: University of Chicago Press, 2011.

Foreman, P. Gabrielle. *The Art of DisMemory: Historicizing Slavery in Poetry, Print, and Material Culture*. Forthcoming.

Foreman, P. Gabrielle. "1857: Dave the Potter's August Pots, Sexual Imagery, and *Dred Scott*." In *Where Is All My Relation? The Poetics of Dave the Potter*, edited by Michael Chaney. New York: Oxford University Press, 2018.

Foster, Hal. "The Archival Impulse." *October* 110, no. 1 (Fall 2004): 3–22.

Foster, Susan Leigh. *Choreographing Empathy: Kinesthesia in Performance*. London: Routledge, 2010.

Godfrey, Mark. "The Artist as Historian." *October* 120, no. 1 (Spring 2007): 140–172.

Goldberg, Arthur F., and James Witkowski. "Beneath His Magic Touch: The Dated Vessels of the African-American Slave Potter Dave." Chipstone Foundation, Ceramics in America, 2006. http://www.chipstone.org/article.php/281/Ceramics-in-America-2006/Beneath-his-Magic-Touch:-The-Dated-Vessels-of-the-African-American-Slave-Potter-Dave.

Golding, Viv. "Creolizing the Museum: Humor, Art, and Young Audiences." In *Museums and Communities: Curators, Collection, and Collaboration*, edited by Viv Golding and Wayne Modest, 195–216. London: Bloomsbury Academic, 2013.

Gomez, Jay Lynn. Interview by Kinsey Lane. Accessed June 24, 2014 (now defunct). http://www.policymic.com/articles/77863/striking-images-reveal-what-it-really-takes-to-live-a-life-of-luxury.

Gomez, Michael Angelo. *Exchanging Our Country Marks: The Transformation of African Identities in the Colonial and Antebellum South*. Chapel Hill: University of North Carolina Press, 1998.

Green, Jonathan. *Gullah Images : The Art of Jonathan Green*. Columbia: University of South Carolina Press, 1996.

Green, Jonathan. *I Made This Jar: The Life and Works of the Enslaved African American Potter, Dave*. Traveling exhibit, curated by Jill Beute Koverman, 1998.

Green, Jonathan. Unpublished interview by P. Gabrielle Foreman. January 28, 2014.

Haley, Alex, and David Olusoga. *Roots*. London: Vintage Classics, 2018.

Hartfied, Ronnie. "Gathering Light in the Gray City: The Chicago Years." In *Gullah Images: The Art of Jonathan Green*. Columbia: University of South Carolina Press, 1996.

Hawkins, Tramaine. "The Potter's House." *All My Best to You*. Accessed July 25, 2020. https://www.allmusic.com/song/the-potters-house-mt0045180997.

Hazelton, Rebecca. "Teaching the Persona Poem: Don't Write What You Know; Write Who You Aren't." Poetry Foundation. May 9, 2014. Accessed August 6, 2018. https://www.poetryfoundation.org/articles/70117/teaching-the-persona-poem.

Hughes, Langston. *The Collected Works of Langston Hughes*. Columbia: University of Missouri Press, 2001.

Hughes, Langston. "The Negro Artist and the Racial Mountain," in *The Collected Works of Langston Hughes*. Poetry Foundation. Accessed October 18, 2021. https://www.poetryfoundation.org/articles/69395/the-negro-artist-and-the-racial-mountain.

Hunter, Tera W. *To 'Joy My Freedom: Southern Black Women's Lives and Labors after the Civil War*. Cambridge, Mass.: Harvard University Press, 1997.

Hurmence, Belinda. *Before Freedom, When I Just Can Remember: Twenty-Seven Oral Histories of Former South Carolina Slaves*. Winston-Salem, N.C.: J. F. Blair, 1989.

Hurston, Zora Neale. "How It Feels to Be Colored Me." *World Tomorrow* 11, no. 5 (May 1928): 215–216.

"In Pictures: Honoring David Drake, a Pioneering Black Poet Who Wrote in Clay." Library of America. February 24, 2021. https://www.loa.org/news-and-views/1786-in-pictures-honoring-david-drake-a-pioneering-black-poet-who-wrote-in-clay.

"Introduction to Praise-Poetry." African Poems. Accessed August 6, 2018. http://africanpoems.net/praise/introduction-to-praise-poetry/.

Jackson, John Andrew. *The Experience of a Slave in South Carolina*. London: Passmore and Alabaster, 1862.

Jackson, John L., Jr. *Real Black: Adventures in Racial Sincerity*. Chicago: University of Chicago Press: 2005.

Jacobs, Harriet A. *Incidents in the Life of a Slave Girl: Written by Herself*. Cambridge, Mass.: Harvard University Press, 1987.

"Jay Lynn Gomez." Charlie James Gallery. Accessed June 24, 2014. https://www.cjamesgallery.com/artists/jay-lynn-gomez.

Johnson, Walter. *Soul by Soul: Life Inside the Antebellum Slave Market*. Cambridge, Mass.: Harvard University Press, 1999.

Koverman, Jill Beute. "The Ceramic Works of David Drake, aka, Dave the Potter or Dave the Slave of Edgefield, South Carolina." *American Ceramic Circle Journal* 13 (2005): 83–98.

Koverman, Jill Beute, ed. *I Made This Jar: The Life and Works of the Enslaved African-American Potter, Dave*. Columbia: McKissick Museum, University of South Carolina Press, 1998.

Mack, Angela D., and Stephen G. Offius, eds. *Landscape of Slavery: The Plantation in American Art*. Columbia: University of South Carolina Press, 2008.

Maryland Commission on Afro-American History and Culture. "A Tribute to Carroll Greene Jr., 1976–1986." 1986.

McGee, Julie L. "Field, Boll, and Monument: Toward an Iconography of Cotton in African American Art." *International Review of African American Art* 19, no. 1 (2003): 37–48.

Mitchell, Angelyn, ed. *Within the Circle: An Anthology of African American Literary Criticism from the Harlem Renaissance to the Present*. Durham, N.C.: Duke University Press, 1994.

Moffett, Ann-Thomas. "Arts-Based Research in Dance." In *Undergraduate Research in Dance: A Guide for Students*, edited by Lynnette Young Overby, Jenny Olin Shanahan, and Gregory Young, 54–62. London: Routledge, 2019.

Moyers, Bill D., et al. *The Language of Life: A Festival of Poets*. New York: Broadway Books, 2001.

Off the Wall and onto the Stage. Columbia City Ballet. Accessed June 16, 2020. https://vimeo.com/257183707.

Overby, Lynnette Young. *Public Scholarship in Dance*. Champaign, Ill.: Human Kinetics Publishers, 2016.

Overby, Lynnette Young, choreographer. *Sketches in the Life of Harriet E. Wilson*. Lauren Wells, composer; Glenis Redmond, poet; P. Gabrielle Foreman, literary historian. First performed at Mitchell Hall, University of Delaware, March 2012.

Poutasse, Marianna. "Jonathan Green's Canvases Bring Dave the Potter to Life." *Winterthur Magazine*, Spring 2000.

"The Power of Poetry: Pre–Civil War to Reconstruction." National Museum of African American History and Culture. Accessed August 3, 2020. https://nmaahc.si.edu/blog-post/power-poetry-pre-civil-war-reconstruction.

"Purpose and Mission." Low Country Rice Culture. Accessed June 16, 2020. http://www.lowcountryriceculture.org/Purpose---Mission.html.

Rambsy, Howard, II. "Catching Holy Ghosts: The Diverse Manifestations of Black Persona Poetry." *African American Review* 42, no. 3/4 (Fall–Winter, 2008).

Rawick, George. *From Sunup to Sundown: The Making of the Black Community*. Westport, Conn.: Greenwood, 1972.

Redmond, Glenis. *Backbone*. Atlanta, Ga.: Underground Epics, 2000.

Redmond, Glenis. "Grave." "I, Master." "Jarring." *Red Rock Review* 35 (Spring 2015).

Redmond, Glenis. *Under the Sun*. Charlotte, N.C.: Main Street Rag Books, 2008.

Redmond, Glenis. "What Hangs on Trees: Legacy and Memory in the Southern Landscape." *Orion Magazine*, October 12, 2012. https://Orionmagazine.Org/Article/Glenis-Redmond-Reads-What-Hangs-on-Trees/, https://orionmagazine.org/article/what-hangs-on-trees/.

Redmond, Glenis. *What My Hand Say: Poems*. Winston, N.C.: Press 53, 2016.

Sajé, Natasha. "Dynamic Design: The Structure of Books of Poems." *Iowa Review* 35, no. 2 (2005): 149–162.

Sajé, Natasha. "Poetry and Ethics: Writing about Others." Association of Writers and Writing Programs, December 2009. Accessed August 6, 2018. www.awpwriter.org/magazine_media/writers_chronicle_view/2241/poetry_ethics_writing_about_others.

Saldanya, Johnny. *Ethnodrama: An Anthology of Reality Theatre*. Walnut Creek, Calif.: AltaMira, 2005.

Saldanya, Johnny. *Ethnotheatre Research from Page to Stage*. New York: Taylor and Francis, 2011.

"Seeking Jonathan Green." Media Library. Jonathan Green Studios. Accessed June 11, 2020. http://www.jonathangreenstudios.com/Media.

Smith, Patricia. "Persona Poetry." In *Poetry Slam: The Competitive Art of Performance Poetry*, edited by Gary Glazner. San Francisco: Manic D Press, 2000.

Stodghill, Ron. "In Charleston, Coming to Terms with the Past." *New York Times*, November 15, 2016. www.nytimes.com/2016/11/20/travel/charleston-south-carolina-past-slave-trade-history.html.

Strobert, Nelson T. *Daniel Alexander Payne, the Venerable Preceptor of the African Methodist Episcopal Church*. Plymouth, UK: University Press of America, Rowman and Littlefield, 2012.

Stuckey, Sterling. *Slave Culture: Nationalist Theory and the Foundations of Black America*. New York: Oxford University Press, 1987.

Thirteen. PBS website. Accessed May 29, 2018. https://www.thirteen.org/wnet/slavery/experience/education/docs1.html.

Thompson, Robert Farris. "African Influence on the Art of the United States." In *Black Studies in the University, a Symposium*, edited by Armstead Robinson, et al., 150. New Haven: Yale University Press, 1969.

Todd, Leonard. *Carolina Clay: The Life and Legend of the Slave Potter Dave*. New York: W. W. Norton, 2008.

Trouillot, Michel-Rolph. *Silencing the Past: Power and the Production of History*. Boston: Beacon Press, 1995.

Vlach, John Michael. "Perpetuating the Past: Plantation Landscape Paintings Then and Now." In *Landscape of Slavery: The Plantation in American Art*, edited by Angela D. Mack and Stephen G. Offius. Columbia: University of South Carolina Press, 2008.

Walker, Alice. "In Search of Our Mother's Gardens." In *Within the Circle: An Anthology of African American Literary Criticism from the Harlem Renaissance to the Present*, edited by Angelyn Mitchell. Durham: Duke University Press, 1994.

Wallace, Maurice O., and Shawn Michelle Smith, eds. *Pictures and Progress: Early Photography and the Making of African American Identity*. Durham: Duke University Press, 2012.

Weems, Carrie Mae. *Three Decades of Photography and Video*. London: Yale University Press, 2012.

Weldon Johnson, James. "Lift Every Voice and Sing." John Rosamond Johnson Music, 1900.

Wentworth, Marjory, and Kwame Dawes, eds. *Seeking: Poetry and Prose Inspired by the Art of Jonathan Green*. Columbia: University of South Carolina Press, 2013.

Wheat, Ellen Harkins. *Jacob Lawrence: The Frederick Douglass and Harriet Tubman Series of 1938–40*. Seattle: University of Washington Press and the Hampton University Museum, 1991.

Williams, Heather. *Self-Taught: African American Education in Slavery and Freedom*. Chapel Hill: University of North Carolina Press, 2005.

Wilson, Harriet E. *Our Nig: or, Sketches in the Life of a Free Black*. Boston: George C. Rand and Avery, 1859.

Wilson, Harriet E. *Our Nig: or, Sketches in the Life of a Free Black, in a Two-Story White House, North. Showing That Slavery's Shadows Fall Even There*. Edited by P. Gabrielle Foreman and Reginal Pitts. New York: Penguin Classic, 2005.

Wilson, Ivy G. *Specters of Democracy: Blackness and Aesthetics of Politics in the Antebellum U.S.* New York: Oxford University Press, 2011.

Wright, Audrey. *Dave the Potter*. Presentation at the biannual meeting of the Council for Undergraduate Research, Washington, D.C., June 2014.

Young, Kevin, ed. *African American Poetry: 250 Years of Struggle and Song*. New York: Library of America, 2020.

Young, Kevin. *The Grey Album: On the Blackness of Blackness*. Minneapolis, Minn.: Greywolf Press, 2012.

Contributor Biographies

KWAME DAWES is the author of twenty-two books of poetry and numerous other books of fiction, criticism, and essays. His collection *Nebraska* was published in 2019. He is Glenna Luschei Editor of *Prairie Schooner* and George W. Holmes University Professor at the University of Nebraska. He teaches in the Pacific MFA Program. He is director of the African Poetry Book Fund and artistic director of the Calabash International Literary Festival. Dawes is a Chancellor of the Academy of American Poets and a Fellow of the Royal Society of Literature. His awards include an Emmy, the Forward Poetry Prize, a Guggenheim Fellowship, the PEN/Nora Magid Award, and the prestigious Windham Campbell Prize for Poetry. In 2021, Kwame Dawes was named editor of American Life in Poetry. In 2021, Dawes was nominated for the Neustadt Prize.

P. GABRIELLE FOREMAN is a poet's daughter and interdisciplinary scholar raised on the South Side of Chicago and Venice Beach, California. She is the founding faculty director of the award-winning Colored Conventions Project, housed in the Center for Digital Black Research/#DigBlk at PSU, where she serves as the center's inaugural codirector. Gabrielle is known for her long-standing commitments to institution and community building and to working in and building collectives. She has also worked for a decade with renowned dance educator Lynnette Young Overby and poet Glenis Redmond to bring Black history to the stage. Foreman is author of five books and editions, which include most recently *The Colored Conventions Movement: Black Organizing in the Nineteenth Century* (2021). She is professor of English, African American Studies, and History at Penn State, where she holds the Paterno Family Chair of Liberal Arts.

JONATHAN GREEN (1955–) Born in Gardens Corner, S.C., Jonathan Green is an internationally acclaimed and awarded professional artist who graduated from the School of the Art Institute of Chicago in 1982. His forty-year track record of creating art and extensive inclusions in museum collections and exhibitions throughout many countries has led to his being considered by numerous art critics and reviewers as one of our nation's outstanding American artists and a highly recognized visual master for capturing the positive aspects of American and African American southern cultures, history, and traditions.

His high level of social interest and cultural commitments and his exhibitions have brought him international recognition through his travels and collections throughout North America, Europe, Central and South America, the Caribbean, Africa, and Japan. It is Jonathan's mastery of color and skillful use of the human figure in rural and urban environments that allows him to preserve and share with the viewer a deep sense of community and how the life challenges of work, love, and belonging are met.

Since 1982 Jonathan has received four honorary doctoral degrees from prestigious universities and numerous awards for his artistic, social, civic, academic, and cultural contributions. In 2017 he was appointed by Mayor John Tecklenburg with the title of Ambassador for the Arts for the city of Charleston, South Carolina.

Jonathan's art and talents have been incorporated into productions of ballet, modern dance, music, opera, theater, literature, film, fashion clothing, and video documentaries throughout the United States. Currently Jonathan resides and paints in his studio located in downtown Charleston, South Carolina. www.jonathangreenstudios.com.

LYNNETTE YOUNG OVERBY is professor of Theatre at the University of Delaware. During her career, she has served with distinction in several leadership roles, including president of both the National Dance Association (NDA) and the Michigan Dance Council. From 2004 to present Lynnette has served as a National Artist Educator from the John F. Kennedy Center for the Performing Arts. She is the author or coauthor of over forty publications and nine books and has a record of over one hundred major presentations and performances. She is a strong believer in interdisciplinary education and in collaboration. She has created four "Performing History" arts-based research projects with English Professor Gabrielle Foreman and a host of artists. Her contributions have earned her more than twenty state, district, and national awards and honors, including the 2000 NDA Scholar/Artist, 2004 Leadership Award, and 2018 Lifetime Achievement Award from the National Dance Education Organization. In 2021 she was selected to serve on the Biden/Harris arts and humanities agency review team.

GLENIS REDMOND is a nationally renowned award-winning poet and teaching artist traveling the world sharing and teaching poetry. She writes about the strength of her Afro-Carolinian roots while exploring their weighted and palpable histories. Glenis is a literary community leader. She is dedicated to coaching and uplifting youth poets' voices. She cofounded a literary program called Peace Voices in her hometown of Greenville, South Carolina, from 2012 to 2019. Glenis is also Kennedy Center Teaching Artist, a Cave Canem poet, and a N.C. Literary Award recipient. In 2020 Glenis became a recipient of South Carolina's highest award, the Governor's Award for the Arts. Her work has been showcased on NPR and PBS and has been most recently published in *Orion Magazine*, the *North Carolina Literary Review*, *Obsidian Literature and Arts in the African Diaspora*, *StorySouth*, *About Place*, and *Carolina Muse*. Her latest book, *The Listening Skin*, was published by Four Way Books in 2022.

EVIE SHOCKLEY, professor of English at Rutgers University, New Brunswick, is the author of *Renegade Poetics: Black Aesthetics and Formal Innovation in African American Poetry* (University of Iowa Press, 2011) and five collections of poetry. The most recent, *semiautomatic* (Wesleyan University Press, 2017), was a finalist for the Pulitzer Prize and the *LA Times* Book Prize and winner of the 2018 Hurston/Wright Legacy Award, which she also won in 2012 for *the new black* (Wesleyan University Press, 2011). She currently serves as editor for poetry at *Contemporary Literature* and is at work on a project investigating the ways Black poets and visual artists negotiate cultural production in an era of colorblindness by creating work at the intersection of text and image.

Index

Page numbers in italic refer to full color plates. Page numbers in bold refer to poems in full text.

ABR (arts-based research), 162
absence of people. *See* hauntings
African American artisans, 8–9
African American Poetry: 250 Years of Struggle and Song (Young, ed.), 14
African resonances, 146
Agency Job (Gleaners) (Banksy; Mills), *192*
All My Relation: Poems for David Drake (Redmond): centering of Drake's perspective, 102; contents, 51; couplets, 102; persona poems, 102–103; praise poem form, 102–103
ancestor artists, 15–17, 121, 137, 186; Redmond on, 113
Ann (enslaved with Drake), 42
apostles of forgetfulness, 133
Art Institute of Chicago, 16, 136
artistic collaborations, 13, 163–164, 179, 203–205; *Dave the Potter* (theatrical production), 161; Green and, 126–127, 129; *Sketches: The Life of Harriet E. Wilson in Dance, Poetry, and Music*, 161–162; visits to Green in South Carolina, 164
arts: Black art, 141–142, 145; Black families and, 128, 149–150; criticism, 130; examination of, 130–131; in historical recovery, 17; self-worth and, 102–103
arts-based research, 162
attention to art, 99; examination of arts, 130–131
authorial partnership, a conversation: Foreman, Gabrielle, 110–132; Green, Jonathan, 110–132; Overby, Lynnette Young, 110–132; Redmond, Glenis, 110–132

Banksy, 191; *Agency Job (Gleaners)*, 192
Bearden, Romare, 8
Bhaba, Homi, 188, 198
Biggers, John, 191, 193, *193*
Black being, 99
Black family, 10
Black histories, 40, 121, 121–122, 157–158, 203; Green's work and, 183–195; healing dimensions in Green's work, 188; held in Black arts and culture, 14; memory, 198; speculative pasts, 188; transmission of oral and visual histories, 186; as utopia, 188
Black labor, 102, 190–191, 193
Black personal history, 100
Black poets: Clifton, Lucille, 114, 146, 153; Dawes, Kwame, 14; Dove, Rita, 130; Drake, David, 14; Finney, Nikki, 112; Horton, George Moses, 14; Redmond, Glenis, 14; Shockley, Evie, 203–205; Smith, Patricia, 10–11; Terry, Lucy, 25; Wheatley, Phillis, 14; Young, Kevin, 14, 19n36
Black vitality, 10
Boneyard (Weems), *196*; *Earth to Earth* (Green) and, 195
"Boy" (Redmond), **152–153**
"Brickmaking: Recipe for Writing" (Redmond), **68**; *Sir Dave*, 51
Brown, Oscar, Jr., 129
Burning Sheets (Green), 155

Carolina Clay: The Life and Legend of the Slave Potter Dave (Todd), 14, 23
"Carry Us" (Redmond), 91–93, **91**, 106; "Embodied" (Redmond) and, 106; Ibo Landing and, 105; Sankofa, 91, 92; *Vessels for Taking Us Home* (Green), 51, 106
Cary, Mary Ann Shadd, 13
"Cash Wanted," 25
"catination," 24
celebration among struggle, 153
Census (1870), 13
Chaney, Michael, 14
channeling art, 123
Charleston's Gibbes Museum of Art, 185
Choreographing Empathy (Foster), 165
"*Christening, The*" (Green), 147, *148*
Christina Cultural Arts Center (Wilmington, Del.), 165
Clifton, Lucille, 114, 146, 153
collaborations, academic, 134–136
collaborations, artistic: collective ownership, 127; Foreman, Redmond, and Green, 110–137; imaginary, 127; Redmond and, 127–128

Colored Conventions, 13
Columbia City Ballet's, 185
community, 7–8, 10, 103–104
Copeland, Huey, 188
cotton, 101–102, 166, 168, 190; cotton slavery, 166, 168; in Drew's work, 190–191; "Field Cotton" (*Dave the Potter* production), 166–168; revisionist plantation painting, 190. See also *Edgefield*
Cotton Pickers (Biggers), 191, 193, *193*
couplets, 107nn8–9
Crossroads (Green), *71*; "How I Walk" (Redmond), 51; "Irony" (Redmond), 51; "Jarring" (Redmond), 51; *Sir Dave* series, 39
cultural kinship, 126–127; Drake and, 132

Dash, Julie, 45
Daughters of the Dust (Dash), 45
Dave. *See* Drake, David
Dave the Potter. *See* Drake, David
Dave the Potter (Green), 18n16, 39, 41, *61*; *Dave the Potter* (theatrical production), 168; girl in red, 42; "I, Master" (Redmond), 51; reading, 41
Dave the Potter (score), "Three Vessels," *109*
Dave the Potter (theatrical production), 161–172; collaborative process, 164–165; "Cotton" (Overby), 166; cotton slavery, 166, 168; dancers, 164; *Dave the Potter* (Green), 168; "Dave the Potter Prelude" (Russell), 166; *Dave's Market*, **171**, 171–172; "Dave's Song" (Russell), 171; Drake's pots, 163; *Dream of Freedom*, 172; *Edgefield* (Green), 166; Emmons, Teresa, 164; "Field Cotton," 166–168, *167*; "Field Cotton" (Redmond), 166; "Field Cotton" (Russell), 166, *167*; Foreman, Gabrielle, 163; goals of, 162–163; Green, Jonathan, 163, 164; Hilliard, Gabrielle, 164; influence on artists, 164; performed, 165; "Praise Dave" (Redmond), 166; Prelude, 166; "Pretty Little Girl," 168–169, *169*; "Pretty Little Girl" (Russell), 168; "Pretty Little Girl" (Thomas), 168; Redmond, Glenis, 163, 164; Russell, Ralph, 164; "Sir Dave," 171; *Sir Dave* (Green), 171; *Sir Dave* (Thomas), 171; *Sir Dave* series, 166; Thomas, Vincent, 164; Wright, Audrey, 164
"Dave the Potter Prelude" (Russell), *Dave the Potter* (theatrical production), 166
Dave's Market (*Dave the Potter* production), 171–172, **171**; "Dave's Market" (Emmons), 171; *Dave's Market* (Green), 171; "Dave's Market" (Russell), 171
"Dave's Market" (Emmons), *Dave's Market* (*Dave the Potter* production), 171
Dave's Market (Green), 18n16, 39, *63*; community, 41; *Dave's Market* (*Dave the Potter* production), 171; girl in red, 41–42; joy, 41; "Market" (Redmond), 51; pots in, 41; reading, 41
"Dave's Market" (Russell), *Dave's Market* (*Dave the Potter* production), 171
"Dave's Song" (Russell), *Dave the Potter* (theatrical production), 171
Dawes, Kwame, 14, 186
death: in *Earth to Earth* (Green), 42; in *From Earth We Came* (Green), 42; in *Vessels for Taking Us Home* (Green), 42
"Deepest Pot" (Redmond), **79–80**, 103; *Earth to Earth* (Green), 51
Dodge Poetry Festival, 146
Dominelli, Darlea, 24
double entendre, 105
double rondeau, 104, 107n5
Douglass, Frederick, 9; as artistic subject, 11; *Narrative of the Life*, 99–100
Dove, Rita, 130
Drake, David, 125; biographical information, 5, 7, 39, 163; after emancipation, 46–47; exhibition of work, 4; human value, 129; inscriptions, 14, 163; as inspiration, 137; likely a typesetter, 124; loss of leg, 7, 39, 47n2, 105; mastering his world, 124–126, 130; performance poet, 120; place in history, 121; signatures, 124, 137; South Carolina and, 158; South Carolina influences, 203; as theologian, 120
—inscriptions: confirmation process, 24; "corrections" of, 23; reverse, 25; signature, 25; translation to page, 24–25
—pottery: 1857 reappearance of, 6; value of, 130. *See also* inscriptions; location of creation
—works about: *All My Relation: Poems for David Drake* (Redmond), 10–11; "Dave" (Dawes), **xv–xvi**; *Dave the Potter: Artist, Poet, Slave*, 3; *Dave the Potter* (theatrical production), 161–172 (see also *Dave the Potter* [theatrical production]); *I Made This Jar: The Life and Works of the Enslaved African American Potter, Dave*, 8–9; *Sir Dave* (Green), 4 (see also *Sir Dave* series); *Where Is All My Relation? The Poetics of Dave the Potter* (Chaney), 14
Dream of Freedom (*Dave the Potter* production), 172, *173*; "Amazing Grace" (Higdon), 172; *From Earth We Came* (Green), 172; Overby, Lynnette Young, 172
Drew, Leonardo, 190, *192*
Dunbar, Paul Laurence, 13–14

Earle, Willie, 157
Earley, Jackie, 113
Earth to Earth (Green), 9, *78*, 103; *Boneyard* (Weems) and, 195; death in, 42; "Deepest Pot" (Redmond), 51; *Grave* (*Dave the Potter* production), 172–173; hauntings, 194–195; pots in, 42, 194
Ebo Landing (Weems), 196, *197*; pot poem, 196–198, **197**
Edenton, N.C., 122
Edgefield (Green), 15, 54, 101–102, 131, 188–190, *189*; in conversation with *Domestic Scenes* (Gomez), 191; cotton in, 45–46; "Field Cotton" (Redmond), 51, 101; fieldwork in, 45–46; haunting of, 190–191
Edgefield, S.C., 13, 131, 163, 171–172, 194–195
Edgefield Hive, 5, 18n6
"Ego Tripping (there may be a reason why)" (Giovanni), 103
ekphrasis, 105, 106–107, 157

Elegba: Green and, 120–121; Tubman and, 120–121
Eliza (friend of Drake), 7, 39
"Embodied" (Redmond), **89**; "Carry Us" (Redmond) and, 106; Sankofa, 89; *Vessels for Taking Us Home* (Green), 106; *Vessels of Sir Dave* (Green), 51
Emmons, Teresa, 164; *Dave the Potter* (theatrical production), 161; "Dave's Market," 171
enslaved Blacks, African-born, 107n6
enslaved life: community and family, 39, 40; forced separations, 6–7, 8; impact on lives of enslaved, 5–8; loan collateral, 39; use of talent and, 5–6; writing and, 5–6
"Epiphany" (Foreman, Kent), **129**
Evolution of Afro-American Artists, The: 1800–1959, 8

family: enslaved life, 40; *Young Dave* (Green), 40
Fetchit, Stepin, 151
"Field Cotton" (*Dave the Potter* production), 166–168; "Cotton" (Overby), 166; "Dave the Potter Prelude" (Russell), 166; *Edgefield* (Green), 166; "Field Cotton" (Redmond), 166; "Field Cotton" (Russell), 166, *167*; "Praise Dave" (Redmond), 166
"Field Cotton" (Redmond), **55**, 103, 131–132; *Edgefield* (Green), 51, 101; hauntings within, 101–102
Finney, Nikki, 112
first lines in this text: "[my mama's] love be like butter churned," 12; "that ingrown South" (Redmond), 11
First Sunday (Green), *144*
Fleetwood, Nicole, 191
flying Africans, 198
"[f]or Mr. John monday," 25
"Forefather" (Redmond), **52–53**, 158
Foreman, Kent, "Epiphany," 129
Foreman, Gabrielle, 4, 15, 162, 163, 203–204; *Dave the Potter* (theatrical production), 161; museum displays, 113; "Slavery's Slippery Touch" (Foreman), **76**, 175
Foster, Susan Leigh, 165
fragments, 131
Frederick Douglass series (Lawrence), 9, 40, 186
From Earth We Came (Green), 9, 42, *81*; darkness, 42; *Dave the Potter* (theatrical production), 172; death in, 42; "Grave" (Redmond), 51; pottery shards, 42, 43

Gee's Bend quilts, 132
Gerima, Haile, 118
Giovanni, Nikki, 103
Gleaners, The (Millet), 191
golliwog, 151
Gomez, Michael Angelo, 17, 17n5
grandmothers, 118–119
Grave (*Dave the Potter* production), 172, *174*, 175; *Earth to Earth* (Green), 172; "From Earth" (Russell), 172–173; "Grave" (Redmond), 172; Hilliard, Gabrielle, 172–173
"Grave" (Redmond), **82–83**, 103–104; *From Earth We Came* (Green), 51
Green, Jonathan, 19n22, 163, 204; absent Whiteness, 124; on art as communication, 112; artistic collaborations, 13, 183–186; Bible in art, 112–113; born with a caul, 121, 135, 147; clothing and textiles in work, 183; *Dave the Potter*, 168; *Dave the Potter* (theatrical production), 161; *Dave's Market* (*Dave the Potter* production), 171; on Drake, 111, 115, 120; on Drake's pots, 112; *Earth We Came* (*Dave the Potter* production), 172; *Edgefield* (*Dave the Potter* production), 166; *Farm Woman*, *184*; *From Earth We Came* (*Dave the Potter* production), 172; *Grave* (*Dave the Potter* production), 172; Gullah heritage, 186; healing dimensions of Black histories, 188; influence on Redmond, 145, 152–156; introduction to Drake's work, 186; on memory, 183; paintings, 18n16 (see also *Sir Dave* series; *and individual paintings*); *Postlude* (*Dave the Potter* production), 179; *Potter's Fragments* (*Dave the Potter* production), 175; on practice, 118; on Redmond, 114; *Requiem for Rice*, 185; *Robert Smalls* series, 183; *Seeking*, 185–186; *Sir Dave* (*Dave the Potter* production), 171; *Sir Dave* series, 4–5, 8–10; on storytelling, 117; *Three Vessels* (Green), 177; *Vessels* (*Dave the Potter*), 177; *Vessels for Taking Us Home* (Green), 177; as young elder, 115, 117. See also *Sir Dave* series
Greene, Carroll, Jr., 8, 186
Griots, 128
Gullah, 16

Hamilton, Virginia, 45
Hammon, Jupiter, 25
Harper, Frances E. W., 13–14
Harriet Tubman series (Lawrence), 186
hauntings, 101, 102, 105; within "Field Cotton" (Redmond), 101–102; within *Sir Dave* series, 45, 46
Hawkins, Tramaine, 20n40
"Heaven-Human-Earth: A Found Poem" (Redmond), **87**; *Three Vessels*, 51
Higdon, Jennifer: "Amazing Grace," 172; *Dave the Potter* (theatrical production), 161, 172
Hilliard, Gabrielle, 164; *Dave the Potter* (theatrical production), 161; *Grave* (*Dave the Potter* production), 172–173
history: art and, 124; embodied sensibility and, 132; poetry and, 122
Horton, George Moses, 5, 25
"How I Learned to Dance and Read the Weather" (Redmond), **143**
"How I Walk" (Redmond), **72**; *Crossroads* (Green), 51

"I, Master" (Redmond), **62**; *Dave the Potter* (Green), 51; *Sir Dave*, 124
"I wonder where is all my relation," *49*, 157–158, 163

Ibo Landing, 45, 102, 105, 198. See also *Ebo Landing*
inscriptions (first line), 4; another trick is worst than this xx, 28; a better thing, I never saw, 27; cash wanted, 25, 29; Catination, 27; Concatination, 27; Dave belongs to Mr. Miles /, 28; Edgefield District, 28; for Mr. John monday, 25, 29; the fouth of July — is Surely come —, 33; Give me silver or; either Gold =, 28; Good for lard or holding - fresh meat, 33; Great & noble Jar, 33; H. Panzerbieter, 35; here is eighteen hundred & fifty nine, 32; horses mules and hogs —, 27; I, made this Jar, all of cross, 34; I made this for our sott, 30; I made this Jar = for cash —, *21*, 30; I made this out of number, & cross ‶, 32; I Saw a leopard, & a lions face =, 34; I saw a leppard, & a lions face ‶, 31; I wonder where is all my relation, 4, 6, 29, *49*; just a mammouth Jar, 29; Ladys & gentlemens Shoes =, 28; Lm says this handle, 25, 29; made at Stoney bluff, 33, 37; Making this Jar = I had all thougts, 30; Mark and, 32; New, 35; nineteen days before Chrismas ——— Eve —, 32; A noble jar, 36; A noble Jar . For pork or beef —, 34; not counted, 29; Over noble Dr. Landrum's head, 32; Ponderosity, 36; a pretty little Girl, on a virge, 30, 41–42; put every bit all between, 27; Rev. W. A. Lawton, 25, 33; the Sun moon and — Stars =, 31, *181*; Think of me when, 35; this is a noble churn, *iii*, 30; This noble Jar = will hold, 20, 31; A very Large Jar = which has 4 handles =, 31; whats better than kissing =, 28, *97*, *201*; when you fill this Jar with pork or beef, *1*, 31; . . . y my chic . . ., 35
integration, 142–143
Intimacy, 131
Ironers, The (Lawrence), *185*
"Irony" (Redmond), **73**; *Crossroads* (Green), 51

Jacobs, Harriet, 25
"Jarring" (Redmond), **74**, 105; *Crossroads* (Green), 51
Jim Crow, 142–143
joy, 10

Koverman, Jill Beute, 8, 116, 136

Landrum, Abner, 5, 40
Landrum family, 18n12
Language of Life, The (Moyers), 146
Lawrence, Jacob, 39–40, 116, 186; *Frederick Douglass* series, 9, 40, 186; *Harriet Tubman* series, 186; *The Ironers*, *185*; *Toussaint L'Ouverture* series, 9
legitimization and money, 134–136
Lester, Julius, 45
literacy, illegality of, 16
"Lm says this handle will crack," 25
location of creation: Horse Creek, 27, 28, 29; Pottersville, 27; Stony Bluff, 29, 30, 31, 32, 33, 34
location of creation (probable): Horse Creek, 35; Stony Bluff, 35
lost lovers, 103–104
Lowcountry Rice Culture Project, 183, 185
Lydia (friend of Drake), 7

"make your own way," 137
"Mama's Magic" (Redmond), 117–118, **153–154**; Green's role, 153
Manzano, Juan, 5
"Market" (Redmond), **64**; *Dave's Market* (Green), 51
Marshland Passage (Green), 18n16, 42–43, *44*, *84*; African cosmologies, 43; birds in, 43, 45; Egyptian divinity in, 43; Middle Passage and, 43; ocean in, 43, 45; pots in, 43; "Tributaries" (Redmond), 51
memory, 183, 198. *See also* ancestor artists; Black histories
Miles, Lewis, 25
Millet, Jean-François, 191
Mills, Jon, *192*
mirrors: absence of mirror texts, 147; instead of windows in education, 133; mirror texts, 113, 123, 155
Moorhead, Scipio, 16
Morrison, Toni, 45
Mother Emmanuel church (Charleston S.C.), 126
mothers, 11–12; "What I Knows" (Redmond), 101
Motley, Archibald, 9
Moyers, Bill, 146
museums holding Drake's pottery: Atlanta History Center (Atlanta, Ga.), 33; Charleston Museum (Charleston, S.C.), 28, 33, 35, 37; Crystal Bridges Museum of American Art (Bentonville, Arkansas), 24, 31; de Young Fine Arts Museum (San Francisco), 24, 27; Greenville County Museum of Art (Greenville, S.C.), 23–24, 28, 29, 30, 31, 35; High Museum of Art (Atlanta, Ga.), 27, 30; Madison-Morgan Cultural Center (Madison, Ga.), 32; McKissick Museum (Columbia, S.C.), 29, 30; Metropolitan Museum of Art (New York, N.Y.), 31; Museum of Early Southern Decorative Arts (Winston-Salem, N.C.), 31; Museum of Fine Arts (Boston, Mass.), 30; National Museum of American History, Smithsonian Institution (Washington, D.C.), 32, 34; Philadelphia Museum of Art (Philadelphia, Pa.), 33; South Carolina State Museum (Columbia, S.C.), 27; Virginia Museum of Fine Arts (Richmond, Va.), 28
music, 128

naming, 12–13, 103
Narrative of the Life (Douglass), and "What I Don't Know" (Redmond), 99–100
narrative painting, 41, 112, 115, 116–117
narratives, centering oneself in, 133, 141–142; Drake, 124–126, 130
"Nature Lesson" (Redmond), **157**

Newman, Vaughn, Jr., 13
"1968 Winters" (Earley), 113–114
nineteenth-century literature, 4
"Notes in the Margin" (Redmond), **94–95**

Off the Wall and Onto the Stage: Dancing the Art of Jonathan Green, 185
Orisha, 120–121
Our Nig (Wilson, Harriet E.), 162
Overby, Lynnette Young, 4, 13, 14, 15, 205; "Cotton," 166; *Dave the Potter* (theatrical production), 161; on *Dave the Potter* (theatrical production), 161–172; *Dream of Freedom* (*Dave the Potter* production), 172; *Shards* (*Dave the Potter* production), 175

Paul Jones Collection, 135
Payne, Daniel, 16
Peace Center (Greenville, S.C.), 13
permission, 137
persona poems, 158
Pinkney, Jerry, 45
plantations in art, 45–46
Poems on Various Subjects (1773), 16
poetics of exile, 196–197
poetry: Black history and, 122; couplets, 3, 25, 58, 102, 104, 163; dope-deuce couplets, 105; as liberation, 128; in other forms, 149; as performance, 135, 137; persona poems, 11, 102–103, 158; power to heal, 146; praise poems, 102–103, 158; Redmond's father and, 149; turns, 129
Postlude (*Dave the Potter* production), *178*; "Carry Us" (Redmond), 179; "Postlude" (Russell), 179; *Sir Dave* series, 179
pots: anthropomorphization of, 25, 105; in *Dave's Market* (Green), 41; in *Earth to Earth* (Green), 42; face jugs, 194–195; in *Marshland Passage* (Green), 43; "Praise Dave" (Redmond), 103; in *Sir Dave* series, 40, 41; in *Young Dave* (Green), 40. *See also* Edgefield, S.C.
pots, Drake's signing, 3, 6, 12, 16, 25; Foreman on, 198; in Redmond's work, 104, 106, 137, 166; in *Vessels for Taking Us Home* (Green), 45, 198
Potter's Fragments (Green), 75, 117; pottery shards, 43; "Remains" (Redmond), 51; "Slavery's Slippery Touch" (Foreman), 51
Pottersville Stoneware Manufactory, 6, 18n8
pottery as centering act, 133
"Praise Dave" (Redmond): *Dave the Potter* (theatrical production), **69–70**, 102–103, 166; *Sir Dave*, 51
Praise Songs, 13
Prelude, 166
"Pretty Little Girl" (*Dave the Potter* production): *Dave the Potter* (Green), 168; *Dave the Potter* (theatrical production), 168–169, *169*; "Pretty Little Girl" (Russell), 168; "Pretty Little Girl" (Thomas), 168
"Pretty Little Girl" (Russell), *Dave the Potter* (theatrical production), 168
"Pretty Little Girl" (score, Russell), *159*
"Pretty Little Girl" (Thomas), *Dave the Potter* (theatrical production), 168

Ra, *44*
racism and stereotypes, 142, 150, 151, 152, 157
Rambsy, Howard, 11
"Read" (Redmond), **66–67**; *Sir Dave*, 51
reading in Green's work, 124; *Dave the Potter* (Green), 41; *Dave's Market* (Green), 41; *Sir Dave* (Green), 41; *Sir Dave* series, 40
Real Black: Adventures in Racial Sincerity (Jackson), 187
Redmond, Glenis: academic background, 145; *All My Relation: Poems for David Drake* (Redmond), 4, 10, 10–12; ancestor artists, 113; artist statement, 158; artistic collaborations, 4–5, 13–15, 164, 204–205; arts in home, 149–150; *Backbone* (2000), 10; on Black being, 99; "Carry Us," 91–93, 179; connection to Drake and Green together, 157; as counselor, 145–146; *Dave the Potter* (theatrical production), 161; on Drake, 110–111, 120; experience with father, 141–143; fibromyalgia, 146; "Field Cotton," 166; "Footnotes" (text of), 10; *Grave* (*Dave the Potter* production), 172; on Green, 115, 152–156; importance of place, 141–157; influence of Clifton, 146–147, 153; influence of Green, 11–12, 145, 147, 152–156; married life, 145; mother and, 149, 156–157; persona poems, 11, 158; as poet, 147; poetry and history, 122–123; on practice, 118; "Praise Dave," 166; racism and stereotypes, 151; role of art, 141–142, 145; on South Carolina, 122, 137, 142, 145, 150, 152–153, 155, 158; "that ingrown South," 11; *Under the Sun* (2008), 10–11; "What I Knows," 11–12; "What My Hand Say," 122; *What My Hand Say* (2016), 10. *See also individual poems*
Redmond, Johnny (Glennis's father), 141–143, 152–153
"Remains" (Redmond), **77**; *Potter's Fragments* (Green), 51
Requiem for Rice, 185
Roots, 150
Russell, Ralph, 164; *Dave the Potter* (theatrical production), 161; "Dave the Potter Prelude," 166; "Dave's Market," 171; "Dave's Song," 171; "Field Cotton," 166, *167*; *Grave* (*Dave the Potter* production), 172–173; *Postlude* (*Dave the Potter* production), 179; "Pretty Little Girl," 168; *Shards* (*Dave the Potter* production), 175; *Vessels* (*Dave the Potter* production), 177

Sajé, Natasha, 19n21, 107n4
Sankofa, 105, 106, 116; "Carry Us" (Redmond), 91–92; "Embodied" (Redmond), 89
Sankofa (Gerima), 118
Sea Island series (Weems), 15, 186, 205; in conversation with *Sir Dave* series, 195–200
"second middle passage," 155

Seeking (Green), 126
Shards (*Dave the Potter* production), 131, *176*; Overby, Lynnette Young, 175; *Potter's Fragments* (Green), 175; score, *175*; "Shards" (Russell), 175; "Slavery's Slippery Touch" (Foreman), 175
shards, funereal: *Boneyard* (Weems), 196; *From Earth We Came* (Green), 42; *Potter's Fragments* (Green), 43; *Sea Island* series (Weems), 195
Sharecroppers, 190
Sharing Our Legacy Dance Theater, 4, 13–14
Shaw Air Force Base, 142
Shockley, Evie, 15, 203–205
Shogun, 120
signatures, 45, 124
Sir Dave. *See* Drake, David
Sir Dave: "Brickmaking: Recipe for Writing" (Redmond), 51; "I, Master" and, 124; "Praise Dave" (Redmond), 51; "Read" (Redmond), 51; reading and literacy, 124–125
"Sir Dave" (*Dave the Potter* production), 171; "Dave's Song" (Russell), 171; *Sir Dave* (Green), 171; *Sir Dave* (Thomas), 171
Sir Dave (Green), 18n16, 39, *65*; *Dave the Potter* (theatrical production), 171; natural world, 41; reading, 41
Sir Dave (Thomas), *Dave the Potter* (theatrical production), 171
Sir Dave series, 39–47, 183, 186; absent Whiteness, 124, 187–188; birds in, 43, 45, 125–126; Black vitality and joy, 187–188, 194; in conversation with *Sea Island* series, 186, 195–200; hauntings within, 43, 45, 46; natural world, 40; nonlinear narrative, 39–40, 186–187; pots in, 40, 41, 42; reading, 40; recovered history, 186; solitude, 42; between spaces, 198; ubiquity of enslaved labor, 188; "vessels," 43. See also *Crossroads*; *Dave the Potter* (Green); *Dave's Market* (Green); *Earth to Earth*; *Edgefield*; *From Earth We Came*; *Marshland Passage*; *Potter's Fragments*; *Sir Dave* (Green); *Three Vessels*; *Vessels for Taking Us Home*; *Vessels of Sir Dave*; *Young Dave*
Sketches: The Life of Harriet E. Wilson in Dance, Poetry, and Music, 161–162; YouTube availability, 162
"Slavery's Slippery Touch" (Foreman), **76**; *Potter's Fragments* (Green), 51
Smalls, Robert, 9; place in history, 121
Smith, Patricia, 11
Sonata Mulattica (Dove), 130
Song of Solomon (Morrison), 45
South Carolina: continuity of African cultures, 195; Drake and, 13, 117, 137, 157; "Forefather" 52; in Green's work, 145, 183, 185; importance to Redmond, 114–115, 122, 155, 156; racism and stereotypes, 142, 150, 152, 157; Redmond and, 158; in Redmond's poetry, 153; slave ports, 5; slavery and, 187; in Weems's work, 195. *See also* Edgefield, S.C.
South Carolina Act of 1740, 18n7
"Steal Away," 101
Stono rebellion, 18n7
storytelling, 106, 117

Terry, Lucy, 25
Thomas, Vincent, 13, 164, 205; *Dave the Potter* (theatrical production), 161; "Pretty Little Girl," 168; *Sir Dave*, 171; *Vessels* (*Dave the Potter*), 177
Three Vessels (Green), 42, *86*; "Heaven-Human-Earth: A Found Poem" (Redmond), 51; pots in, 42
"To S. M. a young African Painter, on Seeing His Works" (Wheatley), 16
Todd, Leonard, 18n6, 20n37, 163; *Carolina Clay: The Life and Legend of the Slave Potter Dave*, 14, 23
Toussaint L'Overture series (Lawrence), 186
"Tributaries" (Redmond), **85**; *Marshland Passage* (Green), 51
Truth, Sojourner, 121
Tubman, Harriet: as ancestor, 135; as artistic subject, 9, 11; Elegba and, 120–121; Orisha and, 120–121; place in history, 120–121

Untitled #25 (Drew), 190, *192*

Vessels (*Dave the Potter* production), *177*; Russell, Ralph, 177; Thomas, Vincent, 177; *Three Vessels* (Green), 177; *Vessels for Taking Us Home* (Green), 177
Vessels for Taking Us Home (Green), 9, 42, 45, *90*; "Carry Us" (Redmond), 51; death in, 42; pots in, 43, 198; signatures in, 198
Vessels of Sir Dave (Green), *88*; "Embodied" (Redmond), 51; pots in, 43
"Vision Is a Complicated Thing" (Redmond), **155–156**; relationship to Green's work, 155
Vlach, John Michael, 188, 190
VTDance, 13

Walker, Alice, 3
Walker, William Aiken, 190
Wanderer, the, 195
Weedman, Richard, 136
Weems, Carrie Mae, 15, 186; Black histories and, 195–200; *Boneyard*, 195, *196*; *Ebo Landing*, 196–198, *197*; *Sea Island* series, 15, 186, 195–200, 205; South Carolina influences, 196;
Wells, Lauren, 162
Wentworth, Marjory, 186
Weston, Trevor, 186
"What I Don't Know" (Redmond), **59–60**; analysis, 99; *Narrative of the Life* (Douglass) and, 99–100; *Young Dave* (Green), 51, 99
"What I Knows" (Redmond), **57–58**; analysis, 99; historical sources and, 100–101; mothers, 101; pots in, 101; religion, 101; *Young Dave* (Green), 51, 99, 100
whats better than kissing =, *97*, *197*

"What's in the Bank" (Redmond), **151**
Wheat, Ellen Harkins, 9
Wheat, Harkins, 186
Wheatley, Phillis, 5, 16, 25
Where Is All My Relation? The Poetics of Dave the Potter (Chaney), 14
whites, erasure of, 10, 11
Wilson, Arline, 24
Wilson, Harriet E., 13, 110, 161–162; *Our Nig*, 162
WPA, 47n10
Wright, Audrey, 164

"You Know You Are Not from Here" (Redmond), **150**
Young, Kevin, 19n36; *African American Poetry: 250 Years of Struggle and Song*, 14
Young Dave (Green), 9, 11, 12, 39, 40, 56; family, 40; pots in, 40; "What I Don't Know" (Redmond), 51, 99; "What I Knows" (Redmond), 51, 99, 100